Ability Grouping in Education

University of Oxfor␣

Short biographies

After a first degree in psychology at the University of Bristol and post-graduate study at Oxford, **Judith Ireson** began her career as a volunteer teacher in Kenya. Since then she has worked in several countries, teaching and researching psychology and education. Her main areas of expertise are in psychological and educational aspects of learning and the influence of cultural contexts on learning and teaching. Her early research was concerned with children's perceptions of drawing and their understanding of emotions. Since then she has researched school processes in curriculum development for pupils with moderate learning difficulty, the teaching of reading in primary schools, support for pupils with literacy difficulties, and social interaction and learning. Her recent work includes several funded research projects on ability grouping, in primary and secondary schools. She has attracted funding for research from the ESRC, DfEE and charitable organisations. In addition, she has undertaken research and published on teaching and learning in formal and informal learning environments.

Susan Hallam trained as a violinist at the Royal Academy of Music after which she spent 10 years as a full time professional musician. An interest in psychology led her to take a BA in Psychology externally with London University. This was followed by a career in teaching. Her PhD studies, relating to the development of expertise in musicians, were completed at the Institute of Education, London University where she became a lecturer in 1991. In 1999 she was appointed Professor in Education at Oxford Brookes University returning to the Institute of Education in 2001. She has received extensive funding for research from the ESRC, DfEE and a range of charitable organisations and LEAs and has published widely in areas as diverse as attendance at and exclusion from school, ability grouping, homework, teaching and learning in secondary, further and higher education, instrumental music teaching and the effects of music on behaviour.

Ability Grouping in Education

Judith Ireson and
Susan Hallam

P·C·P
Paul Chapman
Publishing

Paul Chapman Publishing
A SAGE Publications Company
6 Bonhill Street
London EC2A 4PU

SAGE Publications Inc
2455 Teller Road
Thousand Oaks, California 91320

SAGE Publications India Pvt Ltd
32, M-Block Market
Greater Kailash - I
New Delhi 110 048

A catalogue record for this book is available from the
British Library

ISBN 0 7619 7208 0
ISBN 0 7619 7209 9 (pbk)

Library of Congress catalog record available

Typeset by Dorwyn Ltd, Rowlands Castle, Hants.
Printed in Great Britain by Athenaeum Press,
Gateshead

Contents

Foreword

Throughout the world, governments – across a wide political spectrum – are examining their national systems of education. They appear to believe that a globalised technology-dominated world needs a better educated, more adaptable, work force. At the same time, a number of dissident voices, protesting about the effects of globalisation, the deteriorating environment and what is seen as the selfishness of developed nations squandering the natural resources of the planet, are also demanding better education and the inclusion of environmental issues in national curricula. Both governments and protesters see education as a powerful tool for changing attitudes.

Pupils, however, are affected not just by the content of their curriculum but also by the way learning is organised in their schools. It is the impact of the way that pupils are grouped for learning that this book addresses. Its timing is fortuitous. It is one of the few empirical studies to focus on pupil grouping for more than twenty years and its publication coincides with a resurgence of the idea of meritocracy. There is, it seems, a logic in the notion that a competitive worlds needs a competitive education system and the idea that the cleverest pupils (or at least those who find learning easiest) need to be kept together and given a different educational experience.

In the United Kingdom, two of the most common forms of grouping are streaming (in which pupils are divided into different classes on the basis of their perceived ability) and setting (in which pupils are grouped differently according to their strength in different subjects). There are, however, many variations and combinations of these two forms of organisation. Most are based on the theory that the cleverest pupils will encourage each other and that those who find learning difficult will avoid finding themselves outshone. The theory is highly plausible and is accepted by many pupils, parents and teachers. But, as with so many theories, the proof may be found in the impact of the method of grouping on the pupils' development.

Supported by the Economic and Social Research Council (ESRC), Judy Ireson and Sue Hallam led a team of researchers in the exploration of what pupils and teachers felt about ways of grouping and the impact of different methods on pupils' progress. They questioned, observed and collated test scores to create a large data base of attitudes, behaviours and results for pupils progressing through the early years of secondary schooling. Most importantly, they drew on multi-level analytical techniques to tease out the effects of the organisation over and above factors to do with the pupils or the teachers.

This book does not produce many simple answers and it certainly does not reveal a perfect way of grouping pupils. It does, however, provide rich details of the complex reality in which both pupils and teachers find themselves. It illustrates how findings vary between subjects and how different results emerge for different aspects of the pupils' development. It also emphasises the point that, however seductive the theory, no one system works well for all pupils.

I recommend careful reading of the results. Teachers, and those responsible for the formulation of educational policies, could learn much from them. The research team and the ESRC deserve congratulations for undertaking this detailed study.

Professsor Peter Mortimore
London
May 2001

Acknowledgements

The authors would like to thank all those who contributed to the research on which this book is based. The research was made possible by two grants from the Economic and Social Research Council. Researchers Sarah Hack, Helen Clark, Jane Davies, David Telford and Clare Hurley assisted at various stages of the research and Ian Plewis provided statistical help and advice. Leanne Guillen offered secretarial support and Linda Richards helped with the final stages of editing. Peter Mortimore provided valuable guidance throughout the research. Last but not least we would like to thank all the staff and pupils in the schools, for giving generously of their time and supporting the research. We hope they will find this book of interest.

1

Issues and Context

Selection and ability grouping are issues that arouse strong feelings. They have been hotly debated for over a century. Ability grouping is a thorny issue, tied to fundamental, often conflicting, ideological positions. These are reflected in strong differences of opinion about the merits of selective schooling, which have kept debate alive throughout the twentieth and into the twenty-first centuries. Those against selection argue that it denies equality of educational opportunity to many young people, limiting their life chances and increasing social exclusion. Those in favour argue that selection enables teaching to be more effectively geared for pupils of differing abilities, allowing the most able to reach the highest standards.

Ability grouping appears to offer a simple, rational response to the problem of low attainment. If pupils of similar ability are taught together, it should be possible to tailor teaching to meet their needs and thus raise their attainment. In practice, things are not so simple. There are several fundamental difficulties to be overcome, reflecting the nature of ability and the complexity of schools as cultural systems. These include the difficulty of selecting pupils and placing them accurately and fairly in groups, the expectations of teachers, pupils and parents, and the ethos of the school, which may affect the status of particular groups of pupils and their teachers.

The popularity of selection and ability grouping has waxed and waned over the past century. Several factors contributed to these shifts in the use of ability grouping in education. They include the changing social and economic context in the United Kingdom, changing values in society and the influence of psychological theories of learning and intelligence. In recent years, economic forces and globalisation, combined with international comparisons of pupil performance, have placed educational systems under pressure to demonstrate their effectiveness in producing an educated workforce. These pressures led governments to look for means of raising attainment. In this country, the spotlight has fallen on ability grouping as an organisational solution.

In this chapter we will provide a brief historical account of selection and ability grouping in the United Kingdom. We will then clarify the most common types of grouping arrangements in use at the present time. The final section will outline the remaining chapters of the book.

Historical context

The extent of selection and ability grouping in United Kingdom schools fluctuated during the twentieth century. Selection and streaming were common practice in the middle of the century but then declined rapidly, so that by the 1980s many local education authorities had abolished selection and most schools had abandoned streaming. By the end of the century, however, ability grouping appeared to be gaining popularity once again. In this section we will trace the development of selection and ability grouping from the beginning of the twentieth century to the present day. In the first part, we will chart the rise and fall of selective secondary education. The second part will consider ability grouping within primary and secondary schools.

The rise and fall of selective secondary education

By the beginning of the twentieth century, the elementary school system had been established in England and Wales and the majority of children attended school up to the age of twelve. Only a minority continued their education after the age of twelve in the grammar schools, many of which required the payment of fees. Children from more affluent families were privately educated. Teachers were held responsible for their pupils' progress and were paid according to the number of pupils who passed the end-of-year examinations that allowed them to move up into the next standard. This financial system encouraged teachers to concentrate their efforts on children of a wide range of ability, who were likely to pass the examinations.

Although the Victorian and Edwardian schools have been criticised, it is worth pointing out that teaching at that time was based on the prevailing associationist theories of learning. Although these theories encouraged an overemphasis on rote learning and repetition, they were essentially optimistic about the educability of children and the power of teaching to develop human capacity. They assumed that all children were capable of learning if they were taught appropriately. The challenge for educators was to discover how to bring about that learning. Associationist teaching methods were developed for the inculcation of knowledge, the formation of character and the acquisition of attitudes and habits.

The number of grammar schools gradually increased, but it was not until after the Second World War that secondary education was made available for all children. Even then, the system was tripartite, with the grammar schools continuing to offer access to a classical, academic and arts curriculum for a minority of young people, while the secondary modern schools offered a vocational curriculum for the majority and a small number of technical schools provided a technical education. Entry to the grammar schools remained competitive, with selection of children at the age of 11 years.

The case in favour of selection was supported by the development of the intelligence testing movement. This movement had a profound effect on the education system in this country, as it stressed the limitations of the human intellect. Moreover, the advent of psychometric testing heralded an era in which it was thought that children's intelligence could be measured and their potential achievement predicted. This conception of intelligence was at odds with the associationist view of learning, as it was thought that intelligence placed a limit on the capacity to learn. Intelligence was considered to be a general, innate capacity, not due to teaching or training. The function of the education system was to assess children's intelligence and to provide an appropriate education, which enabled individuals to reach their potential, as predicted by their intelligence quotient. This view was logically compatible with a selective education system and the stratification of pupils through streaming within schools.

Other factors influenced the introduction of selective education and structured ability grouping in schools during the first half of the twentieth century. The system was geared to the requirements of an industrialised society, which required a large number of unskilled labourers and smaller numbers of educated professional people and managers. A selective system provided access to the grammar schools and universities for the minority, while the majority of young people were expected to acquire basic and vocational skills in the secondary modern schools before leaving to take up skilled or unskilled manual or clerical work. In principle, selection allowed intelligent children from working class families a better education and the possibility of entering the universities.

The idea of the all-ability secondary school has been around for most of the century but comprehensive schools were not introduced in this country until the late 1950s. In this respect, England and Wales lagged behind many other countries, which introduced unselective secondary schools more quickly in order to raise the overall level of education. After a handful of local education authorities established comprehensive schools at the end of the 1950s, the number increased rapidly during the 1960s. Many local education authorities scrapped the eleven-plus examination. By then several influential studies had demonstrated that the selective system was not allowing the expected numbers of working class children to gain access to grammar school and to complete school successfully. In addition, there was strong opposition to the view that intelligence was entirely inherited, with mounting evidence that the environment had an important influence. There was increasing concern about the methods used to test intelligence and to select children on the basis of ability (Vernon, 1957).

By the late 1980s, the education system in England and Wales contained a complex mixture of school types. Some local authorities had fully comprehensive systems, while others had selective systems with entry to grammar schools based on tests at the end of junior school. Many authorities had a small number of selective schools alongside a larger number of comprehensive schools. This is still the situation at the start of the twenty-first century. Of the 149 local education authorities with secondary schools, 113 are totally comprehensive in organisation. There are 164 grammar schools, spread unevenly in the remaining 36 local education authorities (Jesson, 2000). In addition, some areas also include selective independent schools. This means that comprehensive schools in areas with grammar schools have fewer higher ability children than schools in fully comprehensive areas. In addition, comprehensive schools have very varied characters, some having been purpose built as comprehensives, while others developed from secondary modern schools, from grammar schools or from amalgamations of schools. Proponents of comprehensive schooling argue that the huge variety of arrangements in the British education system, particularly at secondary level, has come about through a combination of a lack of vision by several governments and civil servants, most notably at the end of the Second World War (Benn and Chitty, 1996).

The 1988 Education Act ushered in the National Curriculum. It also opened the way for the establishment of two types of self-governing secondary school, the Grant Maintained (GM) school and the City

Technology College (CTC). Four years later, the White Paper *Choice and Diversity* encouraged the establishment of specialist schools. These schools were allowed to select pupils on the basis of aptitude in such areas as technology, music or languages.

Ability grouping within schools

The popularity of ability grouping within schools has changed in tandem with selection. At the turn of the century the first elementary schools often had large classes containing children with a wide range of abilities. Grouping children by ability was introduced in United Kingdom primary schools after the *Primary School* report (the Hadow Report, Board of Education, 1930) and continued into the 1960s. Streaming (the formation of classes on the basis of ability) became increasingly common during the first half of the century, so that at the time of the 1944 Education Act it was becoming the standard form of organisation in large primary schools and in secondary schools. Surveys of junior schools in the mid-1960s found that in the schools that were large enough to implement streaming, almost all chose to do so (Barker Lunn, 1970; Jackson, 1964).

By the 1950s the desirability of streaming was beginning to be questioned, although it took some time before it was phased out. It became increasingly unpopular in primary school because it led to low self-esteem and social alienation of pupils in the lower streams (Willig, 1963; Barker Lunn, 1970) and the evidence for its positive effects on achievement was inconclusive (Blandford, 1958; Daniels, 1961b; Barker Lunn, 1970; Ferri, 1971; Gregory, 1984). The Plowden Report in 1967 was a landmark for the primary schools, with its clear encouragement of 'unstreaming'. Its vision of child-centred education, with teaching geared to the individual rather than the whole class, was at odds with grouping on the basis of a general measure of a child's ability. The demise of the eleven-plus examination and the intention to provide equality of opportunity also contributed to the reduction of streaming in primary schools. Theories underpinning primary education also contributed to this change. Piaget's work was translated into English and, together with the work of Montessori and Froebel, contributed to a new vision of child development. Children's learning was seen as fundamentally different from that of adults, requiring much active exploration of the world and the freedom to develop at their own pace. The teacher's role was to offer children a stimulating environment in which they could develop and learn. Many streamed schools reorganised their pupils into mixed ability classes. Primary classrooms were transformed, with rows of individual desks replaced by tables for small groups of pupils.

During the 1960s and 1970s researchers in the United Kingdom also started to question the effectiveness of streaming in secondary schools. There was inconclusive evidence regarding the benefits of streaming on pupils' attainment and the research started to highlight the negative effects, particularly the impact on educational opportunity, achievement and attitudes towards school. Several in-depth studies of individual secondary schools demonstrated that streaming could lead to anti-school attitudes and alienation from school (Hargreaves, 1967; Lacey, 1970; Ball, 1981). Ability grouping was also linked to working class underachievement, with children from working class families being over-represented in the lower ability groups. The research contributed to a shift in educational values away from a focus on individual attainment to concerns about the equality of educational opportunity. Many secondary schools introduced mixed ability classes in the lower school, now years 7 and 8. Some continued mixed ability classes throughout the school, although the majority increased the amount of ability grouping in the later years. In some schools mixed ability form groups or tutor groups were maintained for pastoral support and pupils remained in these groups for some curriculum subjects. They were regrouped into ability groups for other subjects. This remains a popular system of organisation in secondary schools.

Surveys of primary and secondary schools during the 1990s revealed that the vast majority of primary schools organised pupils in mixed ability classes (Hallam *et al.*, 1999; Lee and Croll, 1995; Ofsted, 1998a), but there was setting in at least one subject in the majority of junior schools. Some schools had a high level of setting throughout the primary years while in others children were in mixed ability classes throughout. In many small primary schools, children were in mixed age classes. These surveys also found that within class ability grouping was used in many primary schools. Streaming was rare in secondary schools, but setting was used in many schools, particularly in the upper school (Benn and Chitty, 1996). Following the introduction of the National Curriculum and the testing of pupils at the end of the Key Stages, the use of ability grouping is once again increasing.

With the increasing adoption of mixed ability grouping came a greater awareness of the difficulties involved in mixed ability teaching. Classes, particularly at secondary level, might contain a very wide

range of abilities and some teachers found it difficult to provide sufficiently challenging work for all. Successful teachers of mixed ability
classes use a variety of teaching modes in one lesson, vary the pace
and style of approach, use a range of audio-visual media and encourage a variety of pupil activities (Reid *et al.*, 1982). To support mixed
ability teaching, schools need good backup facilities and resources.
Efforts to confront these challenges were overtaken by the 1988
Education Reform Act (ERA) and the introduction of the National
Curriculum.

The current context

The ERA not only required maintained schools in England and Wales
to adopt the National Curriculum, but also required them to implement a national system of assessment of children at ages 7, 11 and 14.
Pupils are assessed in relation to a framework of attainment targets
within each curriculum subject, organised in levels. The ERA also
introduced principles of the competitive market into the education
system through parental choice and formula funding. To maintain or
increase their level of funding, schools must attract pupils, as funding
is tied to pupil numbers. This places them in competition with neigh-
bouring schools. To help parents make informed choices, schools are
required to publish the results of national tests. Publication of the
results of the Key Stage tests puts schools under pressure to maximise
the attainments of their pupils, so as to attract parents and maintain
their level of funding.

The national pressures to raise children's attainment were fuelled
by the publication of international comparisons of performance in
mathematics and science. Many of these comparative studies over the
years have demonstrated that British children's attainment is low in
comparison with children in other countries, notably those in the
'Tiger' economies of the Far East, such as Japan and Korea (Reynolds
and Farrell, 1996; Keys, Harris and Fernandez, 1996). Many European
countries also outperformed the United Kingdom. In addition, the
United Kingdom figures reveal a worrying level of underachievement
by many children. While the highest achievers compare well with
those in other countries, there is a large proportion of children with
very low scores on these tests. This so-called 'long tail' of underachievement is not a new phenomenon in the British education system, but it is one that must be addressed if the country is to compete
effectively in the global market. It is also a social justice issue, as it is a

tremendous disadvantage for a young person to leave school with no qualifications and limited basic skills. The government's attempts to raise standards of literacy and numeracy are a clear response to this issue.

During the 1990s, changes in the education system were accompanied by recommendations for schools to adopt setting by ability. A report by the National Curriculum Council (1993) argued for greater use of setting to cover the requirements of the National Curriculum and ensure that the objectives of the Education Reform Act were achieved. The government White Paper *Excellence in Schools* (1997) stated that 'Unless a school can demonstrate that it is getting better than expected results through a different approach, we do make the presumption that setting should be the norm in secondary schools and is worth considering in primary schools'. Setting is a system of grouping pupils according to their attainment in a particular subject, so a pupil may be in a high set for one subject and a lower set for another. It differs from streaming, in which pupils are allocated to classes on the basis of a test of general ability and remain with their class for most lessons. Further increases in setting are called for in the Green Paper *Schools: Building on Success* (DfEE, 2001).

Pressures have also been mounting for primary schools to increase the grouping of pupils by ability. The Chief Inspector for Schools, in his Annual Report, reported an increase in setting in primary schools and stated that the inspection evidence indicated that 'setting can help teachers to plan work more precisely and select appropriate teaching methods' (Ofsted, 1999). A further report *Setting in Primary Schools* provided research evidence based on inspection reports and a questionnaire, which indicated that approximately six out of ten junior schools and one-half of primary schools adopted ability setting procedures for at least one subject in some year groups (Ofsted, 1998a). In addition, the introduction of the literacy and numeracy hours has encouraged teachers to make use of ability grouping within primary classrooms.

The move to reintroduce ability grouping appears to have been driven by market forces, rather than by any intellectual shift or change in values. Curiously, recent developments in the theory of intelligence appear to have had little impact. Both Gardner (1983) and Sternberg (1984) propose theories of intelligence that are multi-faceted rather than unitary. Gardner's theory of multiple intelligences includes linguistic, mathematical, spatial, musical, kinaesthetic, interpersonal and intrapersonal intelligence. Sternberg's triarchic theory includes the mental mechanisms involved in intelligent behaviour, the individual's ability to control these mechanisms in everyday life and the impact of an individual's life experiences on both the mechanisms and control processes. Although there are many differences between them, both these theoretical positions suggest that interpersonal and personal intelligence play an important role in learning. They should be given some consideration in relation to ability grouping.

To summarise, streaming was the dominant form of pupil organisation in secondary schools and large primary schools during the middle part of the twentieth century. Its popularity decreased when findings from research demonstrated that it had a negative impact on pupils' self-esteem, attitudes and engagement without any significant positive impact on pupil attainment. Educational values also shifted away from a concern for the attainment of the most able children towards a concern for equality of opportunity and a desire to break down divisions within society. There was also increasing criticism of the tests used to allocate pupils to ability groups. By the time the National Curriculum was introduced, mixed ability grouping was the most common practice in primary schools and also in the first year of secondary school. There are now pressures to increase the amount of ability grouping in primary and secondary schools, particularly through the use of setting, rather than streaming (see overleaf for descriptions of these types of grouping). These pressures are fuelled by the introduction of market forces in the education system and by the competitive global market.

Many in this country have argued that the grammar schools are the jewels in the crown of the state education system. They have served pupils from more advantaged backgrounds very well and the pressure to retain them is easy to understand. However, other countries led the way in reforming their education systems to allow greater opportunity for all children, whatever their backgrounds. In the current context, we must ask whether a fundamental review is needed to give us the education system our country requires in the twenty-first century.

The shifts that have taken place over the course of a century reflect changing priorities in educational aims and values and the changing requirements of the economic context and labour market. A recent statement of educational aims (DfEE/QCA, 1999) is wide ranging and includes promoting pupils' spiritual, moral, social, cultural, physical and mental development and preparing young people to respond positively to opportunities and challenges in a rapidly changing world. It is important, when considering the effectiveness of ability grouping, that we do so in relation to both the academic and non-academic aims and goals of education (Ireson, Mortimore and Hallam, 1999).

Types of ability grouping

Several types of ability grouping have already been mentioned. For the sake of clarity, Table 1.1 provides a list of the main types of ability grouping used in schools. The italicised terms are the American equivalents.

Table 1.1:   Types of ability grouping

Streaming *(tracking)*	Pupils are placed in classes on the basis of a test of their general ability. They remain in their streamed class for most subjects.
Banding	Pupils are placed in two, three or four bands on the basis of a test of their general ability. Each band contains a number of classes and pupils may be regrouped within the band for some subjects.
Setting *(regrouping)*	Pupils are grouped according to their attainment in a particular subject. Setting may be imposed across a whole year group, across timetable halves, within a band or across mixed age classes. Sets may be serially ordered or there may be parallel sets.
Mixed ability *(heterogeneous grouping)*	There is no attempt to group together pupils of similar ability. Pupils may be grouped in such a way as to achieve a range of abilities within the class. Other factors, such as social relationships, gender or ethnic composition, may form the basis for grouping.
Within class ability grouping	Pupils are grouped within the class on the basis of ability. They may be regrouped within the class for different subjects.
Cross-age grouping *(Cross-grade grouping)*	Pupils in two or more year groups are placed in the same class. They may be regrouped by setting or within class grouping or taught as a mixed ability class.

Streaming is the most rigid form of ability grouping. Pupils are placed into a class on the basis of a measure of their overall ability and remain in that class for most subjects. It is based on the assumption that individuals have a fixed level of general intelligence, which predicts their performance across all subjects, and can be measured by objective tests. Streaming reduces the spread of ability within the class, making it easier for teachers to match their teaching to pupils' levels of academic ability. Streaming has been shown to have negative effects on pupils, particularly those in the bottom streams. They may be labelled and stigmatised by staff and by other pupils, and become disaffected with school. Banding is a form of streaming, with pupils allocated to bands on the basis of a measure of general ability. It may be less rigid than streaming, especially when there are fewer bands in a school and each band includes several classes, which may then be regrouped for different subjects.

Setting offers a more flexible way of grouping pupils on the basis of their attainment in particular curriculum subjects. It is consistent with a differentiated view of abilities, and allows for higher attainment of pupils in some subjects than in others. Schools may use setting for some or for all academic subjects. As with streaming, the aim of setting is to reduce the heterogeneity within classes and to enable teachers to match their teaching to pupils' needs. It reduces the negative effects often associated with streaming as pupils are not in the same groups all of the time (Slavin 1987a, 1990a). Sets may be serially ordered, from highest to lowest, or there may be parallel sets. There may be combinations of these; for example, to avoid having a bottom set a school might have one top set and two parallel lower sets. The number of curriculum subjects for which pupils are set also varies from one school to another.

Within class grouping is very common in primary schools. Groups may be formed on the basis of ability, or on attainment in particular subjects, or may be based on working relationships. Some teachers organise pupils in fairly stable groups on the basis of ability. Others seat the children in mixed ability groups and reorganise them according to attainment for English and mathematics. Whichever form of within class grouping is used, it enables the teacher to work with a group of pupils together, rather than working individually. Collaborative work between pupils is also possible, although true collaboration is relatively rare and children mainly work individually while seated in groups (Galton and Williamson, 1992). The advantage of within class grouping over setting and streaming is that it reduces the chances of pupils becoming labelled, but much depends on the ethos of the school and how grouping arrangements are explained to pupils. It has been claimed that, compared with mixed ability teaching, within class ability grouping enables teachers to match work to pupils' needs (Lou *et al.*, 1996). However, there is little firm evidence on this point and much will depend on the range of ability within the class and the amount and type of support provided for the teacher.

Mixed ability classes may be composed on a random basis, by taking the first child on the register and placing him in one class, the second in another class and so on. Alternatively, schools may attempt to achieve a balance of abilities in each class, using available test scores. Other considerations might be to maintain a similar balance of boys and girls in each class, or a similar balance of ethnic groups. In primary schools, the class teacher is responsible for teaching the class for all subjects and the class is a stable unit. In secondary schools, pupils in a mixed ability class are more likely to be taught by subject specialists. Alternatively, the mixed ability class may be together for some subjects but regrouped for others. Mixed ability grouping is based on the recognition that children have different strengths and weaknesses and develop at different rates. It also provides equal opportunity to learn for all pupils, who follow the same curriculum and are provided with the same instruction, resources and learning activities. Mixed ability teaching places greater demands on the teacher and requires good curriculum resources.

In Chapter 8 we will consider each of these types of groupings in turn. Each has both advantages and disadvantages, there is no ideal form or grouping. Some types of grouping may be more suitable for particular types of learning activity or for particular groups of pupil. In Chapter 8, we will also consider alternative forms of grouping arrangement.

Organisation of the remainder of the book

In this book we provide reviews of the research on selection and ability grouping. The literature is extensive and several reviews have appeared recently (Harlen and Malcolm, 1997; Hallam and Toutounji, 1996; Ireson and Hallam, 1999; Slavin, 1987a, 1990a; Sukhnanden and Lee, 1998). Our reviews will concentrate on more recent work undertaken in the United Kingdom. Although the research is extensive, researchers have tended to examine either the effect on pupils' attainment or the impact on social and personal outcomes, such as pupil self-esteem, attitudes towards school and alienation from school. Research on selection, in particular, has been concerned almost exclusively with its effect on achievement in national examinations.

Very few studies have succeeded in analysing the effects of ability grouping on both academic and non-academic outcomes. There has therefore been only limited success in establishing which ability grouping arrangements are most effective in terms of both pupils' achievement and their self-esteem, attitudes to school and alienation. The real questions which now need to be addressed are not what are the overall benefits of different types of ability grouping, but who benefits, how do they benefit, why do they benefit and does anyone else suffer as a result? (Hallam and Toutounji, 1996).

In our own research we have examined the effects of ability grouping on both academic and non-academic outcomes for pupils. We have also explored the implementation of grouping policies in schools, teachers' attitudes and classroom practice in our attempt to understand the factors that may mediate the impact of ability grouping structures on pupils. In the next two chapters, we will consider evidence for the impact of selection and ability grouping on individual pupils. Our research team has recently completed several investigations of ability grouping, in both primary and secondary schools. We will explain how we carried out these projects and describe some of the main findings from them. In Chapter 2 we ask whether selection and ability grouping within schools and classrooms affects attainment in primary and secondary schools. The evidence from research is conflicting, but taken as a whole indicates that ability grouping does not have a strong impact on overall attainment. There is evidence that pupils in selective schools achieve higher grades in national examinations, but these differences disappear when attainment on intake is taken into account. Ability grouping can raise the attainment of those in higher groups, but this is often at the expense of those in lower groups, who do better in a mixed ability environment. Recent research, involving secondary pupils in year 9, indicates that the effect of ability grouping is related to the curriculum subject. In mathematics, ability grouping tends to raise the attainment of the pupils with higher attainment on entry to secondary school and to lower the attainment of those doing less well on entry. There is no impact of setting on attainment in science and English.

In Chapter 3 we consider the impact of ability grouping on pupils' academic self-concept, self-esteem, their feelings towards school and the teasing experienced in school. We will consider the development and differentiation of the self-concept and the relationship between self-concept and attainment. In recent years, considerable advances have been made in the measurement of the self-concept. This has been accompanied by the development of multi-faceted, hierarchical models that include academic and non-academic facets. This work has enabled researchers to arrive at more reliable estimates of the impact of ability grouping on pupils' self-concepts. Recent research demonstrates that pupils' self-esteem is related to the amount of structured grouping in secondary schools, with those in schools with high levels of structured grouping having lower self-esteem. Indicators of pupils' feelings about school also suggest that there is a less supportive climate in schools with higher levels of ability grouping. Pupils in the lower groups report being teased about their ability.

Chapter 4 provides insight into pupils' views of ability grouping. We draw on evidence from questionnaires and interviews with pupils in both primary and secondary schools, exploring their awareness of the grouping arrangements in their school and their experiences of the impact of grouping on teaching and learning in the classroom. This research demonstrates that pupils in both primary and secondary school are aware of the grouping arrangements in their school and can justify the reasons for the adoption of these practices. Secondary pupils preferred setting but their preferences were influenced by the practices in their school, their current placement and their gender. They were aware that those in lower groups could become stigmatised. Pupils' views about which class was best varied, even within a school. Some pupils valued high attainment while others saw being average as being a safe option from teasing and from undue pressure to achieve.

Teachers' attitudes and their classroom practices are key aspects of any grouping plan. Many senior managers are reluctant to impose grouping plans in their schools against the wishes of their staff. In Chapter 5 we discuss evidence from current research on teachers' attitudes towards ability grouping. This research demonstrates that teachers' attitudes relate to the type of school in which they work. Those in mixed ability schools have more favourable views about teaching mixed ability classes. These attitudes may play an important part in mediating the impact of ability grouping on pupils. Teachers' views about mixed ability teaching also depend on the subject concerned, with mathematics and modern foreign languages considered the least suitable for mixed ability teaching and English and humanities the most suitable. Chapter 6 explores teachers' classroom practices with mixed ability classes and classes grouped by ability. There is evidence that pedagogic practices differ with mixed ability classes and classes grouped by ability. Mixed ability teaching is considered to be more demanding, requiring greater differentiation of work in the classroom. When classes are grouped by ability, teachers tend to abandon the methods they use with mixed ability classes. Teaching methods also differ with high and low ability groups, leading to a more stimulating environment, faster pace and more pressure for pupils in the higher groups. There is a lowering of expectations in the lower groups, which appears difficult to counteract.

Chapter 7 considers a number of key practical issues for school managers, including the assessment of pupils for ability grouping, resource allocation and the movement of pupils between groups. We start by drawing on recent research exploring the aims and values underpinning grouping practices in schools. In some schools, strongly held values are in conflict with the current pressures to increase ability grouping. Grouping patterns in primary and secondary schools are also influenced by a variety of factors such as the size of intake, size and availability of rooms, and staffing. Schools adopt a variety of grouping arrangements. In secondary schools, movement between groups generally occurs after assessments, which may be infrequent. Decisions to move pupils to different sets are sometimes based on behaviour, rather than on attainment. Groupings in primary school are often influenced by social factors. We will argue that groupings can create artificial divisions, not based solely on ability, which may have important consequences for pupils who are misplaced.

Having considered some of the issues arising from the adoption of ability grouping practices, we turn to some alternative arrangements in Chapter 8. Here we offer a variety of types of pupil grouping tried by schools in recent years, such as vertical grouping, gender grouping and special activity groups formed for specific purposes, such as literacy teaching or for disaffected pupils. We also consider within class grouping procedures, co-operative learning and mastery learning. We argue that a key issue is the flexibility to meet the changing needs of the learner. In addition, any grouping system should be carefully considered before being adopted and its effectiveness monitored over time.

In the concluding chapter we will draw together the issues and themes of the previous chapters. We question the use of traditional indicators of intelligence as a basis for grouping pupils, especially in view of the tendency for such measures to set limits on pupil achievement. We also argue that school effectiveness can only be judged in relation to educational aims and goals. Schools may be differentially effective in relation to different goals, for particular groups of pupil, in different curriculum subjects and at different points in time. Grouping practices should be considered in relation to the full range of educational aims (DfEE/QCA, 1999), to enable all pupils to learn and achieve and to promote their spiritual, moral, social and cultural development and prepare them for life. Although the academic achievement of young people is of national and personal importance, a narrow concentration on this aim at the expense of the all-round development of young people is likely to be to their detriment and to have a negative impact on social cohesion. A fundamental reconsideration of grouping practices is needed to achieve a constructive alignment between educational aims and goals, practices and pedagogy.

2

Does Ability Grouping Raise Attainment?

The main argument put forward in favour of selecting and grouping pupils by ability is that ability grouping is effective in raising pupil attainment. In this chapter we provide a review of research on the effects of selective schooling and ability grouping within schools. Our emphasis is on the most recent research carried out in the United Kingdom, although we also draw on earlier and overseas research where appropriate. First we consider research comparing the attainment of pupils in selective and unselective, or comprehensive, school systems. Much of this research compares the performance of pupils in selective and unselective local education authorities. We then consider research on ability grouping within primary and secondary schools in this country and overseas. The main questions we consider are whether ability grouping contributes to raising overall standards and whether it benefits particular pupils at the expense of others. Although there is considerable disagreement in the literature, the weight of evidence indicates that selection and ability grouping do not have a powerful impact on the overall attainment of pupils. There do, however, appear to be differential benefits for pupils in selective and unselective systems. Selection and ability grouping tend to work to the advantage of pupils in the higher attaining groups, while unselective systems and mixed ability grouping tend to benefit those in the lower attaining groups. In the final section of this chapter we turn to our own research on the effects of setting, or regrouping, on pupil attainment in English, mathematics and science in English secondary schools. This research indicates that setting influences attainment in mathematics but not in the other subjects. It benefits those entering school with higher attainment, whereas mixed ability grouping benefits those who entered with lower attainment in mathematics. We end the chapter by suggesting factors that might contribute to the discrepancies. These include the complexity of relations between structured grouping and other factors that may operate as precursors to or mediators between the structural aspects of grouping and pupil attainment, such as the ethos of the school, pupils' and teachers' attitudes and values, classroom instruction and the curriculum.

Issues in research on selection and ability grouping

Research comparing the performance of pupils in selective and non-selective schools or schools with and without structured ability grouping is of several different types. Some early research simply compared the examination performance of pupils in areas with and without grammar schools. Research comparing examination results alone is limited, as it fails to take account of pupils' attainment or ability on entry to the schools. Without a measure of prior attainment, there is no way of knowing whether differences existed between the pupils in the two systems before they entered secondary school. As prior attainment is a powerful predictor of later attainment, pupil intake could account for differences in examination performance. In the absence of measures of prior attainment, some of the earlier research used indicators of social class. Steedman (1983) and Gray, Jesson and Jones (1984) both provide very clear analyses illustrating the different conclusions that may be reached when comparisons of selective and unselective local education authorities (LEAs) do or do not take account of social class and pupils' prior attainment. They both demonstrated that differences in examination performance in selective and unselective systems disappeared when pupil intake was taken into account. More recent research has used a variety of measures to take account of differences in pupil intake. These include the results of intelligence tests, performance in standard and standardised reading and mathematics tests, and social class indicators. In the United Kingdom, researchers are now starting to use pupils' performance in national Key Stage tests.

When comparing selective and non-selective schools, care must be taken to compare like with like. For example, comprehensives should be compared with grammar and secondary modern together, rather than with grammar schools alone. Given the diverse mix of schools in different LEAs, this can be problematic. Where an authority is fully selective or fully comprehensive in its organisation, no problems arise. However, where an authority has a mix of grammar schools and so-called 'comprehensives', the selective nature of the grammar schools reduces the proportion of more able pupils in the comprehensive schools. In some cases, the proportion of more able pupils may be severely reduced, making the intake to comprehensive schools more similar to secondary modern schools. The issue of intake is an important one and has been examined in great detail by some researchers. This work shows that the intake to comprehensive schools with and without sixth forms may be quite different, with the schools with sixth forms taking more pupils from families with non-manual occupations (Kerckhoff *et al.*, 1996).

Researchers have used a variety of measures to compare pupils' achievement. These include performance in national examinations, such as those taken at the end of compulsory schooling (for example, GCSE and GNVQ), standardised tests in English and mathematics, or curriculum-based assessments, such as those developed for international comparisons. In the United Kingdom, researchers are now using the results of compulsory testing at the end of Key Stages 1, 2 and 3 of schooling, when pupils are aged 7, 11 and 14. The use of different types of test makes it difficult to compare findings from several studies. However, the development of statistical techniques for meta-analysis (Glass *et al.*, 1981) heralded a number of meta-analytic reviews, comparing research using different measures (for example, Kulik, 1991; Kulik and Kulik, 1982a; 1984; 1992; Lou *et al.*, 1996; Slavin, 1987a, 1990a).

The categorisation of ability grouping is a particular difficulty. As mentioned above, a secondary school in an area with several grammar schools may be called comprehensive, but its intake will not include the full range of ability as the most able children will have been 'creamed off' into the grammar schools. Arguably the comprehensive schools in such areas should be classified as secondary modern schools. Similarly, researchers have difficulty classifying the grouping arrangements within a school, when there may be several different types of grouping operating in the schools at any one time. For example, some schools have banding with mixed ability grouping for pupils in the first year, introduce setting in some subjects in the second year and move to setting for all academic subjects in the fourth year.

Bearing these issues in mind, we now turn to the research to try and establish whether selection and ability grouping raises overall attainment and whether it benefits particular groups of pupils at the expense of others. First we examine research on selective schooling, before considering ability grouping in primary and in secondary schools.

Does selection raise attainment?

Given the passions that are aroused whenever there is a debate about the continuation of grammar schools, there is surprisingly limited research comparing the performance of pupils in selective and non-selective school systems in England and Wales (Crook, Power and Whitty, 1999). The existing research is of two types. The first compares selective and unselective systems, with the unit of analysis being the local education authority. A number of studies compare the attainment of pupils in national tests and examinations in selective and non-selective local education authorities. The second type of research comprises studies comparing selective and non-selective schools.

Comparing selective and unselective systems

Research undertaken by the National Council for Education Standards (Marks, Cox and Pomian-Srzednicki, 1983, 1985) compares selective and unselective systems on the basis of nationally compiled data on pupils' performance in tests and examinations. Using data on the number of 'O' level examination passes per pupil in 54 English authorities, they found that the selective system produced better examination results than the comprehensive system. It is important to note that they only obtained data on the proportion of pupils in low social classes, not their attainment on entry to secondary school. This information was used to form three groups of LEA, which were then assumed to be homogeneous. In addition, in the first study (1983) they did not utilise information on the proportion of pupils in high social classes (Gray, Jesson and Jones, 1984). Furthermore, the sample of LEAs is not representative, as it includes all the selective authorities but less than one-third of fully comprehensive authorities. Bearing this in mind, their analysis demonstrates a large difference between selective and comprehensive systems, with pupils in selective systems obtaining 30–40% more passes in the examinations. In response to criticisms of their earlier study, Marks and his colleagues (1985) included a measure of high social class in a similar analysis and confirmed the findings of their previous research. They demonstrated better examination results for pupils in selective authorities. Of particular note is the finding that pupils in secondary modern schools obtained good results in mathematics and English. As with their previous research, however, this study did not include information on pupil attainment on entry to secondary school. It therefore suffers from many of the weaknesses discussed by Gray, Jesson and Jones (1984), who demonstrated that when prior attainment and social class were taken into account, differences in examination performance in selective and unselective systems disappeared.

Marks (1991) compared trends in 'O' and 'A' level results in Northern Ireland, England and Wales. In England and Wales in the 1970s, when many schools became comprehensive, there was a plateau, whereas in Northern Ireland, where selection continued, examination results continued to improve. This is interpreted as demonstrating that selective schooling improves examination attainment. The explanation may be more complex, however, relating to the disruption in schools during the process of change in England and Wales. The impact of this reorganisation is well illustrated in the study of Treliw, referred to below (Reynolds, Sullivan and Murgatroyd, 1987). Recent figures (1995/6) while indicating high levels of attainment in Protestant grammar schools in Northern Ireland (91% of pupils obtaining five or more GCSEs at grades A–C), showed very low levels (27%) for those attending secondary schools (TES, 1996).

Recent comparisons, drawing on figures from local education authorities where selective education continues, demonstrate that the performance of pupils in grammar schools is not always as good as it should be. In some grammar schools, up to a fifth of pupils do not achieve five GCSE grades A–C (Scheerens, Nanninga and Pellgrum 1989). Very little research comparing examination performance in selective and non-selective authorities has included measures of pupil attainment on entry to secondary school. Recently, however, a 'value added' analysis has been undertaken by Jesson (2000) to evaluate the performance of selective and non-selective systems in England. He identifies 15 'selective' LEAs, which have substantial proportions of pupils in selective schools, and compares these with 134 'non-selective' LEAs. Selective and non-selective LEAs are compared in terms of the school average GCSE/GNVQ points per pupil, taking account of school average Key Stage 3 levels. The multilevel analysis yields standardised residuals both for schools and for LEAs. These enable a comparison of LEAs in terms of the Benchmark framework (SCAA, 1994), which takes account of the particular mix of school types in the LEAs. This comparison reveals the 10 top and bottom ranked LEAs. It demonstrates that none of the top 10 LEAs were fully 'selective', although two in the list had retained some selection (less than 10% of the age cohort was in grammar schools). Four selective authorities and one county LEA, which had retained very limited selection, appeared in the list of the bottom 10 authorities. Jesson concluded that none of the evidence presented supported the view that selective 'systems' provided better outcomes than those with fully comprehensive organisation. He argued that value added performance evaluations should be used in future.

Overall, there appears to be little difference between selective and unselective systems in terms of pupil attainment in national tests and examinations, once intake factors have been taken into account. The research discussed above is based on comparisons between local education authorities. We turn next to research that has taken pupils or schools as the basis for the analysis.

Comparing pupil attainment in different types of school

Several longitudinal studies use data on a cohort of students from the National Child Development Study (Fogelman, Essen and Tibbenham, 1978; Fogelman, 1983; Kerckhoff *et al.*, 1996; Steedman, 1980, 1983). The cohort includes all those born during one week in March 1958. Information was collected from members of the cohort, their parents and the schools they attended when they were 7, 11 and 16 years old. When the members of the cohort were 20 years old, the schools retrospectively provided information about their performance in school examinations. Interviews were conducted with members of the cohort when they were 23 years old. The cohort passed through the secondary school system during the 1970s, a period of rapid change, and they attended grammar, secondary modern and comprehensive schools. A very rich set of data is available on this cohort and the schools they attended, so we have had to be highly selective in the findings we report here, confining ourselves to the main question posed in this section, whether selection raises attainment. We will refer to these studies again in the next section when we consider whether ability grouping within schools influences attainment.

Using data on the cohort referred to above, Steedman (1980, 1983) compared the attainment of children in different types of school. The children were tested and schools were questioned, so that a wide range of information was obtained on the characteristics of the sample at age 11, on entry to three different types of school, grammar, secondary modern and comprehensive. Information on a wide range of academic and social outcomes was also collected at age 16, when the sample left school. Steedman was careful to exclude schools that had recently been established as comprehensives, recognising that schools undergoing reorganisation would be at a disadvantage compared to well-established selective schools. The research showed that the intake of pupils to the comprehensive schools was very similar to that for the secondary modern schools. After controlling statistically for differences in attainment and social composition on intake, there was little difference in the performance of the selective and comprehensive systems. Very able pupils performed equally well in mathematics and reading comprehension. Pupils in the comprehensive schools were more likely to want to stay on at school. Overall, this study demonstrates very little difference between the selective and non-selective schools. Steedman (1983) later obtained information on the pupils' performance in public examinations. The findings presented a very similar picture, with little to choose between the comprehensive and selective systems. An important point made by Steedman, and illustrated through a series of analyses, is that the raw examination results give a very different picture, with pupils in the grammar schools obtaining more passes than those in the secondary modern and comprehensive schools. However, these differences disappear when pupil intake is taken into account.

Research undertaken in Scotland (Gray, McPherson and Raffe, 1983) utilises information from a survey of 40% of 1975–76 school-leavers in four of the nine regions of Scotland. Information was collected on pupils' social class but no measures of ability or prior achievements were available. Detailed information on school structures and local catchment areas was used to classify schools as belonging to selective or unselective sectors. Schools designated as comprehensive that were situated close to selective schools, and therefore deprived of their complement of more able pupils, were classified as belonging to the selective sector. When the achievements of the pupils in the two types of school were compared, little difference was found between pupil attainment in the selective and unselective sectors, although the average performance of pupils in the unselective sector was slightly higher. The authors identified the democratic, community tradition of Scottish schooling as a major force behind the success of the comprehensive education. The lack of any measures of ability or prior attainment and the classification of schools were subsequently questioned by Marks and Cox (1984).

Two further studies examined the performance of children in different types of school. The first used data from the London schools included in the 'Fifteen Thousand Hours' research (Maughan and Rutter, 1987; Rutter *et al.*, 1979). Pupils in selective and non-selective systems were compared, controlling statistically for differences in intake. They found that reading scores at age 14 were significantly higher in the grammar school sample and that examination results, measured in terms of 'points' scored for CSE and O levels, were also better. The difference in examination points was due in part to the fact that the selective schools entered more of their pupils for the examinations. When the higher entry rates were taken into account, by calculating points per entry, the difference between the two types of school was reduced but not eliminated.

The second study compared selective and non-selective schools in Treliw, in South Wales (Reynolds, Sullivan and Murgatroyd, 1987). This area underwent a partial reorganisation of its secondary schools during the 1970s, with two-thirds of pupils reorganised into comprehensive schools and one-third remaining in a selective system of grammar and secondary modern schools. The study provides an interesting account of the difficulties encountered when schools with different status and ethos amalgamate. It also compared the performance of pupils in the two systems. The area was unusual in being relatively homogeneous, so that the pupils entering the two systems were similar in socio-economic background. In addition, the researchers obtained reading, mathematics and intelligence test data for the pupils on intake. There were small differences in favour of the pupils in the selective system on entry, but none of these were statistically significant. When the pupils were in the fourth year they took a test of verbal ability and the results of national examinations were collected the following year. Pupils in the selective system outperformed those in the comprehensive schools in national examinations and the authors found that this difference was particularly marked among pupils in the middle ability range, who would have been in the top streams of the secondary modern schools. The authors argue that the relatively poor performance of pupils in the comprehensives was attributable to within-school factors. These included the difficulties encountered during the amalgamation of the grammar and secondary modern schools to form the new comprehensives and the lack of agreed policies. The headteachers of the new schools had been heads of grammar schools, the majority of heads of department were staff from the grammar schools, while staff from the secondary modern schools were allocated to teaching the lower streams. In effect the new schools had followed the ethos and organisation of grammar schools, resulting in a progressive alienation of pupils in the bottom streams.

The evidence from research based on samples of pupils and schools is very mixed. In some studies there is evidence that selective schooling benefits certain groups of pupils, but the effects are not consistent. Research comparing selective and unselective systems on the basis of examination results alone paints a different picture from research that controls for differences in intake. Greater weight should be given to the research that takes account of intake factors in the analysis, particularly prior attainment and social class indicators, as these are powerful predictors of later attainment. When this is done, the differences between unselective and selective systems are reduced and in some cases disappear. The lack of a consistent pattern of findings suggests that other, uncontrolled factors influence pupil attainment. Features of the local context influence the findings and these features vary from one piece of research to the next. Within-school factors arising from the amalgamation of schools or aspects of the local context of the school may have an impact on pupil attainment.

There is a tendency for selective systems to widen the spread of attainment, to the benefit of the more able pupils but to the disadvantage of the less able, who are left further behind. Unselective systems tend to reduce the spread of attainment, allowing the less able to gain ground (Kerckhoff, *et al.*, 1996). Selective systems affect students' opportunity to learn, by denying some students access to parts of the curriculum. In a review of research examining the relationship between opportunity to learn and student achievement, Lughart *et al.*, (1989) demonstrate the importance of selective systems in accounting for variation in academic achievement between countries, schools and in the classroom. Selective and unselective systems may also affect status hierarchies, thus influencing the position of particular groups of pupils within schools, with the high status groups performing better.

Does ability grouping in schools raise attainment?

As with the issue of selective systems, there are two main questions of interest when we consider whether ability grouping within schools has an impact on pupil attainment. The first is whether it raises the attainment of all pupils and the second is whether it raises the attainment of particular groups of pupils at the expense of others. On both these questions the evidence is mixed, but as a whole, the picture from the research is that ability grouping has little or no effect on average attainment. The impact on particular groups is variable and influenced by a wide range of local factors, making it difficult to draw any firm conclusions. However, more rigid grouping such as streaming disadvantages pupils in the lower groups.

Ability grouping in primary schools

As indicated in Chapter 1, streaming was used in the majority of large primary schools until the 1950s, but was largely phased out following the demise of the 11-plus examination. During the 1960s and 1970s several research studies were completed, demonstrating that streaming had little impact on attainment. The most comprehensive research study in England and Wales was by Barker Lunn (1970), who compared the achievement gains of students in 36 streamed and 36 unstreamed junior schools matched on social class. There were no meaningful differences in achievement between the pupils in the streamed and unstreamed schools. The size and quality of this study provides particularly strong evidence that ability grouping is not by itself a major factor affecting achievement at primary level. Similar findings were reported by Daniels (1961b) who compared achievement in streamed and unstreamed schools over a four-year period. He concluded that lower ability pupils made better progress in unstreamed schools, while the higher ability pupils were not held back. Blandford (1958) found a greater spread of achievement in streamed schools, with the higher ability pupils performing better but the lower ability pupils performing worse. Lower ability children performed better in unstreamed schools. Douglas (1964) examined the progress through primary school of 5,000 pupils born in 1946. Children in the lower streams made much less progress relative to those in the top stream. Several of the studies referred to above also found very little movement of pupils between streams. The research demonstrated that middle class children occupied the top stream while the working class children populated the middle and lower streams. These findings were influential in the destreaming of primary schools.

Slavin (1987a) reviewed the international research using a 'best-evidence synthesis', which combined meta-analysis (Glass *et al.*, 1981) with traditional narrative reviews. He was careful to select research meeting five criteria, as follows:

- the research compared ability grouped classes to heterogeneous classes;
- achievement data from standardised tests or teacher-made tests were presented;

- samples were initially comparable, either through random assignment or through the use of matching procedures;
- ability grouping had been in place for at least a semester; and
- at least three ability-grouped and three control classes were involved.

Slavin concluded that across the 14 elementary studies he reviewed (which included the Barker Lunn study referred to above), the effects of ability grouping were essentially zero. Among the American studies, one by Goldberg *et al.* (1966) stands out as providing particularly strong evidence. This involved 86 Grade 5 classes in New York elementary schools. Pupils were assigned to classes on the basis of IQ scores according to 15 different grouping patterns that varied in homogeneity. They remained in those classes for two years. Most comparisons of achievement showed no difference according to the type of grouping and, where there were differences, it was the pupils in the more heterogeneous groupings that performed better than those in homogeneous classes.

In the United Kingdom, primary teachers implement a variety of grouping strategies in the classroom. They will be considered in more detail in Chapter 7. Within class ability grouping is widely utilised, particularly by schools that are too small to implement setting or streaming. Some schools group pupils from more than one year group or age group to enable regrouping. In the United Kingdom, the recent introduction of literacy and numeracy hours as part of the National Literacy Strategy has been accompanied by recommendations to group pupils by ability in these areas of the curriculum for certain activities. Some teachers group pupils by ability within the classroom for most of the day.

Meta-analyses of the research on within class ability grouping (Lou *et al.*, 1996) and cross-age grouping (Kulik and Kulik, 1992) in primary schools indicate that, when implemented appropriately, they can lead to positive academic effects. Cross-grade grouping can produce positive effects on achievement when it is used for targeted teaching. For example, the Joplin plan is a system of teaching reading in which children in several year groups are regrouped for reading instruction according to their attainment in reading. Kulik and Kulik (1992) reviewed 14 studies in which children were formed into cross-age groups on the basis of their attainment in a particular subject, typically reading. The overall effects on attainment were positive.

The research on ability grouping in primary schools suggests that whereas streaming does not provide gains in attainment overall, other types of grouping have positive academic effects. In particular, groupings that are formed to enable teachers to target specific aspects of the curriculum can raise attainment, providing they are implemented appropriately.

Ability grouping in secondary schools

Research on streaming in secondary schools indicates that it tends to widen the spread of attainment by slowing the progress of the lower ability groups. Early evidence that streaming had a negative impact on pupils in the lower groups was provided by several small-scale studies, based in single schools. Newbold (1977) compared the attainment of pupils in a single comprehensive school with mixed ability and streamed 'halls'. Although the mean scores of pupils were similar for a variety of measures of achievement including standardised tests of ability, examination performance and teacher-devised tests, there were larger standard deviations in the streamed sample, indicating that streaming tended to widen the range of attainment. More differences were reported within the two systems than between them. There was no evidence that high ability pupils were performing differently in the two systems, although the low ability pupils made significant gains in the mixed ability classes. A follow-up study (Postlethwaite and Denton, 1978) demonstrated better overall performance by the less able pupils in the mixed ability situation, without any reduction in the levels of attainment achieved by the more able.

Gregory (1984), in a review of research comparing streaming, setting and mixed ability grouping in secondary schools, noted several contradictory findings. He concluded that the most pervasive finding was the risk of lowered teacher expectations for pupils in low sets and streams. Lacey (1970) also found that pupils in the top group received more attention and resources, leading to higher levels of achievement, and that this had negative effects on children in the lower groups. His research was undertaken in a selective grammar school in which pupils were streamed. In addition, a follow-up study, after the school had introduced mixed ability grouping, showed that the attainment of the most able pupils was unaffected by the change, whereas the attainment of the less able pupils improved (Lacey, 1974). The ability range of the pupils in this study was clearly restricted by the selective nature of the intake to the grammar school.

A longitudinal study referred to in the previous section, using data from the National Child Development Study, compared attainment in reading and mathematics of children in a variety of selective and un-selective schools with streaming, setting and mixed ability grouping (Fogelman, Essen and Tibbenham, 1978; Fogelman, 1983). The type of ability grouping within the schools had little effect on attainment. There were, however, differences in the patterns of entry in national examinations from comprehensive schools, with a higher proportion of lower attaining pupils being entered for national examinations in schools with mixed ability grouping.

A second longitudinal study by Kerckhoff (1986) was based on data collected at ages 7, 11 and 16. Standardised tests of reading and math-ematics were used in addition to verbal and non-verbal scores from a general ability test administered at age 11. The cohort attended four kinds of secondary school: secondary modern, grammar, comprehen-sive and private. Background information collected on the pupils included social class and parental education. Overall, the findings indicated that, between the ages of 11 and 16, ability grouping within schools tends to increase the gap between the higher and lower abil-ity groups. This trend was evident in both mathematics and reading, with pupils in remedial classes losing a great deal of ground, while those in high ability groups increased their average performance. Kerckhoff concluded that there were positive effects of ability group-ing on academic achievement. His research is often cited in the American literature as demonstrating clear, positive effects of ability grouping on academic achievement. His analysis has been criticised by Slavin (1990a), however, on the grounds that there were signifi-cant pre-test differences between pupils in the different types of school that could not be sufficiently controlled by the use of covari-ance techniques. Slavin also claimed that the standardised gains made by the lower ability students were actually greater than those of the high ability group. Kerckhoff himself acknowledged some methodological difficulties in the tests, indicating that there were floor and ceiling effects which would serve to reduce and distort the size of the effects.

Meta-analyses of the research in secondary schools indicate that ability grouping has little or no effect on pupil attainment (Kulik and Kulik, 1992; Slavin, 1990a; Veenman, 1995). Slavin followed the method of 'best-evidence synthesis' used in his previous meta-analy-sis of research in primary schools (Slavin, 1987a). He concluded that across the 29 secondary studies he reviewed, the effects of ability grouping were essentially zero. Most of the secondary school research involved pupils in years 7 to 9. Kulik and Kulik (1992) considered tracking across primary and secondary level and examined research on five distinct programmes described as multilevel classes, cross-age grouping, within-class grouping, enriched classes and accelerated classes. Their findings with regard to cross-grade grouping were discussed above, in relation to primary school grouping. Their meta-analysis also showed positive effects on attainment of enriched classes for children identified as gifted and talented. They concluded that the clearest effects on achievement are obtained in programmes that involve the greatest curriculum adjustment. Generally the higher ability groups benefit, but there do not appear to be negative effects on the achievement levels of the middle and low groups. On the other hand, a meta-analysis of multi-age classes (Veenman, 1995) finds no effects on academic achievement.

The impact of streaming appears more clear-cut than the impact of other forms of ability grouping. Streaming clearly disadvantages pupils in the lower streams, who make better progress in mixed ability groups. It is not yet clear whether other, more flexible, forms of grouping have a similar effect. This is in part because far less research has been undertaken on setting, within-class grouping and other forms of grouping.

Setting (regrouping) in the secondary school

Recent research in the United Kingdom has investigated the effects of setting on attainment. In response to the renewed interest in ability grouping during the 1980s and 1990s, several studies of setting in secondary schools were completed. In 1997, the Ability Grouping in Secondary Schools project was set up to examine the effects of ability grouping on the attainment of Year 9 pupils in English, mathematics and science (Ireson, Mortimore and Hallam, 1999). Given the concerns about the effects of streaming on the social and personal outcomes for pupils, such as their self-esteem and attitudes towards school (which will be discussed in Chapter 3), the research aimed to explore the effects of ability grouping on both academic and non-academic outcomes. It also aimed to provide information on teachers' attitudes and their classroom practice with different types of group and on school practices in allocating pupils to groups, moving them between groups and allocating resources to groups. In this chapter we will provide an overview of the project and the main findings related to pupil attainment. In later chapters we will discuss our findings related to the non-academic outcomes for pupils, teachers' attitudes and classroom practice and to the organisation and ethos of the schools.

The schools

This project provided an analysis of pupils' attainments at the end of Key Stage 3 (year 9), taking account of their attainment at the end of primary school (year 6). A stratified sample of 45 mixed secondary comprehensive schools was selected for the study, representing a range of grouping practices, intake and location. The schools were spread geographically from London and the southern counties of England to East Anglia and South Yorkshire.

The schools were selected to provide a range of ability grouping in the lower school, from completely mixed ability through years 7 to 9, to mainly ability grouping. The sample comprised three levels of ability grouping in the lower secondary school (years 7 to 9), with 15 schools in each level:

'Mixed ability schools' predominantly mixed ability classes for all subjects, with setting in no more than two subjects in year 9.

'Partially set schools' setting in no more than two subjects in year 7, increasing to a maximum of 4 subjects in year 9.

'Set schools' streaming, banding or setting in at least four subjects from year 7.

We checked whether the schools had been inspected during the three years before the start of the project. There were two reasons for doing this. First, we wanted to avoid the risk of including schools that might be inspected during the project as this would put undue pressure on the schools and increase the chance that they would withdraw from the project. Second, schools with unfavourable inspection reports, especially those under special measures, experience an aftermath of activity, which would be difficult to account for in the analysis and might also increase the risk of withdrawal from the project or reduce the availability of the data.

We then took care to balance the three groups of schools in terms of their size and the social mix of their intake, using free school meals as an indicator of social deprivation. The mean number of pupils on roll and mean percentages of pupils eligible for free school meals are displayed in Table 2.1. These figures indicate that the mixed ability schools had a slightly more socially deprived intake than the set and partially set schools. On average, the set schools were slightly smaller than the other two groups. The schools were sufficiently similar for the analysis.

Table 2.1: Size of school and percentage of pupils eligible for free school meals

	Type of school					
	Mixed ability		Partially set		Set	
Mean number and *standard deviation* of pupils on roll	969	212.2	994	212.6	868	181.2
Mean percentage and *standard deviation* of pupils eligible for free school meals	16.3	14.95	13.2	13.99	14.1	12.7

Within the schools, the cohort of year 9 pupils (totalling over 6,000) participated in the research. We collected the results of the Key Stage 3 tests in English, mathematics and science taken during the summer term, when the majority of pupils were aged 14. We also collected the results of the Key Stage 2 tests, taken when the pupils were in year 6, the final year of primary school. We collected these from the secondary school records or, where necessary, from the pupils' primary schools. The secondary schools provided us with information on the pupils' gender, ethnic origin, attendance and whether pupils were eligible for free school meals. Detailed information about the setting arrangements in year 9 was collected from interviews with school managers and from heads of department.

Analysing the data

For each of the English, mathematics and science tests at Key Stage 3, there were 'main tier' tests taken by all pupils and an 'extension' test taken by high attaining pupils. We decided to use only the scores from the main tests as the probability of a pupil taking the extension test was not strongly related to their score on the main test. For English, there was just a single main test and the observed distribution, which was roughly symmetrical, was transformed to a standard Normal distribution for all statistical analyses. For mathematics and science, however, there was more than one test (four for mathematics and two for science), and pupils took just one of these depending on which level their teachers thought they had reached. (There are 10 levels that span the ages of compulsory schooling.) Consequently, it was necessary to construct a single scale for mathematics and science which combined scores from tests at different tiers, and this had to be done in the absence of any published calibration.

The numbers of pupils for whom both Key Stage 2 and 3 results were available were 4,480 in English, 4,337 in mathematics and 4,499 in science. Some schools were unable to provide all the results and a slightly higher proportion of data was available for pupils in the partially set schools, in each subject. Key Stage 2 data were available for approximately 65% of pupils in the partially set schools and for approximately 59% of pupils in the mixed ability and set schools.

The level of setting in each subject varied, with some schools adopting rigorous setting from year 7, while others retained mixed ability grouping or used broad ability groups. We constructed a five-point scale to indicate the amount of setting experienced by each pupil in each subject during years 7, 8 and 9. The five levels of setting are shown in Table 2.2, which also shows the amount of setting in each subject in the 45 schools. As can be seen from the table, the majority of schools taught English in mixed ability classes throughout the lower school. Setting was much more common in mathematics, with science in between. In year 9, some schools adopted rigorous grouping across the year group or timetable halves, whereas others adopted broader types of ability grouping such as parallel sets. A scale point was added if the setting in year 9 was rigorous.

Table 2.2: Strength of setting in English, mathematics and science

		English	Mathematics	Science
0	Mixed ability in years 7–9	20	5	11
1	Set in year 9 only	4	3	5
2	Set in years 8 and 9	6	7	13
3	Set in years 7–9, year 9 broadly set	3	1	2
4	Set in years 7–9, year 9 rigorously set	12	29	14

For mathematics, it can be seen from Table 2.2 that the majority of schools adopted rigorous setting. The partially set schools were more similar to the set schools, with all the set schools and 11 of the partially set schools scoring 3 or 4 on the setting scale. Only 8 of the 15 mixed ability schools scored 0 or 1 on the scale. As only one school scored 3, the scale was collapsed into four levels for mathematics.

There was much less setting in English. All 15 of the mixed ability schools and 9 of the 15 partially set schools scored 0 or 1 on the 5-point scale, while 14 of the 15 set schools scored 3 or 4. In science, 14 of the 15 mixed ability schools scored 0 or 1, 10 of the 15 partially set schools scored 2, and 13 of the 15 set schools scored 3 or 4.

The multilevel analysis takes account of variation in the data at several levels simultaneously. Our model had two levels, the pupil level and school level, so standard multilevel models for continuous responses measured at two levels were used in the analysis. The amount of setting experienced by the pupils in each subject was the explanatory variable of most interest. Each curriculum subject was analysed in turn and, in each analysis, corresponding Key Stage 2 levels were used to control for intake differences, and hence for any differences between the schools. Gender, social disadvantage (indicated by eligibility for free school meals) and attendance were entered into the models as additional explanatory variables. Further details of the analyses are available in Ireson *et al.* (in press).

Setting and attainment

We first analysed the effects on attainment at Key Stage 3 of gender, social deprivation, attendance and attainment at Key Stage 2. These analyses revealed that for English, mathematics and science:

- pupils who do well at the end of Key Stage 2 do better on the Key Stage 3 tests;
- pupils eligible for free school meals make less progress between Key Stages 2 and 3 than those not eligible;
- pupils' progress is related to their attendance;
- girls make more progress than boys in English and this is particularly the case for the pupils with lower attainment at Key Stage 2;
- boys make a little more progress than girls in mathematics and science.

Using the setting scale, we then analysed the data for each subject in turn to see if the extent of setting influenced attainment, taking account of attainment at Key Stage 2, social deprivation (free school meals), attendance and gender. The main findings from these analyses are displayed in Table 2.3.

Progress in English and science was not related to setting. For mathematics, the lower attaining pupils at the end of Key Stage 2 made more progress in schools with more mixed ability grouping, whereas

Table 2.3: Effects of setting on attainment: Estimates (standard errors) by curriculum subject

			English	Mathematics	Science
Fixed effects		KS2 Level [1]	0.79 (0.032)	0.73 (0.017)	0.73 (0.029)
		Gender [2]	0.27 (0.031)	−0.081 (0.022)	−0.087 (0.025)
		KS2*Gender	−0.073 (0.032)	p >0.08	p >0.5
		FSM [3]	−0.18 (0.041)	−0.14 (0.037)	−0.16 (0.04)
		Attendance	0.014 (0.002)	0.010 (0.002)	0.014 (0.002)
		Strength of Setting [4]	0.03 (0.027)	0.061 (0.029)	−0.005 (0.028)
		KS2* Strength of setting	p >0.17	0.061 (0.015)	p > 0.14
Random Effects	**School**	Intercept	0.091 (0.024)	0.025 (0.008)	0.048 (0.015)
		KS2	0.017 (0.007)	0.0028 (0.0019)	0.019 (0.007)
		Covariance	−0.015 (0.010)	0.0044 (0.0028)	−0.011 (0.008)
	Pupil	Intercept	0.51 (0.012)	0.41 (0.010)	0.54 (0.013)
Sample size			3514	3481	3542

Notes:
n.s. not statistically significant at the 0.05 level
(1) mean is zero
(2) boys are baseline group
(3) not eligible for free school meals is baseline
(4) scale values 3 and 4 combined for mathematics

the higher attaining pupils made better progress in schools with more setting. The difference for pupils at level 1 at Key Stage 2 (low attainers) between the least and most set schools was 0.12 standard deviation units. The difference for pupils at level 5 at Key Stage 2 was 0.36 standard deviation units. This indicates that the higher attaining pupils gained more substantially by being in sets than the lower attaining pupils gained by being in mixed ability classes.

These analyses indicate that setting influences pupils' progress in mathematics but not in English or science. In mathematics, the pupils attaining higher levels at the end of primary school make greater progress in sets, whereas pupils whose attainment is low at the end of primary school make more progress in mixed ability classes. For English and science, our findings are consistent with previous research showing little or no effect of ability grouping on attainment. Our analysis adds to previous research in showing that there are differences according to curriculum subject. Attainment in mathematics is influenced by ability grouping, whereas attainment in science and English is not. This conflicts with some of the earlier findings reported above, which do not find different effects on attainment in standardised reading comprehension and mathematics tests (Kerckhoff, 1986; Steedman, 1980). Of the 29 studies considered by Slavin in his review (Slavin, 1990a), 12 report effect sizes for both English and mathematics. Of these, 10 show similar effects for the two subjects, with overall no effect of ability grouping on attainment.

Discussion of our findings

It is possible that the National Curriculum and related assessments have contributed to our findings, specifically the impact of tiered assessments in mathematics. The Key Stage tests may encourage greater differentiation of the curriculum in mathematics than in English or science. At the time of the research, pupils were entered for one of four tests in mathematics, whereas in science there were two tests and in English only one. In the later years of the secondary school, there is further differentiation of work for pupils in higher and lower sets. In years 10 and 11, the curriculum followed by pupils in the lower sets covers different content, designed to enable them to enter for the lower tiers in national examinations (GCSE), whereas pupils in the top sets are prepared for the higher grades. Tiered papers at GCSE have been in place for many years. Pupils entered for the higher paper may obtain grades A to C, those entered for the intermediate paper grades C to E and those entered for the foundation paper obtain grades E to G. Although assessments in English and science are now tiered, these papers have been introduced quite recently so their full impact may not yet have been felt. The more differentiated curriculum may contribute to the greater impact of ability grouping on attainment, leading to a greater spread of attainment (Askew and Wiliam, 1998; Kulik and Kulik, 1982a, 1992). The effect of tiered examinations is to restrict the curriculum offered to pupils entered for the lower papers while allowing coverage of more advanced work in higher tiers.

Several other factors may mediate the impact of ability grouping on attainment. One possibility is that teachers use different teaching methods with mixed ability groups and classes grouped by ability. The impact of ability grouping may be mediated through changes in teachers' classroom methods and practices with groups differing in ability. This is an issue we will take up in Chapter 5. At this point we simply note that teachers in the project schools indicated that the ability composition of classes influences their classroom practice. In mixed ability classes, pupils of all abilities have similar access to the curriculum, participate in the same activities and are taught in the same ways. In classes grouped by ability, lower ability classes have less access to the curriculum and are taught in more structured ways, with more repetition, less discussion and greater use of practical activities.

This information, collected from questionnaires, tells us about teachers' expectations and beliefs and we are aware that teacher reports may not be an accurate account of actual classroom practice. However, we are able to compare the reported practices of teachers who teach both mixed ability classes and sets. This analysis provides further evidence that teachers do alter their practice with groups of differing ability composition. In addition, observational studies of classroom teaching in mathematics and science tend to substantiate this account (for example, Ball, 1981). Hacker and Rowe (1993) found that science teachers altered their pedagogy when they moved from sets to mixed ability classes. With mixed ability classes, teachers provided a greater variety of activities and more differentiated work, whereas they tended to use more whole class instruction with sets. Similarly, Boaler (1997c; Boaler, Wiliam and Brown, 2000) found that in mathematics, teachers took little account of the differences between pupils in sets, treating them as though there were identical in ability. All pupils were given the same tasks and were required to complete them at the same speed. It seems that teachers' expectations are influenced by the formation of ability groups and that they alter their teaching methods accordingly. To date, we have been unable to locate any similar research on the influence of ability grouping on teachers' practices in the teaching of English.

Although we had no data on the primary school experiences of our sample, pupils are more likely to have experienced setting in mathematics in their primary schools. Surveys of setting in primary schools indicate that mathematics is the subject most likely to be taught in classes that are set by ability, particularly in years 5 and 6 (Ofsted,

1998a; Hallam et al., 1999). The effects of setting on attainment in mathematics at the end of year 9 may therefore be reflecting a cumulative effect of setting in the primary school. This is particularly likely to be the case if ability groups are relatively fixed, with little movement of pupils between groups. Evidence from earlier research in primary schools (Barker Lunn, 1970) suggests that this is usually the case. As part of our research project, curriculum managers in the 45 secondary schools provided information on the movement of pupils between groups. Most reported that small numbers of pupils moved groups. In some schools, pupils only moved groups after the end-of-year examinations (see Chapter 7). Placement of pupils in ability groups in primary school with little prospect of movement may therefore add to the progressive differentiation between pupils' attainments in the secondary school.

Some recent studies have linked classroom pedagogy with the attainments of pupils in schools with different ability grouping arrangements. Boaler (1997a, 1997b) studied mathematics teaching in two secondary schools over a three-year period. In one school, pupils were taught in mixed ability classes and in the other school they were taught in sets. The pupils in the mixed ability classes obtained significantly more GCSE grades A–G than those in sets. Another small-scale study in one secondary school also found that a change from sets to mixed ability teaching in science improved examination results (Reay, 1998). Likewise, Cross (1988) reports that the pupils in lower sets in a grammar school performed well below expectation in French. Their scores were comparable with the lower sets in the comprehensive school.

Summary

The weight of evidence from research on both selective schooling and ability grouping within schools indicates that they have rather little impact on overall attainment. Although analyses of school examination results suggest that pupils in some schools perform particularly well, this is very often due to the intake. A school that is able to select pupils by ability should, after all, be high in any league table of examination results. It is essential when making comparisons between schools to take account of pupil attainment on entry.

It is particularly important to include statistical indicators to control for intake when comparing attainment in English and Welsh schools. With the diversity of arrangements in LEAs, from selective authorities to fully comprehensive, and many variations in between, school intake is highly variable. As we have seen, even so-called comprehensive schools differ markedly, some taking a wide range of ability while others are skewed towards the lower range. This is particularly true of schools without sixth forms, whose intakes may be more similar to the old secondary modern schools.

At the beginning of this chapter and in Chapter 1, we noted that research on ability grouping is fraught with methodological difficulties. In spite of the flaws in different studies, the evidence indicates that selection and ability grouping are not, in themselves, particularly effective ways to raise overall attainment. By increasing the extent of curriculum differentiation, it may be possible to raise the attainment of the higher achieving pupils, but this is likely to be at the expense of the lower achievers. This is a counter-intuitive finding, which runs against the usual argument for ability grouping, which is often couched in terms of its effectiveness in meeting pupils' needs. Logically it should be the best way to raise the attainment of all pupils. So what goes wrong?

The conflicting findings of the research and meta-analyses suggest that ability grouping affects pupil attainment indirectly. It may produce its effects on the lower groups by influencing the teachers' and pupils' expectations of attainment, by affecting the opportunity to learn, by influencing pedagogy with groups of differing ability and by offering differential access to resources. We will explore some of these possible explanations in later chapters of this book. Before doing so, we turn to research on the effects of ability grouping on other educational outcomes for pupils.

3

Does Ability Grouping Affect Pupils' Self-image?

Concern about the impact of streaming on pupils' views of themselves was a factor contributing to the demise of ability grouping in schools during the twentieth century. This concern was fuelled by research indicating that streaming had an adverse impact on the self-esteem of pupils in the lower groups. Researchers also found that at secondary level, streaming and tracking can lead to anti-school attitudes and alienation from school. Early British research indicated that primary school children's social adjustment and academic self-image were adversely affected by streaming. In this chapter we will first review the research on the nature and development of the self-concept and on the impact of ability grouping on pupils' self-image. We will then present findings from recent research on the impact of setting on pupils' academic self-concept and self-esteem. This work indicates that the extent of setting in a school has an impact on pupils' self-esteem. It also shows that setting affects pupils' academic self-perceptions in relation to specific curriculum subjects, but that these effects are not uniform. We discuss these findings in relation to differences in the salience of assessment in different subjects and in relation to the ethos that accompanies extensive use of structured ability grouping. In the final part of the chapter we present recent findings on pupils' views about school and the extent to which they experience teasing in school.

Ability grouping and its impact on pupils' self-perceptions

One of the concerns of those who argue against grouping by ability is that placement in the bottom groups has an adverse impact on pupils' self-esteem, self-concept and their attitudes towards school and schoolwork (Gamoran and Berends, 1987; Lacey, 1974; Oakes, 1985). Oakes (1985) argued that for low track students the self-concept becomes more negative as years go by and these students tend to be critical of their ability. On the other hand, Kulik and Kulik (1992) in a meta-analysis of 13 studies found no overall effect of ability grouping on self-esteem. These studies investigated what the authors refer to as XYZ grouping, which includes both streaming and setting. Of the 13 studies, nine examined the effects of streaming. Seven were undertaken in elementary schools and six in junior high schools (middle school or lower secondary school). There was no adjustment of the curriculum to the ability level of the groups. There was no control for teacher and school effects and a variety of measures of self-esteem were used. Perhaps not surprisingly, the overall effect of ability grouping was virtually zero. However, 11 of the 13 studies reported separate effects for high, average and low ability students. They revealed that ability grouping tended to raise the self-esteem scores of lower aptitude students and reduce the self-esteem of higher aptitude students. Streaming and setting may have a levelling effect on self-esteem, with the more able children losing some of their self-assurance when they are placed in classes with children of similar ability.

The differences in these studies may arise in part because many different measures have been used in the research and earlier measures were of questionable reliability and validity. In the next section, we will discuss this issue and turn to research that has used more reliable measures. In addition, the impact of structured ability grouping on self-esteem may be mediated by teachers' attitudes and behaviour (Ireson and Hallam, 1999). Teachers who are committed to ability grouping but teach in mixed ability schools can have an adverse effect on pupils' self-image. Barker Lunn (1970) demonstrated that ability grouping and teachers' attitudes together influence pupils' developing self-image. The strongest effects of streaming on emotional and social development were on the pupils of average and below average ability, who benefited from the non-streamed environment. They also benefited from being taught by teachers who were 'non-streamers', who tended to adopt less formal, more child-centred approaches in their classrooms and to have a greater concern for the all-round development of each pupil. More recent research also provides examples of schools with a strong ethos of meeting the needs of all pupils, where the teachers view students positively and special needs departments provide support for pupils experiencing difficulties in learning. In these schools, both students and teachers talk positively about their experiences (Ireson, 1999; Valli, 1986). Students are encouraged to value diverse cultural backgrounds and to support, rather than exclude and stigmatise, those who have difficulties. It may be that particular school cultures and ethos discourage negative impacts on lower attaining pupils. Strong emphasis on academic success and conformity to strict rules could foster negative attitudes towards those who do not conform. Encouraging a more rounded view of young people could help to encourage more positive attitudes and discourage stereotyping. It is clear that in some schools streaming can have negative effects on pupils in the lower streams. However, it is not clear how general this effect is or how much it is a feature of schools with particular values and ethos.

In our own research we have investigated pupils' views of themselves in schools with a variety of grouping arrangements. At secondary level, we used a measure of self-concept in a questionnaire completed by all year 9 pupils in 45 secondary comprehensive schools. The questionnaire also included items on pupils' views of school and their work in school. In our primary school research we interviewed children in six schools about their experiences of ability grouping and we also asked them about their experiences of teasing. In this chapter we will first report on the findings from the secondary school research and then on the interviews with the primary school children. First, however, we turn to research on the nature and development of the self-concept.

The nature and development of the self-concept

In recent years, considerable progress has been made in understanding the nature and development of the self-concept. In this chapter we will be particularly concerned with the development of academic self-concept and self-esteem. As these are part of the overall development of the self, we will first outline a prevailing model of the structure and overall development of self-concept, before dealing more specifically with academic self-concept in relation to ability grouping.

Much early work measuring the self-concept was based on a view of the self-concept as uni-dimensional. Various scales were designed to measure general self-concept, although much of the research was concerned with students' perceptions of self within an academic context. Findings were inconsistent and conflicting. This was partly due to the fact that the researchers used a variety of measures of self-concept, some of which were of poor reliability. In a review of this work,

Shavelson, Hubner and Stanton (1976) called for construct validation research. Since then there has been considerable work developing and validating measures and models of the self-concept. As a result, the self-concept has been seen increasingly as multi-faceted rather than uni-dimensional.

Marsh and his colleagues have taken up the challenge to develop and validate measures of the various facets of self-concept. Over many years, they have developed a series of Self-Description Questionnaires, which have been widely used in research on students' academic self-concept. These questionnaires contain scales measuring multiple facets of the self-concept (Marsh, 1990). While much of this effort has been directed towards construct validation and testing the structure of the self-concept, some research has explored the relationship between academic attainment and self-concept.

Although there are several models of the self-concept and an enormous research literature, the model that has generated most research on academic self-concept is that developed by Shavelson and his colleagues (Byrne and Shavelson, 1996; Marsh, Byrne and Shavelson, 1988; Shavelson, Hubner and Stanton, 1976). They argue that self-concept represents perceptions of self, derived from self-attributions, interaction with significant others and other experiential aspects of the social environment. The model they propose is multi-dimensional and hierarchical, with global perceptions of self as a person (general self-concept) at the apex and actual behaviour at the base. Working down from the general self-concept, the first split is into two components, academic and non-academic. The academic self-concept then splits into facets for different academic subjects, while the non-academic self-concept splits into physical, social and emotional facets. The academic facets include both descriptive and evaluative aspects of self-perception.

There is much confusion over the terms 'self-concept' and 'self-esteem', which have been used interchangeably in the literature. Self-esteem is thought to be a more limited, evaluative component of the broader self-concept term. However, as yet they have not been definitively identified as separate constructs. Marsh and his colleagues developed their scale for measuring general self-concept from Rosenberg's self-esteem scale (Marsh, 1990) and the scale is often referred to as an indicator of self-esteem. As this is the scale we have used in our own research, we will use the terms 'self-esteem' in place of 'general self-concept'.

The picture regarding the development of self-perceptions is not entirely clear. An early review of the literature (Wylie, 1979) concluded that there was no convincing evidence for developmental change, but in a later review Marsh (1990) found a pattern emerging, with a decrease in self-concept during pre-adolescence and early adolescence possibly followed by a rise in mid-adolescence and early adulthood. The decrease during pre-adolescence is quite well documented, while further evidence is required to establish the rise in late adolescence. Young children's self-perceptions of ability are high but decrease during the primary years (Blatchford, 1997; Nicholls, 1989; Marsh, 1990). There are several possible explanations for this decrease. Nicholls (1989) argued that young children do not differentiate clearly between effort and ability and tend to think that children who try hard are clever. During the primary years, they come to see ability as a normative concept and adopt a culturally defined conception of ability. These conceptions differ between cultures, but in the United States, intelligence is usually thought to be a fixed capacity. Children in primary school begin to see their own ability in this way and to compare their performance with that of others, thus lowering their previously optimistic judgements of their own ability. In addition, Stipek and Daniels (1988) suggest that teachers provide children with more normative feedback, comparing their performance with others in their year group, as they get older and approach transfer to secondary school.

Academic achievement, gender and pupils' self-concepts

It is often assumed that academic achievement and perceptions of self are strongly related. Although this relationship is supported by research evidence, in some cases, the relationships are quite weak. This is especially true of earlier research using measures that were much less valid and reliable than those used in more recent work (Byrne, 1996). More recent work indicates that there are strong relationships between academic attainment and subject-specific self-concept. General measures of self-concept are only weakly correlated with academic attainment, whereas sub-scales of mathematics and verbal self-concept correlate more highly with attainment in these content areas (Marsh, Parker and Barnes, 1985; Marsh and Yeung, 1997). Higher attaining students in mathematics, for example, tend to have higher mathematics self-concepts while higher attaining pupils in English tend to have higher verbal self-concepts.

An important question for educators is whether academic achievement affects self-concept or self-concept affects achievement. Here the evidence is mixed, with some researchers finding that self-concept predicts later achievement and others finding the reverse. Many of the earlier studies used cross-sectional designs, which are not adequate to establish causal direction. Longitudinal studies are necessary to clarify this relationship and, to date, very few have been carried out. Even these arrive at conflicting conclusions, although rather more indicate that the direction of influence is from academic self-concept to academic achievement. It has been suggested that the different measures of academic achievement used in the research may contribute to the discrepant findings, with more association between self-concept and school grades than between self-concept and standardised test scores (Byrne, 1996). It may also be that the relationship between academic self-concept and achievement is reciprocal, with each influencing the other.

There appear to be gender differences in specific aspects of the self-concept. These differences are found among primary school children and during adolescence. Many of the differences counterbalance each other, so that overall gender differences may be small. In a review, Marsh (1990) concluded that there are small differences in favour of males for measures of self-esteem, particularly during early adolescence. Through the late primary years and into secondary school boys tend to view their physical abilities and physical appearance in a more positive light than girls. Differences in academic facets of the self-concept are consistent with sex stereotypes, with boys having higher mathematics self-concepts and girls having higher verbal self-concepts.

Ability grouping and pupils' views of themselves

More recent research using multi-dimensional measures of the self-concept indicate that ability grouping has an impact on pupils' academic self-concepts, but that the impact on general self-perceptions is limited. Byrne (1988) examined the effect of tracking on adolescents' general and academic self-perceptions. She found significantly lower English, mathematics and general academic self-concepts among the lower track students. There were no significant differences between high and low track students' general self-concepts. She suggested that lower track students place more importance on their social and physical competencies and value academic performance less highly. There is a tendency for lower attaining students to have lower self-concepts than their higher attaining peers (Chapman, 1988). Reviewing 21 studies, Chapman found that decrements are apparent by Grade 3. The negative impact of low attainment on academic facets of the self-concept is greater than the impact on general self-concept.

In school, it is argued that students evaluate their academic achievements in relation to those of others. They compare their self-perceptions of their own achievements with the perceived abilities of other students in their frame of reference. A frame of reference is considered to be part of a more general social comparison process. So, students of similar ability who compare themselves with others of high levels of achievement will have lower academic self-concepts than students who compare themselves with others of lower attainment – the Big-Fish-Little-Pond Effect (BFLPE) (Marsh, 1987, 1991; Marsh and Parker, 1984). There is evidence that the average level of attainment in the school may influence pupils' self-concepts, so that pupils in schools with higher average levels of attainment have lower academic self-concepts than pupils of similar ability in schools with lower average attainment (Marsh, 1991; Marsh and Rowe, 1996). The effects appear to be greatest in highly competitive settings and in highly structured settings in which students follow a fixed curriculum and are normatively assessed in relation to common tasks. These situations increase the social comparison processes that may undermine the self-concept (Marsh and Peart, 1988). Social comparison theory would suggest that setting pupils on the basis of their attainment in curriculum subjects would be likely to enhance the salience of the set as the frame of reference. The theory is supported by evidence from Marsh *et al.*, (1995) indicating that pupils who participated in programmes for the gifted and talented experienced a decline in academic self-concept when compared to a matched comparison group. In their review of research, Kulik and Kulik (1982a) reach similar conclusions. However, it is not clear whether similar effects hold for pupils of all attainments.

Self-concept and setting in English secondary schools

As part of our recent research in secondary schools, described in Chapter 2, we examined the relationship between ability grouping and academic self-concept. We used a measure of self-concept adapted from the Marsh Self Description Questionnaire (Marsh, 1990). The SDQ II assesses three areas of academic self-concept, seven areas of non-academic self-concept and a measure of general self-concept developed from the Rosenberg self-esteem scale (Rosenberg, 1979). The general self-concept scale includes self-worth, self-confidence and self-satisfaction in general, not related specifically to school. For the purposes of our research, we used four of the sub-scales from the SDQ II measuring verbal, mathematics, general school self-concept and general self-concept, or 'self-esteem'. In addition, we designed a science self-concept scale, using similar statements to those in the verbal and mathematics sub-scales. Each sub-scale consists of ten statements, presented in a Likert format with respondents being asked to indicate on a six-point scale how true each statement is of them. Options range from true to false. For each sub-scale the possible scores range from a maximum of 60 to a minimum of 10.

As explained in Chapter 2, our sample comprised 45 schools, 15 of which used a substantial amount of setting, 15 that were predominantly mixed ability and 15 partially set. The self-concept scales formed the first part of a questionnaire that was completed by the year 9 pupils during lessons. In most schools the researchers administered the questionnaire during tutor group sessions, but in some schools this was not convenient and another lesson time was chosen. Teachers and researchers assisted any pupils who had difficulties reading the questionnaire. Further information is available in Ireson, Hallam and Plewis (2001).

Marsh's scoring procedures were followed (Marsh, 1990). Where a score was missing for one item of a sub-scale, the mean value from the Marsh manual was inserted. If more than one score for a sub-scale was missing, the data were not included in any further analyses. A total score was calculated for each sub-scale. The reliabilities of the five sub-scales were in the range 0.86 to 0.91, which are very similar to those reported by Marsh. The inter-correlations between the sub-scales are shown in Table 3.1.

Table 3.1: Correlations between the five self-concept sub-scales

	Mathematics	**English**	**Science**	**General school**
English	.11 ** (6622)			
Science	.28** (6623)	.24** (6616)		
General school	.43** (6614)	.55** (6605)	.52** (6610)	
Self-esteem	.40** (6588)	.46** (6582)	.44** (6582)	.80** (6574)

Note: Figures in brackets are the numbers of cases included in each correlation.
  **$p < .01$

Each of the sub-scales correlates significantly with all the others. The lowest correlation is between the mathematics and English facets, which is consistent with previous research. Our science self-concept scale has a moderate correlation with both mathematics and English scales. All three academic facets of the self-concept relate strongly to the measure of general school self-concept, suggesting that pupils' perceptions of themselves in these three aspects of the curriculum form a significant part of the way pupils feel about themselves in school. The strongest relationship is between the general school self-concept and self-esteem sub-scales.

Type of school, school self-concept and self-esteem

We first explored the relationship between the type of school (set, partially set or mixed ability) and pupils' school self-concept and self-esteem, using multilevel modelling. Pupils' level of attainment in the Key Stage 2 tests taken at the end of primary school (year 6) was used to control for differences in the intake to the schools and hence between the three groups of school. Pupils were given a level ranging from 0 to 6 for their attainment in each of the three core curriculum subjects, English, mathematics and science. For the purposes of the analysis a composite score of the levels achieved in the three curriculum subjects (0–16) was used (level 6 was only achieved in mathematics). Gender and social disadvantage (indicated by eligibility for free school meals) were also entered in the model as explanatory variables. Both these analyses were based on 3,199 pupils in 40 schools.

Table 3.2 displays the estimates obtained from multilevel modelling. Further details of the statistical analysis are available in Ireson, Hallam and Plewis (2001). For both self-esteem and general school self-concept we find:

- pupils who do well at the end of Key Stage 2 (year 6) have more positive self-perceptions at the end of Key Stage 3 (year 9);
- boys have more positive self-perceptions than girls;
- pupils from more socially advantaged backgrounds have more positive self-perceptions than those from socially disadvantaged backgrounds.

Taking these factors into account, we then compared general self-concept and self-esteem in the three types of school.

Table 3.2: Estimates (standard errors) by scale

				Self-esteem	General school self-concept
Fixed effects		**Key Stage 2 level**[1]		0.97 (0.09)	1.61 (0.13)
		Gender[2]		-2.35 (0.26)	–1.79 (0.26)
		Free school meals[3]		–0.97 (0.45)	–0.94 (0.46)
		Ability grouping[4]	**Partially set**	1.0 (0.59)	1.40 (0.71)
			Set	–0.48 (0.59)	–0.46 (0.69)
Random effects	**S c h o o l**	**Intercept**		3.50 (1.33)	11.8 (3.32)
		Key Stage 2 level		0.16 (0.07)	0.42 (0.14)
		Covariance		–0.57 (0.28)	–2.05 (0.64)
	P u p i l	**Intercept**		51.5 (1.30)	53.3 (1.35)
Sample size				3199	3199

Notes:
(1) mean is zero
(2) boys are baseline group
(3) not eligible for free school meals is baseline
(4) mixed ability is baseline

The analysis revealed that:
- self-esteem and general school self-concept are higher in the partially set schools than in the set schools;
- general school self-concept is also higher in the partially set schools than in the mixed ability schools.

These analyses support previous research in demonstrating that boys have higher self-esteem than girls in early adolescence. They add to the previous research in demonstrating that socially disadvantaged pupils have lower self-esteem and general school self-concept and that the level of stratification in the school as a whole influences pupil self-esteem and general school self-concept. Overall, the schools with partial setting appear to foster higher self-esteem and general school self-concept than schools with more setting. They also appear to foster higher school self-concept than the mixed ability schools. There is no difference between the mixed ability schools and the partially set schools in relation to fostering pupils' self-esteem. Taken together, these findings suggest that high levels of setting create a less favourable environment for developing pupils' self-image. Pupils in schools with only partial setting (no more than two subjects in year 7 and four in year 9) have more positive views of themselves in school. A note of caution is necessary here, however, as we had no measure of self-concept from the pupils on entry to the schools. It is conceivable that differences in intake may be reflected in our findings. However, the inclusion of controls for prior academic attainment, social disadvantage and gender in our analyses make this unlikely.

Setting and self-concept in English, mathematics and science

We also wanted to know whether setting in English, mathematics and science had any impact on academic self-perceptions of the year 9 pupils. For this analysis we used the scale (from 0 to 4) developed to indicate the extent of setting in each curriculum subject. The scale is described in Chapter 2 and the number of schools in each category is displayed in Table 2.2. This shows that pupils experienced most setting in mathematics and least in English as they progressed through the lower secondary school.

We carried out separate analyses for each curriculum subject in turn. As before, we included pupils' attainment at Key Stage 2, gender and social disadvantage in the multilevel modelling. We found that social disadvantage, as indicated by free school meals, was unrelated to the self-concept scales for English, mathematics and science and it is therefore not included in the analyses that follow. The analyses revealed that:

- in English, mathematics and science, self-concept rises with attainment;
- girls have more positive views of themselves than boys in English, but the difference is small;
- boys have more positive views of themselves than girls in mathematics and science;
- for science, the difference between the sexes was greater for the pupils attaining higher levels at Key Stage 2.

Taking these differences into account in our analyses, we then considered the impact of setting. Here we found some differences between the three curriculum subjects. There was no evidence of any effect of setting in mathematics or science, either alone or combined with Key Stage 2 levels. In English, for pupils average and above at Key Stage 2 (year 6), self-concept fell as setting increased but for pupils below average at Key Stage 2, self-concept rose as setting increased. In English, setting raises the self-perceptions of lower attaining pupils and lowers the self-perceptions of higher attaining pupils. Table 3.3 displays the estimates of the multilevel model.

Table 3.3: Estimates (standard errors) by curriculum subject

			English	Mathematics	Science
Fixed effects		KS2 level[1]	4.95 (0.38)	2.52 (0.24)	3.16 (0.32)
		Gender[2]	0.84 (0.31)	−4.56 (0.34)	−3.96[2] (0.54)
		Ability grouping	−0.20 (0.28)	n.s.	n.s.
		KS2* ability grouping	−0.39 (0.16)	n.s.	n.s.
Random effects	School	Intercept	7.79 (2.09)	4 78 (1.43)	9.80 (2.85)
		KS2	1.28 (0.67)	0.78 (0.49)	0.77 (0.57)
		Covariance	−2.44 (1.01)	−0.36 (0.62)	−2.08 (1.10)
	Pupil	Intercept	82.1 (1.93)	101 (2.37)	98.4 (2.29)
Sample size			3713	3740	3770

Notes:
n.s. = not statistically significant at the 0.05 level
(1) mean is zero
(2) boys are baseline group. The estimate for the interaction between KS2 and gender for science is -0.87 (0.41)

Our analyses indicate that the scales measuring academic facets of the self-concept are sensitive to grouping arrangements in place for particular academic subjects, whereas students' general school self-concept and self-esteem are influenced by the amount of structured ability grouping in the school. The effect of ability grouping on academic self-concept differs from one curriculum subject to another. In mathematics and science, there is no evidence that ability grouping has an effect on the corresponding facets of the self-concept, whereas in English setting raises the self-concept of lower attaining pupils and lowers the self-concept of higher attaining pupils. Ability grouping arrangements in schools influence the social comparison processes. It appears from our analyses that ability grouping is more salient to pupils in English than in mathematics or science. This may be related to the nature of assessment in the three subjects, which may be less frequent and salient to pupils in English than in the other subjects. Pupils may be more aware of their performance, compared to others in their class, in mathematics and science than in English. Answers to questions set in class or for homework are more clearly correct or incorrect in mathematics and science, whereas in English assessment is more in terms of quality of response. This may mean that pupils are more aware of their relative performance in mathematics and science, even in mixed ability classes. A move from mixed ability to setting would therefore have less impact on academic self-concept in these subjects.

In contrast to Byrne's study of tracking, we find that both social disadvantage and gender are linked to self-perceptions, with girls and disadvantaged pupils tending to have more negative self-perceptions than boys and socially advantaged pupils. The influence of the level of stratification in a school on the general facets of the self-concept could arise through processes of social comparison, including the BFLPE. But this is not sufficient to explain why students' general school self-concepts were highest in the schools with a moderate level of setting. This finding is difficult to interpret in terms of the BFLPE or other social comparison processes. We suspect that school values and ethos have an important influence on pupils' views of themselves. For example, it may be that schools with higher levels of setting also tend to be more competitive, thus making set placement more salient and available as a basis for social comparison. This would be consistent with the findings of a recent study of East and West German students following reunification (Marsh, Koller and Baumert, 1999). This research suggests that a competitive environment within schools influences students' self-concepts. We will consider whether our sample schools with higher levels of setting have a more competitive ethos in Chapter 6. Here we simply note that some headteachers in the more highly set schools clearly saw the level of stratification in the school as a reflection of stratification in society. Those in the partially set and mixed ability schools placed a greater emphasis on valuing all the pupils and they adopted a more pragmatic approach towards ability grouping.

Pupils' feelings about school

At primary level, early British studies indicated that attitudes to schools were more positive among children in non-streamed classes, particularly among children of average and lower ability (Barker Lunn, 1970). At secondary level, Fogelman (1983) reported no differences in attitude or motivation in comprehensive schools using streaming, setting and mixed ability groupings. However, he acknowledged that his information on the actual grouping practices in the schools was limited.

In our secondary school research, we included questions about pupils' feelings towards school and school work on the questionnaire completed by the year 9 pupils. Pupils were asked to indicate their level of agreement with a series of statements on a five-point scale from strongly agree to strongly disagree. The questionnaire also included items tapping pupils' feelings about their relationship with their school and their teachers. We compared the responses of pupils in the three types of school, predominantly mixed ability, partially set and set (see Chapter 2 for further information on the three types).

The majority of pupils (70%) either agreed or strongly agreed with the statement 'I am very happy when I am in school' (see Table 3.4). A higher proportion of pupils in the predominantly mixed ability schools strongly agreed with this statement (20%), compared with 11% of pupils in the set schools and 15% in the partially set schools. The differences between the three types of school were small but statistically significant.

Table 3.4: Percentage responses to the statement 'I am very happy when I am at school'

Type of ability grouping	Number of pupils	Strongly agree	Agree	Not sure	Disagree	Strongly disagree
MA school	2270	20.2	50.0	12.6	12.1	5.1
PS school	2064	15.0	56.1	11.1	13.1	4.7
Set school	2245	10.9	56.8	13.0	13.4	6.0
Total	6579	15.4	54.2	12.3	12.8	5.3

Chi-square = 83.54, df = 8, p<.000

About a third of the sample indicated that they strongly agreed or agreed with the statement 'Most of the time I don't want to go to school'. A higher proportion of those indicating a negative attitude towards going to school was in the set schools, with 39% in the set schools, 32% in the partially set schools and 34% in the mixed ability schools (see Table 3.5).

Table 3.5: Percentage responses to the statement 'Most of the time I don't want to go to school'

Type of ability grouping	Number of pupils	Strongly agree	Agree	Not sure	Disagree	Strongly disagree
MA school	2257	11.5	21.0	9.7	36.7	21.2
PS school	1850	9.6	21.9	9.4	37.6	21.5
Set school	2227	11.6	27.1	7.8	35.2	18.3
Total	6334	11.0	23.4	8.9	36.4	20.3

Chi-square = 37.80, df = 8, p<. 000

A similar pattern was evident in pupils' responses to the statement 'This is a good school'. The figures are shown in Table 3.6. Overall, 80% of the pupils agreed or strongly agreed with this statement, with a higher level of agreement in the mixed ability schools. The percentages agreeing or strongly agreeing were 78% in the set and partially set schools and 83% in the mixed ability schools. The differences were statistically significant.

Table 3.6: Percentage responses to the statement 'This is a good school'

Type of ability grouping	Number of pupils	Strongly agree	Agree	Not sure	Disagree	Strongly disagree
MA school	2273	38.5	44.7	7.9	5.6	3.3
PS school	2058	32.1	46.0	9.8	7.8	4.3
Set school	2237	30.3	47.9	9.7	7.3	4.7
Total	6568	33.7	46.2)	9.1	6.9	4.1

Chi-square = 47.09, df = 8, p<. 000

We explored pupils' relationships with their teachers by asking them to indicate how many of the teachers they felt they got on with during the current term (see Table 3.7). A higher proportion of pupils in the mixed ability schools indicated that they got on well with all their teachers with 28% in the mixed ability schools, 25% in the partially set schools and 22% in the set schools.

Table 3.7: Percentage responses to the statement 'This term I have got on well with'

Type of ability grouping	Number of pupils	All my teachers	Most of my teachers	About half my teachers	Less than half my teachers	None of my teachers
MA school	2265	27.9	54.3	11.9	4.5	1.4
PS school	2056	24.8	56.2	12.8	5.0	1.3
Set school	2241	22.0	57.5	13.3	5.7	1.6
Total	6562	24.9	56.0	12.6	5.1	1.4

Chi-square = 24.1, df = 8, p<. 002

We also asked how the pupils felt about their relationship with the school. They were given the stem 'The school and I are like' and asked to choose 'good friends', 'friends', 'distant relatives', 'strangers' or 'enemies'. The majority of pupils (63%) saw their relationship with the school as like a friend or good friend (see Table 3.8). Just under half (47%) chose friends as their response and the percentages were very similar in the three types of school. Overall 16% chose good friends and here the percentage for the mixed ability schools was higher (20%) than for the partially set schools (16%) and set schools (13%).

Table 3.8: Percentage responses to the statement 'The school and I are like'

Type of ability grouping	Number of pupils	Good friends	Friends	Distant relatives	Strangers	Enemies
MA school	2231	19.5	46.0	21.3	6.2	7.0
PS school	2024	16.1	46.9	22.1	7.3	7.6
Set school	2206	12.5	47.0	23.8	8.0	8.7
Total	6461	16.0	46.6	22.4	7.2	7.8

Chi-square = 46.54, df = 8, p<. 000

Two items focused more specifically on pupils' views about the value and importance of their work in school. Almost nine out of ten pupils (88%) felt that the work they did in school was worthwhile. There was slightly stronger agreement with this statement by pupils in the partially set schools (see Table 3.9).

A more marked difference appeared in pupils' responses to a statement about the importance of their work in school (see Table 3.10).

Here, 70% of pupils in the mixed ability schools indicated that work in school was very important, as compared with 65% in the partially set schools and 62% in the set schools.

Table 3.9:   Percentage responses to the statement 'School work is worth doing'

Type of ability grouping	Number of pupils	Strongly agree	Agree	Not sure	Disagree	Strongly disagree
MA school	2259	43.8	43.5	4.3	5.1	3.3
PS school	2037	41.3	47.2	4.0	3.6	4.0
Set school	2230	38.3	49.2	5.2	4.1	3.1
Total	6526	41.1	46.6	4.5	4.4	3.3

Chi-square = 25.3, df = 8, p<. 001

Table 3.10:   Percentage responses to the statement 'To me, the work I do in school is'

Type of ability grouping	Number of pupils	Very important	Quite important	Not really important	Not important at all
MA school	2270	69.5	27.4	2.0	1.1
PS school	2053	65.3	30.7	2.8	1.2
Set school	2238	61.9	34.4	3.0	0.7
Total	6561	65.6	30.8	2.6	1.0

Chi-square = 34.67, df = 6, p<. 000

In all three types of school, there was strong disagreement (91%) with the statement 'School work doesn't help you get a job'. There were no differences between the schools. Similarly, the vast majority of pupils indicated that their parents thought school was important. About 87% agreed or strongly agreed with the statement 'My parents think it is important for me to do well at school' and 95% disagreed with the statement 'My parents think school is a waste of time'.

We were interested in comparing the responses of pupils of differing levels of attainment in the three types of school. As an indicator of attainment we used the total levels achieved at Key Stage 3 in English, mathematics and science. By adding the level obtained by each pupil in these subjects, we obtained a scale from 0 to 24. We then divided this into four quartiles, based on the numbers of pupils achieving each point on the scale, and compared the responses of pupils at each level of attainment in the three types of school. This revealed that more pupils of all levels of attainment in mixed ability schools saw the school as a good friend, compared to pupils in set schools. In both the mixed ability and partially set schools, more of the lower attaining pupils viewed the school as a good friend. Overall, a higher proportion of pupils in the mixed ability schools had very good relationships with the school. In all schools, there were small but worrying numbers of pupils who saw the school as an enemy. These pupils were predominantly, but by no means exclusively, the lower attaining pupils in year 9 (Ireson, Hallam and Hurley, in preparation).

The consistent pattern of these pupils' responses suggests that there are important differences in the climate and culture of the different types of school. In each case, pupils in the mixed ability schools have more favourable affective responses to their school, while those in the more highly set schools have the least. Although each of these differences is quite small, taken together they suggest that mixed ability schools provide an environment that fosters a better affective response from pupils. More pupils report that they are happy in school, fewer do not want to go to school, more think their school is a good school and that school work is very important. Relationships with teachers and the school as a whole are also better, with more pupils getting on well with all their teachers and seeing the school as a good friend. Overall, their views about school are more positive. These affective responses to the ability grouping structures in the schools suggest that structured ability grouping does in some sense reflect the ethos and values of the school. We must interpret these findings with caution, however, as we have no information about the attitudes of the pupils on entry to the schools, so it is possible that we have simply uncovered an existing difference in intake. This seems unlikely, given that the intake to the mixed ability schools had slightly lower average Key Stage 2 attainment in English, mathematics and science and contained more socially disadvantaged pupils.

Labelling, stigmatisation and teasing

Labelling, stigmatisation and teasing in school all have the potential to influence pupils' developing self-esteem. Hurtful teasing can undermine confidence and sense of self-worth. Labelling and teasing about ability can also accentuate the salience of ability, making it more likely to feature in processes of social comparison that affect self-esteem. Labelling and stereotyping are both common human responses in complex social situations. Stereotyping helps us to reduce the complexity of the social world and to make it manageable. Teachers work in a highly complex social environment and it is therefore not surprising if they tend to stereotype their pupils as a way of managing this complexity. Over-use of stereotyping can, however, be disadvantageous especially if it limits teachers' expectations of their pupils.

In schools with streaming or tracking, pupils tend to be labelled and stereotyped according to the stream they are in (Hargreaves, 1967; Lacey, 1970; Keddie, 1971; Ball, 1981; Schwartz, 1981; Burgess, 1983; Metz, 1983; Page, 1984). Schwartz (1981) reports teachers' stereotyped description of pupils as thick, bright, slow, difficult, etc. Pupils themselves also have stereotyped descriptions, such as teacher's pet, brain, dumb, stupid. Burgess (1983, 1984) found that students not taking external examinations were the subject of teachers' negative jokes. Most of the teachers in the school regarded them as 'scruffs' although the teachers who taught these students viewed them positively and attempted to bring them up to the schools' academic goals. As the Elton Report suggested, bad behaviour can occur in lower streams because of pupils' recognition of their place in the scheme of things – at the bottom (DES, 1989).

Teasing experienced by pupils in primary school

Our recent project on ability grouping in the primary school aimed to explore the rationale given for the adoption of different grouping practices, how the grouping arrangements were implemented and resources provided, and the pupils' experiences of learning within different types of grouping. A sample of six primary schools was selected to represent a variety of grouping arrangements, ranging from a high level of structured ability grouping (streaming or setting) to predominantly mixed ability groupings. Table 3.11 provides information about the grouping arrangements in each school. School 1 was an unusually large primary school which, at the time of the research, streamed pupils on entry to the reception year and kept them in their streams through to year 3. From year 4, the pupils were in mixed ability classes, but set by ability for English, science and mathematics. This school had the most ability grouping and School 6 the least, with a variety of combinations in between.

We will report on findings from this research in several later chapters. Here we refer to evidence collected about teasing experienced by the pupils. In the six case study primary schools, pupils from years 3 to 6 were interviewed in mixed gender pairs and were selected on the basis of ability by their class teacher. Three pairs were interviewed from each year group (above average, average, below average). They were asked for their views of ability grouping and also about their experiences of teasing. In the secondary schools, pupils were interviewed in small groups.

Table 3.11: Ability grouping arrangements in the six primary schools

School 1 720 on roll	Streaming for KS1 and year 3. Mixed ability classes from year 4, with setting for the core National Curriculum subjects, English, science and mathematics.
School 2 283 on roll	Mixed ability classes with within class ability groups at KS1. At KS2 pupils are streamed into 3 mixed age classes based on ability.
School 3 342 on roll	Mixed ability classes with within class ability grouping. Pupils are set for mathematics and English from year 1.
School 4 405 on roll	Mixed ability with within class ability grouping. Pupils are set for mathematics from year 4.
School 5 70 on roll	Pupils are in 2 mixed age classes according to Key Stage. Cross-age setting for English and mathematics.
School 6 420 on roll	Same age, mixed ability classes. Some within class ability grouping.

Previous research has indicated the stigmatisation of pupils in the lower streams as a problem created by streaming. Pupils in higher ability groups are also the subject of naming and teasing, but the language used to refer to high and low ability children has a different quality. Derogatory terms are often used to refer to lower ability pupils, wheareas terms such as 'boffin' or 'brainy' are used when referring to those of high ability. 'Boffin' means a person engaged in scientific research, a term that does not have negative connotations in everyday life. Both groups of pupils can be victims of teasing which may be malicious in intent. This occurs at primary and secondary level and with pupils at both ends of the ability spectrum.

> I don't like it when people poke fun. It doesn't happen that often . . . not quite a lot, but a couple of weeks ago, people laughed at me and sometimes they call you thick. (Primary pupil)

> People say like 'You're silly' and all that . . . it makes me feel sad. (Primary pupil)

> I get teased a lot at the bottom end of the school I get beaten up and kicked . . . they throw pebbles and sand at me and call me fatso and all that. (Primary pupil)

Some children in the top sets are show offs and they say 'Oh, I'm brainier than you'. (Below average ability, primary)

Mixed ability classes are better because you could learn more things from other people and other people won't take the mick out of you. (Secondary pupil in a set school)

I get teased and called the professor because I'm one of the cleverer ones . . . it bothers me. (Primary pupil)

Sometimes people might say things but they're not really being nasty . . . they say things to make you laugh like you've got a really good brain . . . it's so big it's popping out through your ears. (Primary pupil)

I'm in set 3 and I'd like to move to set 2 because it isn't too hard but you still have to be pretty intelligent. You don't get teased as much as in the top set. (Secondary pupil in a set school)

Primary-aged pupils sometimes reported the teasing to teachers who generally took action to resolve the situation.

Joan sometimes says that I can't do anything . . . I tell the teacher and she sometimes puts her in detention. (Year 3 average ability, primary)

Sometimes they say 'You don't know what to do and you're a baby . . . you've got to go to Mrs B' . . . I tell the teacher and she tells them off sometimes. (Year 4, below average ability, primary)

Teachers are not always perceived as being supportive and in some cases may also make comments.

I prefer mixed ability classes as no one gets the mickey taken out of them and teachers can't make their horrid remarks. (Secondary set school)

Some pupils are very aware of the sensitivities of the situation.

I think mixed ability is best because it would be embarrassing if you were in the bottom group or set. (Mixed ability school)

Over 40% of pupils interviewed from the six primary schools reported either having been teased or having witnessed teasing that was related to grouping practices or academic ability. For some, the teasing was interpreted as 'playful', particularly for those children in the higher ability groups, but many found it upsetting. Table 3.12 summarises the responses from the pupils who were interviewed.

Table 3.12: Teasing reported by pupils interviewed in the six primary schools

School	Teasing reported
1	30% of pupils interviewed claimed they had been teased because of their placement in streams or sets. Many of these were children of lower ability. All of them indicated that they found the teasing hurtful.
2	29% of pupils interviewed indicated that they had been teased and most reported that they found this hurtful. Most of these pupils came from lower ability classes.
3	33% of pupils claimed they had been teased, the majority being of lower ability.
4	52% of pupils interviewed indicated that they had been teased about their allocation to a group and 75% of these indicated that they found the teasing hurtful.
5	8% of pupils interviewed indicated that they had been teased. They reported that the teasing was playful in nature.
6	33% of pupils interviewed indicated that they had been teased because of their allocation to groups. The majority reported that the teasing was playful in nature.

There was a tendency for teasing to focus on children of different ability in different schools. In School 1, which had both streaming and setting, no child of above average ability reported being teased. In this school 43% of average ability and 57% of below average ability children interviewed had been the target of teasing. The reverse pattern occurred in School 6, where there was a commitment to mixed ability teaching. In this school, 50% of the above average ability group reported being teased, 37% of the average ability group and only 13% of the low ability group. The incidence of teasing was low in School 5, even though the pupils were aware of the ability groupings in place. This suggests that ability grouping is not the only relevant factor. Teasing about ability appears to be related to the grouping practices adopted and the values espoused within the school.

Summary

Our research suggests that ability grouping has an impact on pupils' self-esteem, academic self-concept and their emotional responses to school. This relationship is not entirely straightforward, however, as many different factors are interrelated. When considering the impact of school organisation, it is important to take account of the multiple facets of students' self-perceptions, social disadvantage, developmental changes and gender differences. Our research indicates that in the lower secondary years, socially disadvantaged pupils and girls have less positive self-esteem than socially advantaged pupils and boys. When students' academic self-perceptions are considered, however, gender differences remain, while social disadvantage is not an important factor. Boys have much more positive views of themselves in mathematics and science, even when attainment is taken into account, while girls have more positive views of themselves in relation to English, although the difference is smaller. These findings are consistent with previous research and perhaps reflect more general perceptions of mathematics and science as 'masculine' subjects. However, the gap between the self-perceptions of girls and boys, particularly those of high attainment, is of some concern, especially as emotional factors may influence their choice of subjects in later years of education.

Overall, pupils in schools with more structured grouping feel less positive about school. Pupils in the schools with less structured grouping had more positive relationships with the school and their teachers. The differences are small but consistent. Teasing is one factor that contributes to pupils' feelings about school. Pupils of all abilities may be teased, but for those in lower ability groups, teasing can reinforce pupils' negative views of their academic attainment. Taken together, the evidence we have presented in this chapter indicates that pupils have lower self-esteem in schools that have higher levels of ability grouping and they feel less positive about the school as a whole. It is likely that there are differences between the schools in each of the three groups, which we have not yet uncovered in our analysis.

Positive attitudes towards learning and positive self-concepts are important elements fostering a disposition to learn in the future. It is important for schools to beware of becoming too seduced by a technical approach to ability grouping and to ensure that all pupils are supported and encouraged to develop these dispositions. While the emphasis in previous research has been on the negative impact of ability grouping on lower attaining pupils, our research indicates that structured ability grouping may also have a negative effect on more able pupils' self-concepts. Moderate levels of regrouping may be beneficial for pupils' self-esteem, whereas higher levels of setting may be less advantageous. We suspect that it has to do with the ethos and values espoused by the school, teachers' attitudes and expectations of pupils, the extent of social mixing experienced by pupils, or the differences in the competitive climate in structured ability groups. These will be explored in later chapters.

4

Pupils' Perspectives on Ability Grouping

In this chapter we will bring together the findings of several recent research studies that have explored pupils' views of working in school in structured and mixed ability groups. The evidence from these studies demonstrated that children at primary and secondary school can justify the reasons for the adoption of different grouping practices and are able to evaluate critically the benefits and drawbacks of them. Overall, pupils preferred setting to other grouping practices but their perceptions and preferences were influenced by the practices currently adopted in their school, their current placement in an ability group and gender. Pupils of all ages demonstrated sensitivity to the effects of structured ability grouping, in particular the stigmatisation that can occur in relation to pupils in the lower ability groups and the teasing which may have to be endured by those in the top set. The main stated reason for preferring setting at primary and secondary level was that it enabled work to be set at a level of an appropriate standard. From the pupils' perspective this matching process was often inaccurate. Pupils' perceptions of the 'best' class as perceived by most pupils in their school revealed that within any single school different cultures could exist which placed different values on academic achievement. Some pupils valued attaining the highest level of academic achievement, others saw being 'average' as offering a safe option from teasing and an opportunity to have fun and be under less pressure. In both these cultures, being in the lowest groups was seen as stigmatising.

Previous research

Previous research has considered the personal and social effects of grouping on pupils' attitudes towards school and particular subjects, pupils' self-esteem, friendships, the extent of their involvement in school activities and the impact on particular groups of children, of different social class, ethnicity and birth date. It is only recently that there has been an interest in pupils' own perceptions of structured ability grouping and its effects on them as individuals (Boaler, 1997a, 1997b, 1997c). Issues relating to self-esteem and attitudes towards school have already been considered in Chapter 3. This chapter will focus on pupils' perceptions of and attitudes towards different grouping practices and how they may impact on the self-perceptions of some groups of children and social cohesion within the school.

Expectations

One of the perceived negative effects of highly structured ability grouping highlighted by previous research is its influence on the expectations of pupils regarding their prospects (Gamoran, 1986; Kerckhoff, 1986). In the USA, students in college tracks are expected to enter college, while others are expected to enter the workforce immediately on leaving school. Students in the lower vocational tracks generally hold lower expectations (Berends, 1995) and in the United Kingdom, when streaming was commonplace, those in high streams received more encouragement to stay on at school (Hargreaves, 1967; Lacey, 1970). Gamoran and Berends (1987) argue that because of the symbolic importance of track and stream positions, students and others hold these differential expectations regardless of actual performance or potential. However, not all of the research supports this view. The National Child Development Study showed no differences between streamed and non-streamed schools in their pupils' self-ratings, motivation or plans for the future (Essen, Fogelman and Tibbenham, 1978; Fogelman, 1983). Nevertheless, high and low track students view the top tracks as offering a better education and more prestige (Rosenbaum, 1976). In the United Kingdom, setting not only limits expectations but sets very real limits on examination entry and possible attainment (Boaler, Wiliam and Brown, 2000).

Effects on friendships

One of the perceived benefits of mixed ability grouping has been its promotion of social mixing among pupils. However, a number of studies have suggested that at both primary and secondary level pupils tend to choose friends of similar social class, ability and ethnic grouping (Barker Lunn, 1970; Postlethwaite and Denton, 1978;

Gamoran and Berends, 1987). Johannesson (1962), Deitrich (1964) and Neave (1975) found no differences between mixed ability and streamed groups in their friendship patterns. In the United Kingdom, at primary level, Barker Lunn (1970) found that children in streamed and non-streamed schools tended to choose those of similar ability and social class as friends, although a greater number of mixed social class and ability friendships were observed in non-streamed schools. At secondary level, Newbold (1977) suggested that the form unit provided the basis for friendships to develop and that this outweighed any long-standing influence of former primary school associations unless these were linked. The children studied tended to associate with others of similar ability and social class but this was less marked in mixed ability forms. Several studies have confirmed that students' friends tended to be in the same stream (Ball, 1981; Hargreaves, 1967; Lacey, 1970; Rosenbaum, 1976; Schwartz, 1981). As the majority of pupils' time at school is spent in the classroom, this is to be expected. The adoption of setting procedures, where pupils regroup for different subjects as they progress through school, can split friendship groups and reduce the social support that pupils have developed. Some pupils reported anxiety related to having to work with different pupils and fit into new structures (Chaplain, 1996).

Cohesion within the classroom

It has been suggested that mixed ability teaching can lead to greater social cohesion in the classroom. The argument is that pupils will help each other and that the more able will provide encouragement and support for the less able by their example (Findlay and Bryan, 1975; DES, 1978; Reid et al., 1982; Eilam and Finegold, 1992; Scottish Office, 1996). Peverett (1994), observing the teaching of 9–11-year-olds, found little evidence that lower ability pupils benefited from the presence or support of higher ability pupils. Studies in the USA report that pupils enjoy lessons more when they are grouped with others of similar ability (Kulik and Kulik, 1982a).

There may be differences in the quality of peer interactions in low and high ability groups. Oakes (1982, 1985) found that students in higher ability groups reported behaviour between peers which was more supportive when compared with lower ability classes where pupils' interactions were often characterised by hostility and anger. Behaviour is often more disruptive in the lower sets (Oakes, 1982; Findley and Bryan, 1975; Berends, 1995) whereas in mixed ability classes lower ability pupils tend to behave better (Slavin and Karweit, 1985). Slavin and Karweit argue that this is because every class has a norm for appropriate behaviour. Mixed ability classes are likely to have higher morale and place a higher value on learning than bottom sets, streams or tracks.

Social cohesion within the school

The evidence regarding social cohesion within school as a result of structured ability grouping is complex. At primary level, early British studies indicated that social adjustment, social attitudes and attitudes to peers of different ability were 'healthier' among children in non-streamed classes (Willig, 1963; Barker Lunn, 1970). Barker Lunn also found more positive attitudes to school and greater participation in school activities among children in non-streamed classes, particularly in those of average or below average ability. This finding is supported by Jackson's (1964) reports of more co-operative atmospheres in non-streamed schools. Neither school organisation nor teacher type (streaming or non-streaming) had much effect on the social, emotional or attitudinal development of children of above average ability but they did affect those of average and below average ability (Barker Lunn, 1970). The poorest attitudes were found among pupils in non-streamed schools who were taught by teachers who were streamers. Boys of below average ability had the most favourable relationships with typical non-streamer teachers in non-streamed schools.

At primary level, the more streams the more negative the attitudes of those in the lower streams and the greater the possibility of them regarding themselves as socially segregated with the humiliation which this implied (Barker Lunn, 1970). Moreover, children of below average ability who were taught by typical streaming teachers in non-streamed schools were friendless or neglected by others. Their teacher's emphasis on academic success and dislike of the below average may have been communicated to other pupils who, in turn, rejected the below average child. Chaplain (1996) reported similar perceived negative effects on pupils in the lowest groups in secondary schools related to the number of sets. The negative effects on pupils in the lower ability groups in relation to their social standing and the stigma that is attached to being in a low group have constituted one of the strongest arguments for not adopting structured ability grouping.

The evidence regarding the effects of different kinds of grouping on pupils' attitudes towards school is equivocal. Rudd (1956) found no differences related to ability grouping but reported that streamed children made fewer contributions and paid less attention in lessons. Their behaviour was also more aggressive than non-streamed children. An NFER study of 12 schools found greater participation in school life among non-streamed boys but not girls, although the girls were more involved in school teams (Ross *et al.*, 1972). Newbold (1977) found that pupils of early secondary school age were more socially integrated if they were in mixed ability classes but it was only the low ability children who tended to have a more positive attitude to school life when they were in mixed ability systems. The differences in attitudes towards school within one system were as great as the differences between systems. In a follow-up study, Postlethwaite and Denton (1978) showed that pupils in the mixed ability system had more positive attitudes towards the school as a social community. The National Child Development Study showed no differences between streamed and non-streamed schools in their pupils' self-ratings, motivation and/or behaviour at school (Essen, Fogleman and Tibbenham, 1978; Fogelman, 1983). Similarly, Hargreaves (1967), Lacey (1970) and Ball (1981) found that some pupils were more pro-school than others even within the same stream.

More recent work suggests that setting tends to have a detrimental effect on the attitudes of those pupils who find themselves in the low sets (Devine, 1993; DES, 1989; Taylor, 1993; Boaler, 1997a, 1997b). Pupils in the high sets tend to fare better (Devine, 1993) although Boaler (1997a, 1997b) suggests that some pupils in the top sets for mathematics find learning stressful because the pace is too fast, they do not have time to develop a deep understanding, and they dislike the competitiveness and high expectations which they find anxiety-provoking. Other students, in contrast, find the pace too slow and the competition and high expectations motivating. These studies indicate that individuals may not respond to structured groupings in the same way. An alternative approach, adopting within class ability grouping, seems to lead to more positive attitudes towards the subject being taught (Lou *et al.*, 1996).

Alienation from school

Much early research on structured ability grouping focused on the way that streaming or tracking engendered anti-school attitudes and alienation from school. Where whole peer groups felt alienated anti-school cultures developed. Streaming, it was argued, played a major role in polarising students' attitudes into pro- and anti-school camps (Hargreaves, 1967; Lacey, 1970; Ball, 1981; Schwartz, 1981; Gamoran and Berends, 1987; Abraham, 1989). High ability pupils in high streams tended to accept the school's demands as the normative definition of behaviour, whereas low stream students resisted the school's rules and attempted to subvert them. Over time, streaming fostered friendship groups (Hallinan and Sorensen, 1985; Hallinan and Williams, 1989), which contributed to polarised stream-related attitudes, the high stream pupils tending to be more enthusiastic, those in the low stream, more alienated (Oakes, Gamoran and Page, 1991). As noted in Chapter 3, a major question, as yet unresolved, is whether negative school attitudes result from streaming, setting and tracking or whether grouping procedures merely reflect existing attitudes. What appears to be an outcome of streaming may be a reflection of class alienation.

In the USA, Vanfossen, Jones and Spade (1987) noted that students from academic tracks reported fewer disciplinary problems in their schools and were more likely to describe their teachers as patient, respectful, clear in their presentations and enjoying their work. They suggest that these ethos differences may have contributed to differences in achievement and other outcomes and may be related to the proportion of students in the school in academic rather than vocational programmes.

In the next sections we will report on findings from two recent studies, one at primary and one at secondary level, which explore pupils' perceptions of different aspects of ability grouping within the current United Kingdom educational context. (The secondary school research was outlined in Chapter 2 and the primary research in Chapter 3.) Pupils' perceptions were explored through questionnaires and interviews. At secondary level pupils responded to questions which asked:

- which kind of grouping they believed was best and why;
- whether they wished to move group in mathematics, science or English and if so why;
- which group most people thought was the best and why.

The questionnaire data was supplemented with interviews with groups of pupils in different ability groups.

At primary level pupils from Key Stage 2 in each of the six case study schools were interviewed in mixed-gender pairs selected on the basis of ability by their class teacher. Three pairs were interviewed from each year group (above average, average, or below average).

Pupils were asked questions about:

- the way that their teacher organised the class and why he or she did it in this way;
- whether all the children did the same kind of work and why;
- whether there were some groups that they found difficult to work in and did not like;
- whether they would like to be in a different group;
- whether other children ever said things to them because they were in a particular group;
- which group they thought their teacher would put them in if he or she was dividing the children into clever, moderately clever and children who needed extra help.

The findings are reported in the next sections.

Pupils' perceptions of the benefits and limitations of different types of grouping

Despite the wide age range of the pupils taking part in the two studies (7 to 14) and the variety of schools they attended, there was considerable agreement regarding the benefits and limitations of different kinds of grouping. The main benefits of setting were perceived to be matching work to pupil needs and allowing for differential attainment in different subjects. The benefits of mixed ability classes were seen to be in relation to the extent to which pupils could help and learn from each other and the avoidance of stigmatisation of those in the bottom sets and to a lesser extent those in the top sets. The sections below explore these issues and others that emerged.

Matching work to pupils' needs

By far the most common reason stated for preferring setting to mixed ability classes was that work could be tailored to the level required. At secondary level pupils indicated:

> Sets mean that you are in the right set for your ability with people who are of the same ability and doing work that meets your ability.

> Sets are best because it puts people into groups which are right for them.

> Sets are best because all the people in your group are the same ability.

At primary level, responses to a question about the way their teacher organised the class and why reflected similar perceptions.

I think they decided to do that so that the children could get the best education that they need . . . then the teachers who are good at different subjects can help the children who need it . . . they can help the children who are good at something and the children who are different . . . I think that I prefer setting because I know that with the setting I will be given the best education that I need because when we were doing it as a whole class there were some children who had different abilities from us to them and the teacher sometimes needed to help them more. During the setting they mainly focus on your actual ability so the work is really suited to what you can do . . . it's better when everyone is about the same because then you don't waste your time.

I think they put you in sets so that the work is right for you and that people can work at the same pace instead of some people having to wait for the slower children and the slower children having to keep up with the faster children . . . so I think it's so that we get more work done and to help us.

The role of national testing in the adoption of particular procedures was very evident to the primary school pupils. This was demonstrated in their responses to the rationale for setting and how they would organise the groups. In the quotations below, the pupils refer to SATs meaning the Key Stage tests taken by all children in the United Kingdom when they are 7, 11 and 14 years old.

It's for the SATs . . . they want to see who's clever . . . they don't want to put everyone in one set because it will be too hard for some people.

Well maybe you could split the people into different groups for maths and English and the people who didn't need much help could go and work with similar people and people who need help can go with another teacher . . . it's preparing them for their SATs as well.

Comments regarding the purpose of setting as matching work to student need were made across all subjects, at primary and secondary level and by pupils who were often not in the higher level sets.

I am in set 8 and I would like to stay there because I find everything at my level of understanding. (Secondary, mathematics)

I'm in set 5/6 for science and I want to stay because I am happy where I am. (Secondary)

I'm in set 8 for English and it is just right for me. (Secondary)

I'm happy in the top sets for everything. (Above average pupil at primary school)

It's the bottom set but to tell you the truth I wouldn't want to be in the middle set because I think I couldn't do it. (Below average pupil at primary school)

Pupils raised two issues in relation to the matching of work to needs: understanding and pace of work. Most of the comments about understanding were framed in relation to general ability.

Sets are best because if you put people into mixed ability classes some are going to be bright some dim . . . so if a teacher is teaching a lesson the bright person might find it really easy and the dim person might find it really difficult so if you put them in all different sets they are going to be able to understand. (Secondary)

When he goes over things I understand it better . . . I think it's a really good way to work because if we didn't have sets then people who don't understand the hard sums say in maths well they'll get confused and they need something easier so it's better to be in a group that you know that is right for your brain. (Primary)

Primary school pupils were very aware of the differences in work that were being undertaken by different sets.

At lunchtimes sometimes they're talking about what they do and the rest of us are sitting there and we haven't even heard of the sums.

Sometimes when we come in there's something still on the board for maths top set and I just think oh dear I don't know how to do that.

The other benefit of sets was in relation to the pace of work. Pupils felt that sets allowed them to work at a speed commensurate with their ability.

Sets are best because the people who are good in a subject get pushed further and the people not so good work at a slower pace. (Secondary)

Because some people can't learn as fast as us so they have to put them in a slower group to learn things. (Primary)

Some people do get far ahead but we start off on the same page . . . in maths it's the same as English it depends how fast you work . . . we start on the same page and then some people might do two pages and some people might do 3 pages. (Primary)

Related to the different pace of work for different sets some pupils commented that having structured ability groups saved time and avoided repetition.

> I think that sets are best because then you can learn something new every time . . . when you're in mixed groups you go over the easy stuff over and over again. (Secondary)

> There are three different groups, red, blue and green. Blue is the middle, green is the hardest and red is easiest. The teacher decides who is in which group by how they can spell . . . and what kinds of words they can spell. Teachers put us in the groups so that they don't have to spend so much time . . . for example, she wouldn't give silent letters on the first Monday to people in the blue group and she wouldn't give three-letter words on the first day to people in the green. We might get 5 or even 6 letter words. (Primary)

However, some pupils pointed out that mixed ability teaching could save teacher time as the more able pupils could support the weaker students and the teacher would therefore be needed less.

> Mixed ability is best because if the teacher is helping somebody else the other students who need help can get it off students who know what they're doing which saves time. (Secondary)

According to the pupils, the main reason for ability grouping was to match work to pupils' needs so as to facilitate understanding, enable pupils to work at the fastest pace possible and save teacher time. Later, we will explore the extent to which the actual practice of setting was able to achieve these ends.

Differential attainment in different subjects

Another reason given by the pupils for sets, as opposed to streaming or banding, was that they enabled students to be put into different groups for different subjects. This rationale was less evident in the primary school where setting was less frequent and often restricted to only one subject, mathematics. Typical responses follow:

> Some pupils may be really really good in some subjects but pretty bad at others so they need to be in the right group for each subject so they can understand properly most things that they do. (Secondary)

Sets are best because it's not because of your overall ability . . . if I was rubbish at French and excellent in science . . . French would hold me back. (Secondary)

At secondary level, where the practice of setting is common, a key issue is the extent to which pupils actually are put in different set levels for different subjects. There was also an appreciation in some students that setting might be better for some subjects than others, although comments such as these were infrequent. (DT refers to Design and Technology, PE to Physical Education.)

I think mixed ability classes are good for art, food, DT and textiles and PE . . . sets are good for science, maths and humanities. (Secondary)

The evidence indicates that pupils not only understand the rationale for different kinds of grouping but also perceive the complexity underlying decisions about how to group pupils. This is well illustrated in the examples from primary pupils below outlining how they would group pupils. Issues relating to the level of work, subjects taught, behaviour, pupils' support for each other, pupils' ages and teacher control are raised.

Well I don't know whether I'd have the year 4s all on one table and the year 3s all on another table but I don't actually agree with girls all on one table and boys all on another table. I think it should be a mixture . . . not just a load of boys and one little girl it should be a proper mixture of boys and girls . . . I think that the real clever year 3s should go on and try and go on their own separate tables and the not so clever ones should go on another set of tables. I'd put the year 3s that were clever . . . I wouldn't put them all together so that they could help the other children. I might put the clever year 4s with the year 3s that were not so clever so that they could help them. (Year 3 primary pupil in a mixed age class)

I'd get some really clever and some not so good, group them in and then get some of the medium ones so that the people who are better can help the ones that have got problems and then all the silly ones . . . I'd put them on a table close so you could just watch them and then they could all do it. I'd mix up the not so goods with the people who can help them. I would do that for science and maybe geography and history. I think for maths if we had to have groups I would have partners. I'd just let them sit with whoever but if I was left with one person who was not so good then I'd say 'Can I put so and so in with your group please?'

If I was the teacher, I would have some brainy ones with some people that aren't up to the standard that they should really be and I'd have the really good people next to someone who's having problems and the really good boys and I would put them on a desk right at the back and all the good girls right over on the other side and if some people aren't really good, I'll have them on a table and if some people are really bad I'd have them on a little table right at the front by my desk so that I could see them and check what they're doing. I'd have the boys and girls separate.

These young pupils have learnt much about the complexities of the way teachers group pupils from their personal experiences in the classroom. They demonstrate acute awareness of the issues and the problems that teachers face.

Behaviour

Behaviour emerged as an important issue in relation to grouping. At secondary level it was used by some pupils as a justification for setting.

Sets are best because you don't get held back by people who don't want to work and muck about.

If you are in mixed ability classes for English, science and maths and there's a really disruptive person in the class you won't learn a thing.

However, pupils in mixed ability classes also recognised that there were differences in behaviour between mixed ability classes, as one pupil described.

Our form group is best because it's better behaved and we are quite far ahead.

At primary level pupils' descriptions of how they were grouped and seated within the class and how they might group pupils themselves acknowledged the importance of good behaviour and the teacher's use of groupings to help achieve it.

I'd put the brainy ones not near me but where I could still see them and the people who don't act their age and they do know a lot but they don't get on with it . . . they'd be near me so if they don't get on with it I could tell them off.

Some people at the front don't concentrate so Sir has to keep an eye on them at the front . . . that's how he gets them to concentrate.

The teacher was perceived to have a role in ensuring that children worked well together and spent time on task.

I would have them in twos . . . I wouldn't put good friends together because they'd be talking too much but I wouldn't put two people together who hated each other . . . I'd have people who know each but are not really friendly . . . I would have someone who's not so clever and someone who's clever but if I had two people who were both really good at say history then I'd swap the class around a bit . . . I'd have different pairs for different things I think.

I would sit them in special groups . . . I would let them choose their friends and then if they talked too much I would find some different tables.

I'd let them pick where they wanted to sit for two weeks and see how they are and if they're not getting on with their mates I'd move them around on tables . . . I'd have a table of year 6s on their own and a table of year 5s on their own and then the rest can be mixed . . . because you might get some people who would mess around so you should try them out with a different year 5 or year 6 and see if they was alright with that.

Pupils appreciated the difficulties facing teachers.

In our class if you said sit where you want there'd always be someone who'd be cheesed off because the most popular person sits down and then everyone flocks to that table and then there's never enough room for everyone and people are left out . . . I don't think that's a good idea but it's a tricky problem.

Mixed gender groups were viewed as one way in which teachers could maintain an optimal working climate.

I'd let them pick and see if they got on and then I'd probably put boy, girl, boy, girl . . . I'd only do that if they were naughty though.

If anyone's being naughty I'd sit down and think about swapping the naughty children and the good children around the tables because sometimes I would put some naughty boys on the girls' table so that they'll be mixed up.

I think that boys can get silly with boys and the girls might be more sensible so I'd put some of the girls with the boys.

At primary level the manipulation of groups within the classroom was seen as a way of reducing class conflict and promoting optimum working relationships.

We do the same topic but sometimes we have different work . . . I think that she looks at who gets on well and will work well together.

We stay on the same table groups all the time unless we don't get on very well then the teacher might move us.

Now I don't really like working together . . . I prefer to work single because usually if we work as a group . . . if people have different ideas then there might be a fight.

I was in this group and it was just like all boys and they were really naughty and they would like pull faces . . . the teacher thought I might calm them down I suppose but it didn't really work . . . nothing would calm them down. (Primary girl)

At secondary level pupils did not refer to the teacher manipulating groups within the class to promote effective working and good behaviour. Perhaps it is a rare occurrence or as pupils have different teachers for each subject they may not be aware of any individual teachers' rationale for grouping. However, the evidence indicates that grouping plays a role in the control of behaviour. In the case of structured ability grouping pupils may be put into lower ability groups because of their behaviour as in the example below.

I am in set 5 and would like to move to set 3 because that was the set I was in when I was in year 7 and then I started to behave badly and stopped learning.

Motivation and effort

In addition to issues surrounding behaviour, some pupils at secondary level believed that particular types of grouping could influence motivation and effort.

I prefer setting because it sorts out the more intelligent people and makes the less intelligent people have a goal to reach.

Setting is best because it gives people motivation to be in a better set
. . . makes people proud to be in that set . . . helps pupils achieve their
best and mix with people of their own ability.

I like setting because I think I work well with people of good ability
because I compete with them which pushes me to do well.

Sets are best because it's fair that if you work hard you should be in a
better set than someone who is lazy.

Pupils from schools that adopted only mixed ability grouping suggested that mixed ability classes promoted motivation and effort.

Mixed ability grouping is the best type of grouping because the less
clever get pushed to do better.

I think mixed ability is best because it can help some people try harder
and get better at doing things they aren't good at.

From the pupils' perspective, motivation and effort can be promoted
through either kind of grouping.

Changing sets

For setting to act as a motivator for pupils there has to be the possibility of changing sets. Some pupils at secondary level pointed out that
this was not easy.

I'm in set 3 and I would like to be in set 1 or 2 because I can work quite
well but it's hard to move up.

I am in set 3 and would like to be in the top set . . . in the year and in
exams I have been well ahead of the class and have not changed . . . I
feel held back.

At primary level changing set seemed to occur more often and pupils
were aware that movement between sets was possible and knew the
mechanisms through which this could be achieved, although this was
not always the case.

They have tests and if your test is level with the bottom set work then
you go to the bottom set and if your test result is medium then you go
to the middle set and if you got every single one right then you go to
the top set.

At the end of the autumn term they give us a few maths tests to see where we are with our ability and they might put you somewhere else . . . lower or higher.

They wait until you get really good before you go to a higher group.

Some people in my group if they're not very good at spelling and they keep getting things wrong then they have to move down because it's no good being in a higher group if you can't do the spellings. So you keep going up and up and when you're in the top group if you get some spellings wrong then they move you down again.

Parents were seen as one means of facilitating change between sets at primary level. This was not raised at secondary level.

Do children move from group to group very much? No . . . but sometimes if their mum or dad think that they're in the wrong class then they might move to another class or another school.

My Dad talked to the headmistress as well and they moved me up and I felt pleased because I wasn't with the people that I didn't like very much and I felt that I was moving up to my level.

Teacher attention

Pupils also thought that a reason for different kinds of groupings was to allow the teacher to focus attention on particular groups of pupils. Generally, in mixed ability classes there was a perception that the lower ability pupils would receive most attention but there were exceptions.

People get chances to show the teachers how they do in their lessons . . . if we did not have sets and we were mixed the children who had more ability would get all of the attention. (Secondary)

I prefer setting because people with higher ability can be concentrated on to make more out of them and people with lower ability can be in the lower set so they can be taught in their own time . . . you tend to find that in mixed ability classes the teacher concentrates more on the lower ability students and higher ability students don't get much of the teacher's time. (Secondary)

In sets teachers can concentrate on all the class instead of a few that need a lot of help. (Secondary)

This issue was not raised by any of the primary pupils.

Pupils' reasons for preferring mixed ability teaching

The main reasons given for preferring mixed ability teaching related to the ways that pupils could help, inspire and motivate each other while avoiding those in the lower sets becoming stigmatised.

Helping each other

Pupils made direct reference to the way they supported each other in their learning and what could happen if they did not. This was particularly well illustrated in one of the case study primary schools where there was a firm commitment to mixed ability teaching because of the perceived importance of encouraging social inclusion.

> Working in a group you can get ideas from other people and some people work together.

> I like working as a group because if you're stuck on something you can ask who's sitting next to you and they can help you out.

> Once I was with a group and I couldn't get my sums right and nobody would help me and I didn't know how to do them, but I was too frightened that if I said something I would get into trouble, so I just sat staring at my work.

> Does it help to work as a group? Yes because if you get two children, you have double brain power.

Similar reasons for within class groupings were given at secondary level but in some cases the language was more derogatory.

> Mixed ability grouping is best because if someone is thicker than you, you can help them. If someone's brainier than you, they can help you.

> Mixed ability because then you know more people and if you're thick the clever people can help you.

> Mixed ability because if you mix intelligent people with some dumb people the dumb can learn from the brainier people.

The ways that pupils could learn from each other was not always framed as direct helping but sometimes in relation to the indirect ways that working with people who are more experienced or expert can raise standards.

> Mixed ability is best because then it gives the less able people a chance to work more with more ability pupils bringing their standard up. (Secondary pupil in set 1 for everything)

I think mixed ability is best because the more intelligent pupils encourage the less intelligent pupils to do better.

Social inclusion and equality of opportunity

Closely related to the issue of helping each other was that of social inclusion and the opportunities that mixed ability grouping provided for getting to know pupils from a range of backgrounds.

> I think mixed ability classes are the best type of grouping because it helps you because when you go out into the open world you may have to work with people of different ability. (Secondary)

> Because it's helping you to work with other people as well ... if you have to do a science project or a DT project then you have to work with other people even people you don't like that much which helps you to learn a lot about them. (Primary)

> Because as well as working at this level of your ability you also get to work with people different to you which helps your social skills. (Secondary)

> I think mixed ability is the best type of grouping because pupils get to mix with people they would not normally be with and pupils with a higher ability would be able to help lower ability pupils because sometimes an explanation is better coming from another person of your own age who can put it into better words. (Secondary)

At secondary level pupils demonstrated an increasing awareness of issues relating to equal opportunities and discrimination, particularly in the schools where there was a commitment to mixed ability teaching.

> Mixed ability is the best grouping because it gives everybody an equal opportunity to do well. (Pupil from a mixed ability school)

> I don't know which is best but it is discrimination if you had top sets for everything. (Pupil from a mixed ability school)

> Mixed ability teaching is best because the weaker children will get more opportunities. (Pupil from a mixed ability school)

> People shouldn't be split up because of their ability. (Pupil from a mixed ability school)

There was also an emphasis on including pupils who were perceived as less able in the mixed ability schools.

Mixed ability is best because it enables the students which cannot do as well in subjects to feel more confident because they know they are not in the class for the slow kids. (Pupil from a mixed ability school)

Mixed ability is best because everybody should be in the same class not just for their ability they should be mixed or other people might just think they were thick. (Pupil from a mixed ability school)

Mixed ability is better for the not so clever people because they don't get left out . . . everyone does the same. (Pupil in a middle set)

Highlighting and legitimising differences between pupils

The issue of inclusion was related to the notion that putting pupils in structured ability groups made pupils more aware of their differences and provided an opportunity to enable pupils to establish where they were in the pecking order.

I prefer sets because then you know where you are compared to every-one else. (Pupil from secondary set school)

Sets are best because it gives you a better picture of how you are doing in each subject. (Pupil from secondary set school)

I prefer mixed ability classes because then no-one gets picked on because they're too clever or too dumb . . . in mixed ability classes no one really knows that much who's cleverest and who's not. (Pupil from a mixed ability school)

Allocating pupils to sets legitimises differential treatment of pupils. It acknowledges that there are differences in ability and that it is accept-able to treat pupils with different abilities in different ways, which carry advantages for some pupils.

Mixed ability doesn't split anyone up and doesn't show the people who are better or worse. (Pupil from a mixed ability school)

Mixed ability is best because then there isn't a brainy set and a dumb set. (Pupil from a set school)

In our old class the teachers used to put the clever ones in a higher group and that was a bit upsetting because you knew that you weren't going to go in there . . . I won't say the thick ones but the ones that weren't so clever we were in a lower group and that made you feel uncomfortable . . . I think they should be mixed . . . half the clever peo-ple and half the not so clever people so that then you don't feel upset. (Primary)

The unspoken values behind ability grouping as perceived by the pupils emerged in subtle ways. One pupil described how:

> I'd put people in groups and the not very clever ones could be a darker colour and the clever ones could be a brighter colour.

As we saw in Chapter 3, this legitimisation of differences in ability can lead to teasing and stigmatisation. Although there is an assumption amongst adults that pupils are aware of the pecking order of ability within their class, whether that class is mixed ability or a set, the evidence from the primary study suggests that children are perhaps not as aware as we have believed. The children were asked to assess themselves academically and this revealed that the majority of pupils demonstrated a self-perception in accordance with that of their teachers. However, there were differences between schools ranging from 52% to 76%. The most accurate estimates were made in the school with the greatest degree of streaming and setting. The least accurate were made in the school which adopted mixed ability teaching in Key Stage 1 and streaming for the whole curriculum in years 3 to 6. In this school 52% of the pupils gave an accurate estimation, 13% underestimated their ability and 35 % overestimated. In the school that was committed to mixed ability teaching, 66% of pupils gave accurate estimations, but with one exception the lower ability pupils overestimated their ability. This overestimation continued throughout the age range into year 6. Of those who overestimated their ability, 64% were boys in comparison with 36% of girls. Of those who underestimated their ability, the greatest proportion were girls (55%). These gender differences are consistent with the research reported on self-esteem in Chapter 3.

How can we explain the differences in these estimations between schools? Structured ability grouping, when it is visible, makes perceived differences in ability transparent. Where pupils are taken out of classes or move to different rooms for setting procedures, the groupings become apparent to everyone. The status of the child in relation to ability is then legitimised. This can lead to teasing and the stigmatisation of the lower ability pupils.

Primary pupils' perceptions of different types of grouping

At secondary level pupils were asked which type of class grouping most people believed was best and why and which type of grouping they preferred and why. At primary level, pupils were asked to state the advantages and disadvantages of the kinds of ability grouping with which they were familiar.

At primary level, the majority of pupils had an accurate awareness of how they were grouped. The younger respondents in School 1 tended to be unaware of the streaming implemented up to year 3, although children in the top stream seemed to know that they were expected to work at a faster pace and higher level than their peers. At Key Stage 2, most pupils in all schools were aware of how and why they were grouped. As we have seen in the previous sections, some demonstrated a mature insight into the differences. They generally felt that the ways in which they were grouped were effective and most pupils (55%) indicated that they would not make any changes to the practices in place in their schools although there was considerable variation between schools. Just over 25% indicated that they would like to move into a different group to do harder work, while 12% wanted to move groups to be with their friends. None of this variation was related in any systematic way to the grouping policies adopted. Only 2% overall wished to be in a lower group or to have easier work. These children tended to be in the schools with higher levels of streaming and setting.

The main perceived advantage of setting was that work was set at an appropriate level. This view was expressed by 27% of the pupils. 13% indicated that setting provided opportunities to work with different pupils, 10% indicated that it enabled better teaching and explanations from teachers, and 8% said that when classes were set the work given was at a harder level. Other advantages, mentioned by a very small numbers of respondents, included having opportunities to work with other teachers, having the opportunity to gain status by being in a high group, having opportunity to get a higher grade in the Key Stage tests, and not being held back by other pupils. Very few pupils responded in relation to the advantages and disadvantages of streaming, as few had experience of it. Of the responses made, the greatest number raised the issue of work being set at an appropriate level.

The main disadvantages of setting as perceived by the primary school pupils were the stigmatisation of the pupils in the lower sets (23%) and the teasing of pupils in higher sets (5%). The disadvantages of streaming were seen as not being in the same stream as friends (17%), the work being too easy (8%), the top streams having more interesting work and being of higher status (8%), and the pressure of being in the top streams (8%). Other disadvantages raised were the low status of the bottom stream, teasing related to being in a lower stream, and pupils' abilities in different subjects not being catered for.

Secondary pupils' views about which type of grouping is best

In our secondary study just over 6,000 pupils responded to the question 'Which type of grouping do you think is best?' Of these, 62% indicated a preference for setting, 24% for mixed ability classes, and 2% each for streaming, banding or an unspecified other. 7% said that they didn't know. These figures differed according to the type of school that the children attended. The preference for mixed ability classes was greater where the pupils had experienced more mixed ability teaching (37%) and was identical for those schools that had been classified as mainly adopting setting or a mixture of setting and mixed ability classes (17%). Setting was the preference of 71% of the pupils in set and partially set schools and 41% of the pupils in mixed ability schools (see Figure 4.1).

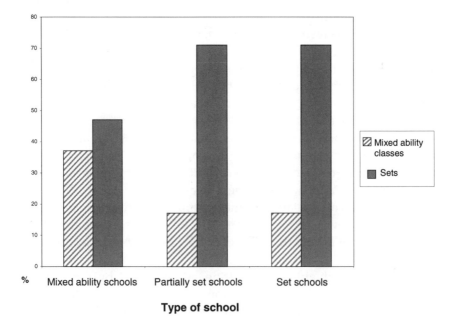

Figure 4.1: Pupils' preferences for different types of ability grouping by types of school

These overall figures obscure very wide diversity. Within the set schools the highest preference for setting was 83% and the lowest 40%. In the partially set schools the range was smaller, 82% to 58%. In the mixed ability schools the picture was confused. Only three of these schools solely adopted mixed ability classes with no setting at all. Most had some setting, with an increase as the pupils progressed through school. In the three schools where there was no setting, the pupils showed stronger preferences for mixed ability teaching with a range of 72% to 50%. In the remaining schools in the mixed ability group there was a preference for setting with a range from 42% to 64%. In some schools there was little difference in the percentage of pupils choosing setting as opposed to mixed ability with differences as small as 4%. In other schools the difference was as great as 37%. This suggests that in some schools there was greater cohesion within the pupil body. This may indicate variations in levels of alienation. Pupils acknowledged that their preferences depended on their own experiences. Most, by year 9, had experience of both setting and mixed ability classes at secondary school but this was not the case for all pupils.

Which type of grouping is best? Differences between groups

There were marked differences in the preferences of pupils from higher and lower ability groups for different kinds of grouping. A greater proportion of those in the lower sets for mathematics (the most frequently set subject) preferred mixed ability classes (39%) when compared to those in the middle sets (21%) or top sets (16%). The order of preference for setting was reversed, with 73% of pupils in the highest sets preferring setting, 66% of those in the middle sets and 44% of those in the lowest sets. These figures were supported by an analysis of preferences by Key Stage 3 test scores, which also indicated that those with the highest scores have the greatest preference for setting.

There were also gender differences in grouping preferences. Girls had a slightly greater preference for setting (65%) than boys (61%). Boys were more likely to prefer mixed ability classes (26%) than girls (21%). When the data were further broken down by the sets that the pupils were in for mathematics, 79% of boys in the top sets preferred setting while 11% preferred mixed ability; in the middle groupings the percentage preferring setting fell to 65% and in the bottom sets to 43%. For the girls the pattern was similar: 80% of girls in the top sets preferred setting, falling to 70% in the middle sets and 47% in the lowest sets. There are then two interweaving patterns, a slightly greater preference of girls for setting alongside an increasing preference for setting if you happen to be in the top set. Figure 4.2 illustrates the gender differences in relation to the set that pupils were in.

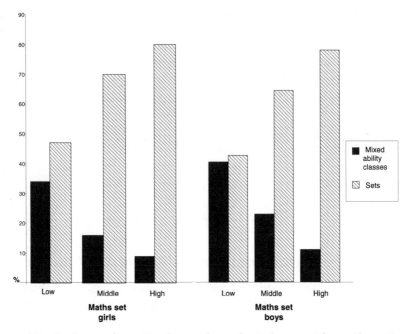

Figure 4.2:   Preference for setting by gender and set placement for mathematics

There were also social group differences. Although there are known limitations on the credibility of free school meals as a measure of social class, they do provide an

indication of those who are not only eligible for free school meals but who are prepared to face the possible stigmatisation involved in taking them. The data revealed that there was a greater preference for setting amongst children not taking free school meals: 64% preferred setting and 22% mixed ability. For those taking free school meals, the figures were 55% and 32% respectively. There was insufficient data to assess whether ethnicity was a factor in grouping preferences.

Satisfaction with current ability group

The secondary pupils responded to two questionnaire items asking about their set placement. They were 'If you could choose, would you like to be in a different class or set?' If the answer was yes, the pupils were asked 'Which class or set would you like to be in?' These questions were repeated for English, mathematics and science. While the evidence above indicated an overall preference for setting amongst secondary school pupils, a sizeable proportion of pupils were not happy with the set that they were in and wanted to move to a different set. The largest proportion wanting to change set was in mathematics (39%), followed by science (32%) and English (26%). Table 4.1 displays the number of pupils wanting to change set by type of school. Those in the schools with less setting overall were consistently less likely to want to change set.

Table 4.1: Percentage of secondary pupils wanting to change set by type of school

	Mathematics	**Science**	**English**
MA school	37	29	22
PS school	43	32	25
Set school	39	35	30

In mathematics, of the 39% of pupils who wanted to change set, just over a quarter (28%) wanted to be in the top set and almost half (49%) in another higher set. Overall, 77% of those pupils who wanted to move set wanted to be in a higher set. Only 17% wanted to move down. 2% wanted to be in a parallel set. In science, of the 32% who wanted to change set, almost a third (31%) wanted to be in the top set and approximately two-fifths (41%) wanted to be in another higher set. Overall 72% of those wanting to move set wanted to move up. Only 14% wanted to move down, while 8% wanted to move to a parallel set and 6% wanted to move to an unspecified other group. Of the 26% wishing to change set in English, almost a third (30%) wanted to be in the top set and just over a third (35%) in another higher set. Two-thirds (65%) wanted to move in an upward direction, 12% wanted to move to a lower set, 13% to a parallel set, and 10% to another unspecified group. Overall, a substantial proportion of pupils were unhappy with their placement in sets and the majority of those wanted to be in a higher set.

Pupils' responses differed according to the type of school they attended (see Table 4.2). In mathematics, in the set schools 79% of pupils who wanted to change set wished this change to be in an upward direction. In the partially set schools this was slightly less,

76%, and in the mixed ability schools 73%. In the set and partially set schools, a much greater proportion of pupils wanted to move to a higher set but not the top set. This finding may be because those in the lower sets in these schools see it as unrealistic to be in the top set or it may be that in those schools the pressure or teasing in the top set is such that pupils wish to avoid it. In the mixed ability schools the percentages of pupils wishing to be in the top set or another higher set are very similar. Regardless of the type of school, it is in mathematics that the greatest proportion of pupils wish to move down to a lower set.

The proportion of pupils wishing to change set in science also varied by type of school, being greater in the set schools. In science the pattern differed from mathematics. Here the greatest proportion of pupils wanting to move into the top set was in the partially set schools (37%). Again in the set schools more pupils wanted to be in another higher set (44%) rather than the top set (37%). The smallest proportion wanting to move up was in the mixed ability schools (31%) as was the smallest proportion wanting to move down (11%). In the mixed ability schools, 27% of pupils wanted to move to parallel (27%) or other (15%) sets or classes.

Table 4.2: Which class or set would you like to be in? Percentages of response according to type of school

	Top set	Other higher set	Lower set	Parallel set or class	Other type of change
MATHEMATICS					
MA school	37	36	17	4	6
PS school	25	51	18	1	4
Set school	23	56	17	2	3
SCIENCE					
MA School	31	16	11	27	15
PS school	37	44	15	1	3
Set school	27	53	15	2	4
ENGLISH					
MA school	22	6	5	38	30
PS school	39	30	12	14	6
Set school	29	49	15	3	5

In English the pattern was very similar to science. In the mixed ability schools the greatest proportion of pupils wanted to move to a parallel (38%) or other (30%) set or class. In the partially set schools 69%

wanted to move up, 39% to the top set, and in the set schools 78% wanted to move up, almost half of these to another higher set.

There were also gender differences in preference for moving set (see Table 4.3). Far more boys than girls wanted to be in the top set in all subjects. In mathematics 82% of the boys wanted to move into a higher set as opposed to 68% of the girls. This difference arose because a larger proportion of boys (34%) as opposed to girls (19%) wanted to be in the top set. In science 78% of the boys wanted to move to a higher set. This figure fell to 65% for the girls. Again the difference was in relation to being in the top set (boys 37%, girls 24%). In English the difference was much smaller. Here 71% of boys wanted to move up compared to 68% of the girls. In all subjects the girls were more likely to want to move down to a lower set. This was particularly marked in mathematics (girls 23%, boys 13%). There were no marked differences in relation to movement to a parallel set between the genders.

Table 4.3: Set preferences: percentages of response by gender

	Top set	Top or other higher set	Lower set	Parallel
MATHEMATICS				
Males	34	48	13	1
Females	19	49	23	3
SCIENCE				
Males	37	41	10	6
Females	24	41	19	9
ENGLISH				
Males	33	38	8	13
Females	27	31	18	13

Reasons given for wanting to move into a different set

What reasons did pupils give for wanting to change set or remain in their existing set? There were several main reasons including status, to do harder or easier work, aspirations, to be with friends, the poor behaviour of classmates, and the skills or personal qualities of the teacher.

Status

The importance of status was indicated in relation to the direct question asked about which set individuals would prefer to be in. It also emerged in response to the question about the set which most people believed to be 'the best set'. Status issues emerged in relation to wanting to be in the top set but also in relation to not being in the bottom or very low sets:

> I am in set 1 for maths and want to stay there because I like to be quite good at all subjects. Set 1 is best because the people who are best at maths are in that set and some people think it is a measure of intelligence but it's not. (Set school)

> I am in set 1. I want to stay there. Set 1 is best because people in set 1 find maths easier than others. (Set school)

> I'm in set 2. I would like to be in the top set because I want to be the best in the year. (Set school)

> I am in set 8 for maths and would like to move up as set 8 is a very low set and I would like to be higher. (Set school)

To do work at a more appropriate level

One of the most common reasons for wanting to change set was to undertake work at a more appropriate level.

> I am in set 11 for maths and would like to move to set 9 because set 11 are too slow and I understand what they do really clear when I've finished they're still doing the work. I don't want to be in set 10 because some of my mates are in there and I'll just talk too much. (Set school)

> I am in set 9 for maths and would like to change to 6 or 7 because the work is too easy. (Set school)

> I am in set 5 for science but would like to be in set 3 because I am a fast paced worker in science and always get high marks. (Set school)

> I am in set 4 for English and would like to move to set 2 because the work we do is quite boring most of the time. (Set school)

> I'd like to be in a higher science set . . . I'd like some harder work . . . in my set we have to do things like colouring in and sticking and tests and stuff but it's really easy . . . I want to get more brainy and go higher I'd be delighted if they put me in a higher set . . . I wouldn't mind doing harder work. (Primary, below average pupil)

Some pupils wanted to move down a set because they found the work too difficult. This was not restricted to those in the higher sets.

I am in set 3 for maths and would like to be in set 4 because I sometimes find maths hard and think I would like to go a bit slower so I fully understand what I'm doing. (Set school)

I am in set 10 for maths and I would like to be in set 12 because the work is easier. (Set school)

I am in set 1 for English. I would like to move to set 2 because the work is a bit easier. (Set school)

This suggests that the matching of work to pupils' needs is not necessarily satisfied through structured ability grouping.

Aspirations

Other reasons that pupils gave for wanting to move into a higher set included the opportunities that opened up to pupils in the higher sets.

I would like to be in set 1 for English because there is more chance of having a successful future. (Set school)

You need to be in a high set as maths is very important for getting a job. (Set school)

I would like to be in a higher group for science because I need to know a bit of science because I want to be a mechanic. (Primary pupil).

Other pupils specified getting better grades in examinations that in turn would open up better career opportunities.

I would like to be in a higher set to learn more harder mathematics to get a better grade. (Set school)

I am in set 11 for English and would like to move to set 6 so I can get a better grade. (Set school)

I'm in set 10 for English but I would like to be in set 1 because I could get a better mark in my exams. (Set school)

Setting also placed limitations on pupils' career aspirations and what they thought they were capable of.

I'm in set 8 of 12 . . . I think it is right for me because if I was clever enough to be moved up I would have gone up. (Set school)

I am in set 12 and I would like to be in set 11 because I am learning and I work hard but my English teacher says I do it all wrong. (Set school)

I'm in set 7. I would like to be in set 4 because I think it's about the most I could handle. (Set school)

Social reasons

Not all the reasons that pupils gave for wanting to change set related to academic matters. Some wanted to change because they felt they did not get on with other people in the class or their friends were in a different class.

I'm in set 5 and I would like to move to set 4 because there are certain people in my set who I don't get on with. (Set school)

I'm in set 2 and I sometimes would like to be in set 1 because my best friends are there but my standard is set 2. (Set school)

I am in set 6 but would like to be in set 5 because that's where all my friends are. (Set school)

Sometimes comparing notes with friends in other groups led pupils to believe that they were in the wrong group.

I'm in set 10 but I'd like to be in set 9 because I got the same grade as my friend but he is in set 9. (Set school)

I'm in set 8 and I would like to move to set 6 or 7 as most friends don't have difficulty with the work and I do . . . it sounds easier . . . we study harder things than them sometimes so it feels like I'm in a higher set than my friends. (Set school)

Teachers

Some pupils wanted to move set or class because they didn't like their present teacher.

I'm in set 3 and I would like to be in set 2 because I don't like my science teacher. (Set school)

I'm in set 5 and I would like to move because I don't really like the teacher, it's not the set that bothers me it's just that he never lets us ask him a question . . . he's too pushy . . . he always goes shhhhhh when we ask him a question or ignores our hands up in the air when he does that I call him and he just shakes his head and goes 'No, work quietly'. (Set school)

I'm in set 5 for science and I would like to move anywhere because I hate the teacher I've got now. (Set school)

Others wanted to stay in their current set or class because they liked their teacher, or to move to another class because they liked the teacher in a different class.

> I'm in set 9 for English and I would like to stay there because I have a good teacher. (Set school)

> I would like to move to Mrs C's class ... we don't have sets but she explains maths well and she's funny. (Mixed ability school)

> I would like to be in science 1 because I know I could do the work and my current teacher cannot control the class or explain things well. I feel I could do a lot better with a different teacher. (Set school)

Some primary school pupils liked the opportunity setting offered to experience teaching from a variety of teachers.

> I like the sets because you go to different rooms and have different teachers instead of having the same teacher all the time ... you don't get bored with the same teacher for everything ... it's good. (Primary, above average ability)

Others commented on the stability of being in the same class.

> I liked being in a class all the time because you were more settled and you knew what you were doing for the week. (Primary, below average ability)

For one primary pupil gender was an issue:

> I'd like to be in Sir's class because I want a boy to be my teacher.

The frequencies of responses for each category are given in Table 4.4. There were many similarities between the responses for mathematics,

Table 4.4: Reasons for wanting to be in a different set (percentages)

Reason	Mathematics	Science	English
Status	10	6	7
To do harder work	25	20	18
To do easier work	13	9	8
To be with friends	3	8	8
Because of poor behaviour of classmates	2	2	3
Because of the skills of the teacher	2	3	2
Because of the personal qualities of the teacher	3	4	7
Other	36	41	40
Combination	6	7	7

science and English. The single major reason given for wanting to move set was the fact that the work was of an inappropriate level. This particularly applied in mathematics (38%), followed by science (29%) and English (26%)

Table 4.5: Reasons given for wanting to be in a different class by type of school

Reason	Mathematics (%)			Science (%)			English (%)		
	MA	PS	Set	MA	PS	Set	MA	PS	Set
Status	16	7	7	21	26	29	6	9	7
To do harder work	24	23	29	5	2	5	5	16	25
To do easier work	14	14	13	6	5	6	6	7	10
To be with friends	5	3	3	6	1	2	22	4	5
Because of poor behaviour of classmates	1	2	2	1	1	1	6	3	1
Because of the teacher's skills	1	2	2	2	2	2	3	2	2
Because of the personal qualities of the teacher	3	3	4	6	2	2	10	8	6
Other	31	41	35	43	51	42	30	45	39
Combination	7	7	6	10	12	11	13	6	6

Set and class preferences: school and gender differences

The secondary school students' reasons for wanting to be in a different set varied across type of school as well as subject (see Table 4.5). For instance, in mathematics status seemed to be more important in the mixed ability schools than the other schools, although this trend was reversed for science and English. Perhaps this is because mathematics was often the only subject that was set in the mixed ability schools. While mathematics was overwhelmingly the subject where people wanted to do harder work this was the case in the set schools for English and to a lesser extent in the partially set schools. In most of the mixed ability schools English was taught in mixed ability classes. In science the main reason for wanting to change set in all types of school was related to status. In all types of school a large proportion of cases were not easily classified.

Table 4.6:   Gender differences in reasons for wanting to change group

| | Mathematics (%) | | Science (%) | | English (%) | |
	Male	Female	Male	Female	Male	Female
Status	12	7	8	5	9	4
To do harder work	26	24	21	18	19	16
To do easier work	11	17	7	12	6	11

At secondary level, in most categories there were no substantial gender differences with the exception of status and doing harder or easier work. The girls were consistently less status conscious than the boys. They were also slightly less likely to want to change sets to do harder work and more likely to want to change to do easier work. This applied across mathematics, science and English. Table 4.6 gives the details.

Primary school pupils' desire to change group

In the case study primary schools that adopted same age ability grouping, the main reason for wishing to change groups was to have harder work. In the school where mixed ability teaching was the norm most pupils did not want to change groups (86%). In the school where there was cross-age setting the main reason for wishing to change groups was to be with friends. A small proportion of pupils across most schools wished to move down to be in a lower set and have easier work, but most wanted to move to a higher group and have more difficult work (see Table 4.7).

Which set is best and why? Secondary pupils' views

In examining the reasons given for pupils wishing to change set or class, it became apparent that there were substantive differences at primary and secondary level in response to this question dependent on the type of grouping being adopted. In addition, the evidence from the secondary school pupils' responses to the question exploring which type of grouping they preferred (even within types of school) suggested that there were important differences in the ethos of the school which led pupils to make different responses. The next section explores secondary pupils' responses to being asked 'which set or class do people think is best and why? in an attempt to understand some of these differences. Many of the reasons given were similar to those given for wishing to move set.

The top set is best

The reasons given for the top set being best were based on references to superiority, ability, aspirations to do well in examinations and future employment prospects.

There were a number of examples of pupils expressing the view that being in set 1 set them or others apart in a superior position because it was 'higher'.

> Set 1 is best because you are the best in your year group, better than anyone else. (Set school)

> Set 1 is best because all the 'bofs' are in there and it is the highest set. (Set school)

In some cases set 1 was seen as best because to be in it one had to be 'brainy'. There was also an indication that in some schools this was seen as better by the teachers.

> Set 1 because pupils in set 1 can understand things in science more easily. (Set school)

> Set 1 because if you're in set 1 you are considered hard-working and brainy. (Set school)

> The teachers say sets 1–4 are the best. 'Why can't you have the brains like them?' So in this set they are apparently meant to be really brainy and we should be like them. (Set school)

Other responses indicated that pupils thought the top set or other higher sets are best because they may offer privilege in relation to taking examinations early or being entered for higher tiers.

> The best set academically is set 1 but otherwise set 2 is best. In set 1 you get to take GCSE a year early which is a real privilege but I don't think that most people would want to be in this set. (Set school)

> Set 1 because we are doing our GCSEs a year early and always do well in tests. (Set school)

Table 4.7: Primary pupils' desire to change groups

School	Wish to move to a higher group/have harder work (%)	Wish to move to a different group to work with friends (%)	Wish to be in a lower group/ have easier work (%)	Wish to move to a different group to be with a particular teacher (%)	No desire to change groups/ happy with groups (%)
1 Streaming up to year 3, setting for core curriculum for rest of KS2	35	6	6	6	47
2 Mixed ability/ within class ability grouping in KS1, streaming for whole curriculum in KS2	21	17	4	4	58
3 Setting for mathematics and English from year 1, mixed ability/within class ability grouping for the rest of the curriculum	30	20	10	10	30
4 Setting for mathematics	33	0	6	6	61
5 Cross-age for mathematics and English	11	33	0	0	56
6 No setting, mixed ability/ within class ability grouping	14	0	0	0	86
Overall percentage (n = 85)	26	12	2	5	55

Sets 1 and 2 are best because in year 10 when the sets are spread out set 3 get put into set 6 or 7 and when the work is given to lead up to our GCSEs set 6 get the higher tier and set 7 get the foundation tier so we are put in the middle. This is why set 1 or 2 is better. (Set school)

Being in the top set was seen as offering better long-term prospects, while being in a low set was seen as being on course for unemployment.

Set 1 is seen as best because if you're in this set you can get a better job. (Set school)

Set 1 is best because they are brainy and will get good jobs and lots of money when they are older and the lower sets will be left for unemployment. (Set school, pupil in set 8)

Overall, there tended to be something of a halo effect operating in relation to the top set. Some pupils thought that pupils in the top set had the best of everything.

Set 1 is best because this is the set with the best teachers, best textbooks and we are allowed to do more creative practicals. (Set school)

Middle sets are best

A large number of pupils viewed the middle sets as best because they offered anonymity which protected against teasing, the work was neither too hard nor too easy and there was usually an enjoyable atmosphere which was not too competitive.

Sets 3 and 4 are seen as best because it is not really difficult nor really easy. It sounds good that you are in set 3 or 4 and you're not a total boffin or really dense. (Set school)

Set 4 is seen as best because it is not too hard but not too easy. (Set school)

Set 8 or 9 is best (for maths) because they have the coolest people or teacher. Set 5 is the best (for science) because all the nice boys are in our set. Set 9 is best for English because of the people in it they make the class more fun. I would like to be in set 5 because my class is boring and we never do anything fun. (Set school, female pupil)

Some pupils' responses indicated alienation from the values of the school.

> Set 2 or 3 are best because people consider people in set 1 to be 'bofs' and sad and it's cool to get bad grades and have an attitude problem. (Set school)

Other pupils interpreted such responses as a defence against being rejected by the school's academic values.

> Obviously people think the lower sets are a laugh but everyone really would like to be in sets 1 or 2 because they want to become clever and get a good education so that they can get a good job. (Set school)

The different values held by pupils within the school are illustrated by the following statement:

> If you mean for academic reasons then set 1. If you mean for most fun then 3 or 4. In set 1 you get to take your GCSE a year early which is a real privilege if you can handle it. Set 3 or 4 is most fun because you can have a laugh in the lessons as well as work . . . there is less pressure on you. (Set school)

Other pupils expressed the view that their class was the best. The reasons for this were various. As in relation to moving sets, the role of teachers was crucial. This was in some cases related to their teaching skills and in others in relation to their personality. What was very clear from the pupils' responses was the importance of the individual teacher.

> Set 7 is best because the teacher takes it slower and does not rush through the subjects and it gives you more time to understand the subject you are doing. (Set school, pupil in set 8)

> Set 3 is best because one of our teachers is really good and he makes learning interesting but our other teacher is a waste of space so we muck around a lot. (Set school)

> Set 4 is best because they have a nice teacher who does not set much homework. (Set school)

> The best set is set 7 because it's got everyone's favourite teacher. (Set school)

> Set 4 is best because there is a really cool teacher. (Set school)

In some subjects the status of sets was perceived in relation to the activities that were undertaken in them. Top sets seemed to have a range of privileges that were not afforded to other groups. This particularly applied to English and science.

> The top set is best because we get to go on trips and others don't. (English, MA school)

> The top set is best because you are allowed to be more creative. (English, MA school)

> Set 1 is best because we do interesting work. The teacher communicates well with us. We are allowed to express our own views. (English, set school)

> The top set is best because you get to go on trips, get nice teachers and better grades. (English, MA school)

> Set 1 is best because you do more practical work and more experiments. It sounds like fun. (Science, set school)

> Set 1 is best because you learn the most and get to do interesting things like dissecting things. (Science, set school)

> Set 1 is seen as the best because you learn about more interesting science. (Science, set school)

These findings confirm what has been observed in studies in the USA (Oakes, 1985). However, some students indicated that the top set did not always do the most interesting work. There are school and teacher differences.

> Set 2 is best because in this lesson the subject is gone into slightly more depth and you can do the practical in pairs instead of the teachers doing it all the time. (Set school)

> Set 2 is best because you get to do a lot of practical work. (Set school)

Which set do most people think is best? Subject differences

Secondary pupils were asked 'Which set do most people think is best?' in English, mathematics and science. In all subjects the single largest response category was the top set. In mathematics the top group was perceived as best by 46%, the top or other higher class by 17%, a lower set by 12% and a parallel group by 1%, 17% thought that their set was the best and 7% said that they did not know. In science the top set was seen as best by 40%, another top set by 15%, a lower class by 9%, a parallel group 2%, 21% believed that their set was the best group and

13% didn't know. In English the top set was perceived as best by 35%, a top or other high set by 11%, a lower set by 8%, a parallel group by 4%, 24% thought their own set was best. In English a large proportion simply did not know (18%). The data is displayed in Figure 4.3.

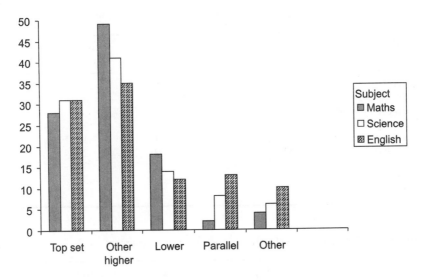

Figure 4.3:   Which set is best and why: subject differences

For all subjects, status was the single main reason given for a set or class being seen as best. The effect was strongest in mathematics followed by science and then English. In English, perhaps because of the nature of the material being taught, the personal qualities of the teacher seem to take on more importance (see Table 4.8).

Which set is best and why: school type and gender differences

There were differences between type of school in the responses made to the question 'Which class or set do most people think is best?' The top set was perceived as best by 49% of the pupils in mixed ability schools, 47% of those in the partially set schools and 43% in the set schools. In the set (19%) and partially set (19%) schools there was a greater proportion of pupils indicating that another top or higher set was the best than in the mixed ability schools (12%). The figures for preferences for the lower sets or classes were similar (between 11% and 13%). In the mixed ability and set schools 'my own' class was seen as best in 18.5% of cases. In the partially set schools this fell to 13%.

There are differences in pupils' perceptions between the three types of schools. Status was again the main single reason given for the choice of 'best' group. Status was cited by 34% of pupils in the mixed ability and set schools and 28% in the partially set schools (see Table 4.9).

Table 4.8: Reasons for a particular set being seen as best: subject differences

Reason	Mathematics (%)	Science (%)	English (%)
Status	32	26	22
To do harder work	4	4	4
To do easier work	6	5	5
To be with friends	1	3	3
Because of poor behaviour of classmates	1	1	1
Because of the skills of the teacher	2	2	3
Because of the personal qualities of the teacher	2	3	7
Other	39	45	46
Combination	13	11	9

Table 4.9: Choice of best set: school type differences (percentages)

	Top	Other higher set	Lower	Parallel	Mine
MATHEMATICS					
MA school	49	12	11	3	19
PS school	47	19	13	0	13
Set school	43	19	13	0	18
SCIENCE					
MA school	31	6	7	9	26
PS school	43	17	10	0	18
Set school	41	17	10	0	21
ENGLISH					
MA school	16	1	3	13	33
PS school	39	11	7	3	23
Set school	39	14	10	2	23

In line with other responses there were gender differences in preference for different sets. Here, 51% of boys and 40% of girls said that the top set was best in mathematics, 43% of boys and 36% of girls in science and 38% of boys and 31% of girls in English. Girls indicated across all subjects that the top or other higher set was best (see Table 4.10). There was also a tendency for more girls than boys to select 'my set' as being the best in mathematics and English.

Table 4.10: Which class do most people think is best: gender differences (percentages)

	Top	Top or other higher set	Lower set	Parallel	My set
MATHEMATICS					
Males	51	15	12	1	15
Females	40	19	13	1	19
SCIENCE					
Males	43	12	9	2	21
Females	36	18	10	2	21
ENGLISH					
Males	38	10	7	4	23
Females	31	12	9	3	27

Status was the main single reason given for the choice of best set, cited more often by boys than girls (see Table 4.11). There were few responses relating to the level of work, friendships, behaviour or teacher skills. The skills of the teacher again emerged as important in relation to teaching English.

Table 4.11: Gender differences in reasons given for choice of best set

	Mathematics (%)		Science (%)		English (%)	
	Male	Female	Male	Female	Male	Female
Status	34	29	28	24	25	20
To do harder work	5	4	4	3	4	4
To do easier work	7	6	6	5	5	4
To be with friends	1	1	3	2	3	3
Because of inappropriate behaviour in the class	1	1	1	1	1	1
Teacher skills	1	2	2	2	4	3
Teacher personal qualities	2	2	3	3	8	7
Other reason	37	41	44	47	43	48
Combination	12	15	9	13	7	11

Summary

The majority of pupils at secondary level reported that they preferred setting to mixed ability classes. This preference was influenced by the school that they attended and their experiences of different types of grouping. Pupils in schools where mixed ability teaching was the predominant way of organising classes showed a preference for learning in mixed ability classes. In schools where setting was the predominant form of grouping pupils expressed a preference for setting. There were differences between pupils of different abilities, with pupils in low sets and those who did not attain high scores in their national tests at Key Stage 3 showing a greater preference for mixed ability groupings. These differences were overlaid with gender differences, with girls showing a greater preference for setting, and boys for mixed ability classes. Pupils who had free school meals were also likely to prefer mixed ability classes. There was too little data regarding ethnicity to explore whether there were different preferences from different ethnic groups. At primary level pupils demonstrated understanding and acceptance of the rationale for grouping adopted by their school and were able to outline the advantages and disadvantages of different kinds of grouping.

The main reason for pupils expressing a preference for setting were related to having work matched to their needs. However, a substantial proportion expressed a wish to move to a different group because the work was not well matched, most feeling it was too easy. Pupils also expressed the wish to move to higher sets to gain status, get better marks in examinations and enhance their opportunities for employment. Moving to a lower set was related to being given work more suited to individual needs. Teachers were important in pupils' desire to move classes – their teaching skills and personal characteristics were both cited. Some pupils wanted to move to be with friends. These factors emerged at primary and secondary level. Mixed ability teaching was viewed positively for the opportunities it gave to work with others and its contribution to social integration and equal opportunities.

Where structured ability groupings were adopted, they legitimised and made more transparent differences in pupils' attainment. Contrary to popular belief, pupils at primary level were not always aware of the extent of the differences between them. This was particularly true of the boys who tended to overestimate their ability especially when they were in mixed ability classes. The process by which pupils' attainment level becomes public through structured grouping leads to teasing of high and low ability pupils. This was unpleasant for both. The nature of language adopted, such as 'thick' or 'dumb', with its negative connotations stigmatised those of lower ability. Perhaps as a result of this, two parallel cultures appeared to have developed in some schools, one held by teachers and shared by some pupils in which high academic attainment was valued, the other where pupils valued being 'average', not being in the top set, having fun and not being too pressured. This culture is likely to have developed out of the perception by the majority of pupils that they were not valued by the institutional school culture of high attainment. There were differences between schools in the degree of preference for different types of grouping within similar school type. This suggests that the ethos of the school may be crucial in mediating the effects of different types of grouping. This will be explored further in Chapter 5.

There are clear practical implications from these findings. Firstly, if setting is to be adopted, schools must ensure that work is really matched to students' level of attainment. Related to this they must ensure that mechanisms are in place to facilitate movement between sets based on pupils' achievements. Given the negative impact of setting in relation to teasing and stigmatisation, schools need to ensure that an emphasis on high academic attainment is not paramount and that the skills of all children are valued. Schools might, for instance, emphasise effort, good behaviour, good attendance, sporting prowess, artistic or musical achievement or creativity. Teachers need to be aware of the messages that they are giving to their pupils about what they value and ensure that all pupils feel valued.

5

Teachers' Attitudes to Ability Grouping

In this chapter we will consider teachers' attitudes towards different kinds of pupil grouping and the factors that affect them. We will argue that teachers hold strong attitudes towards ability grouping, that these vary according to the type of school in which they work and also the subject that they teach. After reviewing the literature, we explore teachers' beliefs about the impact of structured ability grouping on the academic progress and self-esteem of pupils, whether ability grouping benefits particular groups of children, and the impact of ability grouping on the behaviour of pupils in the classroom. We then turn to teachers' views about the suitability of different curriculum subjects for mixed ability teaching. In both primary and secondary schools in this country there is a view that mathematics is the least suitable subject for mixed ability teaching, closely followed, in secondary schools, by modern foreign languages.

Research on teachers' attitudes

Surveys of teachers' attitudes towards ability grouping in the USA (NEA, 1968; McDermott, 1976; Wilson and Schmidts, 1978), Sweden (Husen and Boalt, 1967), England (Daniels, 1961a; Jackson; 1964, Barker Lunn, 1970) and Israel (Ministry of Education, 1965; Guttman et al., 1972) have revealed generally positive attitudes towards teaching classes where pupils are grouped by ability. However, there are variations based on teachers' prior experience and the subject that they teach. In the UK in the 1970s, when mixed ability teaching was innovatory, teachers who had direct experience of it tended to hold more favourable attitudes (Newbold, 1977; Reid et al., 1982). The advantages of mixed ability teaching were seen largely in social terms, while the disadvantages related to the difficulty of providing appropriate work for pupils of high and low ability in the same class. Criticisms suggested that mixed ability teaching failed to motivate and increase the achievement of the highly able, although the less able were perceived to benefit. Experienced teachers appeared to be more supportive of mixed ability teaching (Clammer, 1985) but they often found it more difficult to put into practice than those who had been recently trained to adopt such practices (Reid *et al.*, 1982).

At primary level, Barker Lunn (1970) reported that the attitude of the teacher towards mixed ability teaching was crucial in relation to its implementation in the classroom. Teachers classified as 'typical streamers' were 'knowledge'-centred, with an emphasis on the acquisition of knowledge and the attainment of a set of academic standards. They were particularly interested in and concerned for the bright child, concentrated on traditional lessons, gave more emphasis to literacy and numeracy, encouraged competition and approved of the selective examinations. Firm discipline was seen as important as the classroom atmosphere was formal. The typical non-streamer was more child-centred, with a greater concern for the all-round development of each pupil. Teaching tended to stress self-development, learning by discovery and practical experience. A more co-operative environment was encouraged, where pupils worked in groups and helped each other. There was also a more permissive classroom atmosphere. These teachers disliked streaming and selective examinations.

Reid *et al.* (1982) found that attitudes varied depending on the teachers' working environment. Where worksheets and other resources were readily available, mixed ability teaching was viewed more positively, but as external examinations approached and pressures increased, teachers felt more uncomfortable with mixed ability classes.

At secondary level, there appear to be differences in teachers' attitudes towards mixed ability teaching depending on the subject that they teach. Where subjects are structured in such a way that learning builds on previous knowledge, for example mathematics and modern foreign languages, teachers seem to favour streaming. Reid *et al.* (1982) found that subject domains were perceived as varying in their suitability for mixed ability teaching. The humanities were perceived as suitable whereas mathematics and modern foreign languages were perceived as inappropriate (90% of language teachers were sceptical of the possibility of mixed ability teaching). Scientists occupied a middle position perceiving some difficulties. Those subjects where mixed ability teaching was perceived as problematic tended to require correct answers and a grasp of abstract concepts. This may explain the greater number of studies specifically examining the effects of streaming and mixed ability teaching on achievement, or classroom interaction, in science (Frost, 1978; Plewes, 1979; Harvey, 1981; Lawrence and Munch, 1984; Hacker and Rowe, 1993). The research, with the exception of that of Frost (1978), found in favour of streamed groups.

Teaching preferences

Where a system of streaming or setting is in operation, the research suggests that teachers generally prefer to teach the high ability groups (Hargreaves, 1967; Lacey, 1970; Findlay and Bryan, 1975; Ball, 1981; Finley, 1984). Finley (1984) found that teachers competed against one another to be able to teach the advanced classes. Several researchers have suggested that teachers avoid teaching the low streams because of pupils' negative attitudes towards school and poor behaviour in the classroom which make them more difficult to teach (Hargreaves, 1967; Schwartz, 1981; Finley, 1984; Taylor, 1993).

There is also evidence that teachers of high ability streams tend to be more enthusiastic about teaching (Rosenbaum, 1976) and that teachers feel more efficacious when they teach higher ability classes (Raudenbush, Rowan and Cheong, 1992). This effect disappears when the level of pupil engagement is controlled. Perhaps teachers find it difficult to interest pupils in lower streams and the resulting lack of engagement undermines their sense of efficacy. Other research has shown that those teachers who consistently teach low ability groups tend to become demoralised over a period of time (Hargreaves, 1967; Finley, 1984).

Teachers' attitudes towards teaching low ability streams may contribute to the alienation of pupils in those streams. Pupils from high streams exhibit pro-social behaviour and it is this, rather than their academic accomplishments, which seems to shape teachers' behaviour towards them (Hargreaves, 1967; Lacey, 1970; Ball, 1981; Finley, 1984). Teachers also interact with high ability groups more frequently and positively than they do with low ability groups (Harlen and Malcolm, 1997; Sorenson and Hallinen, 1986; Gamoran and Berends, 1987). However, in some schools, teachers of low stream students do view them positively (Burgess, 1983, 1984). Teachers who perceive their role specifically relating to pupils with Special Educational Needs may have more positive attitudes (Ireson, 1999).

Teachers' beliefs about the impact of ability grouping

The projects reported here explored teachers' attitudes towards different types of ability grouping and the factors that affected those attitudes. Data were collected through a questionnaire survey of over 1,500 secondary school teachers in the 45 secondary comprehensive schools. Twenty-three per cent of the sample were between the ages of 20 and 29, 23% between 30 and 39, 35% between 40 and 49 and 16% over 50. Just over half of the sample were female (53%). Most of the teachers were educated to degree level, 59% had a PGCE, 21% a Certificate in Education and 13% a higher degree. Teachers in the six primary school case studies were also interviewed regarding their attitudes to ability grouping.

Perceived effects of ability grouping on academic progress

At both primary and secondary level most teachers believed that teaching pupils in structured ability groups raised academic standards. Table 5.1 sets out the rationales given by each of the six case study primary schools for the grouping practices that they adopted. Improvement in Key Stage tests was seen as crucial in all cases, although schools also took account of the perceived effects on pupils' self-esteem, albeit to different degrees, and their current resources.

Effects of different grouping systems on able children

In the questionnaires teachers in the secondary schools were asked to indicate the extent to which they agreed with a number of statements about the effects of pupil grouping on the more able pupils. In addition, in the interviews and open questions in the questionnaire, teachers volunteered their own views about the effects of different types of ability grouping on able children. Here we include comments from both primary and secondary school teachers.

> I have a few reservations about mixed ability teaching because the higher ability pupils are not stretched to their full potential. However, we do very well with the lower ability in the classroom. (Science teacher, mixed ability school)

> I would move towards more setting because it enables pupils' curriculum needs to be better matched, reduces brighter children being inhibited by peer pressure or slower children having self-esteem affected,

Table 5.1:   Rationale for the adoption of particular grouping practices

School	The perceived benefits of the grouping practices adopted
School 1 Streaming at KS1 and in year 3, setting for core curriculum for rest of KS2	• Improving all pupils' academic achievement • Improving Key Stage test results • Encouraging more focused, whole class teaching • Avoidance of creation of a 'sink' group by grouping pupils at KS1 in streams ABB to cater for wide ability range but with no C stream • Easing transition from KS1 to KS2 by maintaining streaming in year 3 • Catering for individual strengths and weaknesses while avoiding stigmatisation • Maximising the use of subject specialists
School 2 Mixed ability/within class ability grouping in KS1, streaming for the whole of the curriculum in KS2	• Improving academic performance • Extending more able pupils • Supporting less able pupils in smaller teaching groups • Reducing the range of differentiation • Raising the quality of teaching and learning • Improving general school performance • Responding to Ofsted recommendations following inspection
School 3 Setting for mathematics and English from year 1. Mixed ability/within class ability grouping for the rest of the curriculum	• Improving Key Stage test results • Catering for the extremes of the ability spectrum • Improving the clarity of planning and schemes of work • Alleviating potential problems caused by mixed age classes • Reducing ability range in classes for mathematics and and English
School 4 Setting for mathematics from year 4. Mixed ability/within class groupings for the rest of the curriculum	• Catering for the wide range of needs in mathematics • Enabling each pupil to achieve his/her full potential • Enabling settling into KS2 by not setting in year 3 • Enabling better allocation of pupils to sets by allowing time for assessment by not setting in year 3 • Taking advantage of subject specialisms of staff • Avoiding demoralisation of children in the lower sets by not setting for English
School 5 Cross-age setting for mathematics and English	• Raising levels of achievement • Catering for individual needs • Enabling all pupils to achieve their full potential • Reducing differentiation within classes • Providing children at the top of KS2 with the opportunity to work with same age peers • Maximising available space in the school
School 6 No setting. Mixed ability/within class grouping	• Improving Key Stage test results • Increasing the confidence of the children • Providing opportunities for pupils to work collaboratively • Providing access to peer models • Providing access to peer support

increases student (and teacher) motivation. (Mathematics teacher, partially set school)

I have reservations about mixed ability practices. One student in my tutor group, a straight A student when he arrived in year 7, is now a school refuser because of bullying and negative peer attitudes towards him. (Music teacher, mixed ability school)

I think that certainly the top groups have activities that will stretch them a little bit more now they are set. (Primary teacher in a set school)

Setting really released the more able children to be able to move on. I think because we have so many children with additional needs it's easy to teach too low here if you're not careful. The predicted grades for the end of year . . . 4 and level 4b and one or two 4as which we've never had before. (Headteacher, primary school)

Table 5.2 provides details of the statements in the secondary school questionnaire and gives the overall frequency counts for all of the teachers in response to these statements. It also provides a breakdown by the type of grouping practices adopted within the school.

Teachers tend to believe that there are benefits to the academic progress of the more able pupil when set grouping procedures are adopted. There was less agreement that able pupils are held back in mixed ability classes. Over half of the respondents indicated that setting prevented bright children being inhibited by negative peer pressure. There were also significant differences in the responses to these statements from teachers in schools adopting different kinds of ability grouping procedures. Teachers working in schools adopting mixed ability practices tended to view mixed ability teaching as less likely to inhibit the progress of the more able. Similar differences in response were also evident in relation to setting being advantageous to the academic progress of the able child and the inhibiting effects of negative peer attitudes, but they were less strong.

Perceived effects of ability grouping on personal and social development

In the interviews and questionnaires, in addition to indicating their level of agreement with statements about the effects of ability grouping on personal and social development, teachers volunteered their own views. Most teachers were aware of the possible negative effects of highly structured ability grouping on self-esteem and the way that mixed ability teaching might avoid them.

Table 5.2: Percentage responses to statements related to the academic performance of able pupils by different types of ability grouping practices

Statements	Type of ability grouping	Strongly agree	Agree	Neutral	Disagree	Strongly disagree
Bright children are	MA school	7.7 (39)	33.4 (169)	15.8 (80)	32.8 (166)	9.7 (49)
neglected or held back	PS school	15.2 (77)	41.6 (210)	15.2 (77)	20.8 (105)	5.1 (26)
in mixed ability classes	Set school	12 (73)	36.5 (222)	20.7 (126)	26.8 (163)	3.1 (19)
P = .0001	Total	11.7 (189)	37.1 (601)	17.5 (283)	26.8 (434)	5.8 (94)
Setting ensures that	MA school	14 (71)	40.7 (206)	18.6 (94)	22.5 (114)	4 (20)
brighter children make	PS school	26.1 (132)	47.5 (240)	13.5 (68)	9.9 (50)	2 (10)
maximum progress	Set school	26.5 (161)	50.5 (307)	12.8 (78)	8.4 (51)	1.6 (10)
P = .0001	Total	22.5 (364)	46.5 (753)	14.8 (240)	13.3 (215)	2.5 (40)
Setting prevents brighter	MA school	8.9 (45)	40.1 (203)	22.7 (115)	21.3 (108)	5.5 (28)
children being inhibited	PS school	19 (96)	42 (212)	18.4 (93)	16 (81)	3 (15)
by negative peer pressure	Set school	16 (97)	42.4 (258)	21.4 (130)	18.6 (112)	1.5 (9)
P = .0001	Total	14.7 (238)	41.6 (673)	20.9 (338)	18.6 (301)	3.2 (52)

I believe that it is too early in year 7 to label pupils as bottom set. This will have a negative effect on their self-esteem. (Geography teacher, set school)

Mixed ability teaching because the social and personal development of the students would outweigh any academic deficiencies, if any. (Humanities teacher, mixed ability school)

In my experience mixed ability promotes self-esteem and motivation and encourages lively differentiated teaching. Co-operative skills are developed between students – more able students consolidate their knowledge by helping less able and less able have positive role models while covering the same ground. (English teacher, mixed ability school)

All groups in this school are mixed ability. The price paid for setting or banding is too high, i.e. reduction in self-esteem, sink groups, fear of failure. Students' needs can be met successfully with good, well-planned, differentiated work with clear targets. (Biology teacher, mixed ability school)

I prefer mixed ability teaching largely for social development. The less able benefit greatly, the more able benefit less, whilst in setting the less able don't benefit academically and the more able are only stretched a little more. I don't think it's worth it considering the benefits socially. (Science teacher, mixed ability school)

Years of experience have convinced me that this (mixed ability) is the most effective system academically, socially and personally. High self-esteem is in my opinion at the heart of successful learning and living. (English teacher, mixed ability school)

Some teachers were also aware of the polarisation that could occur through the adoption of rigid ability setting.

If you go for rigid streaming although there is no political bias to that I feel that you're producing a sink group, you're producing a group who think they're high flyers in everything and it's not necessary . . . to add to the social climate of the school we go for setting which I think is a compromise that should be there. (Headteacher, set school)

I have quite a lot of reservations about the current system (setting) as it results in social barriers and an ability class system within the school. The more able pupils are seen as swots and squares and less able pupils are seen as thickies, idiots, etc. Stereotyping leads to low self-esteem in lower groupings and an air of arrogance with the able. (Religious education teacher, set school)

I believe that the classroom environment should reflect real life where pupils learn about individual needs . . . and empathise. Where classes are set pupils become isolated within their own ability. Communication between different class groups breaks down and barriers are built. Able pupils can become overly confident and so under-achieve and less able lose motivation altogether believing themselves to be useless. (Religious education teacher, set school)

Table 5.3 gives a detailed account of the frequencies of the responses made in relation to questionnaire statements relating to self-esteem, stigmatisation, children's perceptions of their own ability, social adjustment and motivation. The responses to most of these statements are differentiated by the kind of ability grouping structures which are operating in the school where the teacher works. Those working in schools where there are mixed ability grouping procedures tend to view setting in a more negative light in relation to the social outcomes of education, particularly those relating to self-esteem and social adjustment.

There was general agreement that grouping practices affect self-esteem. There were no significant differences between responses from teachers of different types of school for this question. When the question referred to setting having a damaging effect on the self-esteem of those in the lower sets the responses were significantly differentiated. In the set and partially set schools a much larger proportion of

Table 5.3: Percentage responses to statements related to the perceived personal and social effects of different kinds of ability grouping

Statements	Type of ability grouping	Strongly agree	Agree	Neutral	Disagree	Strongly disagree
Pupil self-esteem is	MA school	1.2 (6)	11.3 (57)	20.2 (102)	45.5 (230)	20.8 (105)
unaffected by ability	PS school	1.6 (8)	12.9 (65)	24.2 (122)	45.5 (230)	14.5 (73)
grouping	Set school	.8 (5)	13.2 (80)	22.5 (137)	49 (298)	13.7 (83)
NS	Total	1.2 (19)	12.5 (202)	22.3 (361)	46.8 (758)	16.1 (261)
Setting has a damaging	MA school	18.4 (93)	40.5 (205)	17 (86)	19 (96)	4.3 (22)
effect on the self-esteem	PS school	9.7 (49)	34.1 (172)	20 (101)	30.3 (153)	4.4 (22)
of those in lower sets	Set school	9 (55)	36.3 (221)	20.2 (123)	30.4 (185)	3.3 (20)
p = .0001	Total	12.2 (197)	36.9 (598)	19.1 (310)	26.8 (434)	4 (64)
Setting children	MA school	27.1 (137)	36.6 (185)	12.8 (65)	19 (96)	3.2 (16)
stigmatises those	PS school	11.1 (56)	38.6 (195)	18.4 (93)	23.8 (120)	6.7 (34)
perceived as less able	Set school	9.7 (59)	45.1 (274)	15.8 (96)	22.2 (135)	6.3 (38)
p = .0001	Total	15.6 (252)	40.4 (654)	15.7 (254)	21.7 (351)	5.4 (88)
In mixed ability classes	MA school	6.5 (33)	32.4 (164)	16.4 (83)	32.4 (164)	10.7 (54)
the less able pupils are	PS school	7.9 (40)	40.8 (206)	17.8 (90)	26.1 (132)	6.5 (33)
more aware of what they	Set school	6.9 (42)	43.4 (264)	17.8 (108)	25.5 (155)	4.4 (27)
are unable to do. They are						
aware that other pupils						
are doing different work						
p = .0001	Total	7.1 (115)	39.2 (634)	17.4 (281)	27.9 (451)	7 (114)
Less able children	MA school	2.2 (11)	37.4 (189)	20.8 (105)	34 (172)	5.1 (26)
compare themselves	PS school	6.1 (31)	44.2 (223)	22 (111)	22.8 (115)	3 (15)
unfavourably to more	Set school	4.1 (25)	42.4 (258)	27.5 (167)	23.7 (144)	1.3 (8)
able children in mixed						
ability classes						
p = .0001	Total	4.1 (67)	41.4 (670)	23.7 (383)	26.6 (431)	3 (49)
Mixed ability grouping	MA school	15.8 (80)	47 (238)	20.8 (105)	13.2 (67)	2 (10)
leads to better social	PS school	9.7 (49)	43.4 (219)	27.9 (141)	15.2 (77)	2.8 (14)
adjustment for the less	Set school	7.1 (43)	43.6 (265)	28.9 (176)	16.3 (99)	3.3 (20)
able pupils						
p = .0001	Total	10.6 (172)	44.6 (722)	26.1 (422)	15 (243)	2.7 (44)
Mixed ability grouping	MA school	18.6 (94)	44.3 (224)	22.5 (114)	11.7 (59)	1.2 (6)
leads to better social	PS school	7.9 (40)	41.6 (210)	27.9 (141)	18 (91)	2.8 (14)
adjustment of all pupils	Set school	5.8 (35)	41.3 (251)	32.4 (197)	17.8 (108)	1.6 (10)
p = .0001	Total	10.4 (169)	42.3 (685)	27.9 (452)	15.9 (258)	1.9 (30)
Overall motivation is	MA school	8.7 (44)	28.9 (146)	29.6 (150)	26.9 (136)	5.3 (27)
higher when pupils are	PS school	4.2 (21)	15.8 (80)	34.7 (175)	33.9 (171)	9.7 (49)
in mixed ability classes	Set school	3.3 (20)	18.8 (114)	31.9 (194)	36.3 (221)	8.9 (54)
p = .0001	Total	5.3 (85)	21 (340)	32.1 (519)	32.6 (528)	8 (130)
Knowing they are in a	MA school	12.3 (62)	34.2 (173)	17.8 (90)	29.2 (148)	5.5 (28)
low set leads to pupils	PS school	7.1 (36)	28.5 (144)	16.8 (85)	39.4 (199)	6.5 (33)
giving up	Set school	6.9 (42)	31.1 (189)	17.1 (104)	38.2 (232)	5.8 (35)
p = .0001	Total	8.6 (140)	31.3 (506)	17.2 (279)	35.8 (579)	5.9 (96)

teachers disagreed with this statement than in the mixed ability schools, although overall the majority of teachers believed that setting did have a damaging effect. A similar pattern was in evidence regarding the stigmatisation of pupils in the lower sets. Similarly, teachers in set and partially set schools were more likely to agree that pupils are more aware of their academic limitations in mixed ability classes and compare themselves unfavourably with more able children. However, there was overall agreement that social adjustment is better for both low ability and all children in mixed ability structures, although this effect was more marked in responses from teachers in mixed ability schools. Where motivation was concerned there was overall agreement that setting has a negative effect on those in the low sets but the response was stronger in the mixed ability schools.

Perceived inequity of ability grouping

Teachers were asked to respond to statements about the benefits and costs to different groups of pupils of different types of ability grouping. In the interviews and the open-ended questions in the questionnaire they also volunteered their own views. Most opinions offered acknowledged the possible inequities of structured ability grouping.

> I feel it should be mixed ability up to year 9 to allow pupils to develop at a rate that suits their learning styles. All student development rates vary. As a student I remember the iniquity and trouble caused to me by being set. (Science teacher, mixed ability school)

> It's a school that does really practise or *has* practised what it's preached about valuing all students. It hasn't traditionally liked the ethos of setting. It's not liked what is created by, you know, a bottom group, in inverted commas, mentality. The difficulties of coping with that, the elitist approach to *top* sets or *top* groups, again in inverted commas; that's been very much a view I think shared by all staff here. There's a good consensus about this issue I think across the staff as a whole. That's been the reason for the approach. And the feeling that the differentiated approach in an all ability setting, where groups are kept relatively small in numbers because I think you need that to make it work. That's been the ethos. And the school got its best ever GCSE results two years ago . . . 57%. So the strength of it is that most faculties feel it has worked for them. (Headteacher, mixed ability school)

> It is felt very strongly that all kids get a fair crack of the whip if they're in the all ability groupings and there's a tendency to concentrate on top groups in many schools where they're setting, streaming or banding

and that's something that I think teachers here feel very strongly about. (Mixed ability school)

The children in the lower streams had had quite a difficult time because they'd had a lot of supply teachers and they weren't moving on very well. The children in the top streams had always had the most experienced teachers and it just wasn't equality of opportunity at all and so we moved away from that to mixed ability groups. (Headteacher, primary school)

Table 5.4 displays the responses made by the teachers in the secondary schools in relation to the effects of grouping structures on pupils of differing ability. Overall, there was a general tendency to disagree that setting benefits the more able pupils at the expense of the less able, that mixed ability teaching in reality only benefits the average child and that mixed ability teaching benefits the less able pupils academically at the expense of the more able. There was very strong agreement that mixed ability classes provide the less able pupils with positive models of achievement.

Table 5.4: Percentage responses to statements concerning perceptions of issues of equity in relation to the grouping of pupils by ability

Statements	Type of ability grouping	Strongly agree	Agree	Neutral	Disagree	Strongly disagree
Setting benefits the more able pupils at the expense of the less able $p = .0001$	MA school	8.3 (42)	30 (152)	12.8 (65)	32 (162)	15.8 (80)
	PS school	6.9 (35)	17.2 (87)	15.2 (77)	35.2 (178)	24.2 (122)
	Set school	5.8 (35)	22.7 (138)	16.8 (102)	32.1 (195)	22 (134)
	Total	6.9 (112)	23.3 (377)	15.1 (244)	33 (535)	20.8 (336)
Mixed ability grouping gives each child a fair chance $p = .0001$	MA school	10.3 (52)	35.6 (180)	18.2 (92)	26.5 (134)	8.9 (45)
	PS school	5.7 (29)	20.6 (104)	20.6 (104)	33.7 (170)	17.8 (90)
	Set school	2.8 (17)	20.2 (123)	22.2 (135)	38.5 (234)	15 (91)
	Total	6.1 (98)	25.1 (407)	20.4 (331)	33.2 (538)	14 (226)
Mixed ability teaching in reality only benefits the average child $p = .0001$	MA school	3 (15)	18 (91)	19.4 (98)	42.3 (214)	16.4 (83)
	PS school	3.4 (17)	25.5 (129)	21 (106)	36.8 (186)	11.9 (60)
	Set school	1.8 (11)	22.7 (138)	26.3 (160)	40.3 (245)	7.9 (48)
	Total	2.7 (43)	22.1 (358)	22.5 (364)	39.8 (645)	11.8 (191)
Mixed ability classes provide the less able pupils with positive models of achievement ns	MA school	11.1 (56)	51.8 (262)	21.5 (109)	13.4 (68)	1.6 (8)
	PS school	8.3 (42)	47.7 (241)	22 (111)	18 (91)	3.6 (18)
	Set school	8.4 (51)	51.3 (312)	21.7 (132)	15.6 (95)	2.1 (13)
	Total	9.2 (149)	50.3 (815)	21.7 (352)	15.7 (254)	2.4 (39)
Mixed ability teaching benefits the less able pupils academically at the expense of the more able $p = .001$	MA school	1.2 (6)	18.6 (94)	22.7 (115)	48 (243)	9.1 (46)
	PS school	3 (15)	22.6 (114)	27.1 (137)	38.6 (195)	6.9 (35)
	Set school	1.6 (10)	24 (146)	27.6 (168)	41.3 (251)	4.1 (25)
	Total	1.9 (31)	21.9 (354)	25.9 (420)	42.6 (689)	6.5 (106)

There were significant differences in response from teachers from schools adopting different ability grouping structures, particularly in relation to issues of opportunity and fairness. Teachers working in mixed ability schools were more likely to agree that mixed ability grouping gave every child a fair chance, while those working in set schools were more likely to disagree. Those working in mixed ability schools were also more likely to agree that setting benefits the more able at the expense of the less able and disagree that it benefits the less able academically at the expense of the more able.

Perceived effects of ability grouping on discipline and disaffection

Teachers indicated that setting could have an impact on disaffection and several suggested that mixed ability teaching could overcome this.

> Mixed ability is best. Pupils already know between them the ones with low and high ability. Grouping them only serves to emphasise the lack of ability of those in the lower ability classes. These pupils then become disaffected at a very early stage and I would like to avoid or delay their disaffection to as late as possible. (Mathematics teacher, mixed ability school)

> Having had experience of both mixed ability and set teaching and having seen a lot of excellent mixed ability teachers I believe this is the best way to ensure that no one fails or drops out. This is particularly important for students for whom English is a second language who may be bright but have limited English. It prevents labels which can prevent growth. (English teacher, partially set school)

> I've worked in several schools where there's heavy setting, ten sets, start the most able in set 1 and the least able in 10. Nobody wants to teach set 10, well probably sets 8, 9 and 10 don't feel very good about themselves at all. It often concentrates behaviour problems. The big challenge of setting is setting by ability rather than by behaviour. I think you get that problem a great deal. The students end up in the bottom groups or sets because of their attitude to work or behaviour, rather than ability. The kids tend to rattle around in these groups of quite challenging youngsters for the whole of their time, virtually from the minute they come into school and I think you end up with a real problem about disaffection. And I think all ability teaching gets over that. That's one of the main advantages as far as I can see it. (English teacher, mixed ability school)

There could also be difficulties in mixed ability classes when the particular group of pupils did not work well together.

> You've got some extremely good groups of students who work very, very well together, and that's fine when that happens. When you get a mix of kids who don't work quite so well together they are together so much of their time that it begins to have an impact, a negative impact on achievement and some of the heads of faculty are asking for, you know, blocking to enable them to regroup. English have asked for this to regroup students in year 8 or 9 on the basis of a better mix of kids in terms of work ethic, not in terms of ability. (Headteacher, mixed ability school)

Teachers acknowledged that pupils were sometimes placed in sets because of their behaviour.

> There are anomalies which exist. Behaviour and peer relationships are sometimes taken into account, which on rare occasions can lead to potentially able pupils being placed in sets lower than their potential ... measured by CATs ... suggests they should occupy. (English teacher, partially set school)

Table 5.5 displays the responses to statements about the effects of different kinds of ability grouping on discipline and disaffection from school. There was strong agreement across all types of school that there are more discipline problems in the lower ability classes when setting procedures are adopted. In contrast opinion was divided as to whether there are more discipline problems in mixed ability classes. The strongest agreement with this statement came from teachers in the partially set schools. Opinion was generally neutral over the effects of different grouping practices on truancy and exclusion, although slightly more teachers agreed that there were more exclusions from pupils in the lower sets. This tendency was more marked in the set schools.

Subject domains considered appropriate for mixed ability teaching

At primary level, mathematics is the subject that is most often taught in sets. Our primary school survey showed that 24% of schools were setting for mathematics by year 6, 3% for science and 17% for English. In the case study schools, school 1 streamed from years 1 to 3, and then set for the National Curriculum core subjects. In school 2 the children were not set but streamed. In school 3 pupils were set for mathematics and English, school 4 set for mathematics only, school 5 adopted flexible setting as and when possible and appropriate and school 6 adopted no setting. At primary level, mathematics and English are considered the main subjects where it is appropriate to adopt setting procedures.

Table 5.5: Percentage responses to statements related to the effects of different kinds of ability groupings on discipline and disaffection

Statements	Type of ability grouping	Strongly agree	Agree	Neutral	Disagree	Strongly disagree
In general there are more	MA school	5.5 (28)	23.3 (118)	21.1 (107)	26.3 (133)	21.5 (109)
discipline problems in	PS school	8.5 (43)	28.3 (143)	22.8 (115)	27.7 (140)	10.3 (52)
mixed ability classes	Set school	5.8 (35)	21.2 (129)	24.2 (147)	34.2 (208)	12.2 (74)
p = .0001	Total	6.5 (106)	24.1 (390)	22.8 (369)	29.7 (481)	14.8 (235)
Where classes are set	MA school	23.5 (119)	39.3 (199)	17.6 (89)	14.6 (74)	3.8 (19)
there are more discipline	PS school	17.6 (89)	42.8 (216)	14.5 (73)	18.2 (92)	5 (25)
problems in the lower	Set school	20.4 (124)	44.2 (269)	15.3 (86)	16.3 (98)	3.9 (24)
ns	Total	20.8 (332)	42.2 (684)	15.3 (248)	16.3 (264)	4.2 (68)
Where classes are set	MA school	5.1 (26)	25.3 (128)	41.7 (211)	17.4 (88)	6.1 (31)
there is more truancy	PS school	4.4 (22)	18.2 (92)	39.2 (198)	26.7 (135)	6.9 (35)
from pupils in the lower	Set school	3.9 (24)	20.6 (125)	40 (243)	25.7 (156)	5.1 (31)
sets						
p = .007	Total	4.4 (72)	21.3 (345)	40.3 (652)	23.4 (379)	6 (97)
Where classes are set	MA school	4.9 (25)	26.7 (135)	43.5 (220)	16.6 (84)	3.6 (18)
there are more exclusions	PS school	4.8 (24)	23.8 (120)	37 (187)	23.2 (117)	3.8 (19)
of pupils in the lower sets	Set school	4.1 (25)	30.1 (183)	40.1 (244)	19.4 (118)	2.5 (15)
ns	Total	4.6 (74)	27.1 (438)	40.2 (651)	19.7 (319)	3.2 (52)

At secondary level, teachers were asked which subjects they felt were suitable for teaching in mixed ability classes in years 7, 8 and 9, in years 7 and 8 only, in year 7 only or not at all. Figure 5.1 illustrates the responses for all of the subject domains. English and humanities were the subjects considered most suitable for mixed ability teaching. Those considered most unsuitable were mathematics and modern foreign languages. However, there was a tendency for those teachers working in schools where mixed ability teaching was the grouping structure in operation to support mixed ability teaching more than those in the schools with more setting.

When the analysis was undertaken separately for the teachers of each subject the differences were more marked. 54% of English teachers thought that English could be taught through years 7, 8 and 9 adopting mixed ability teaching methods. Only 13.4% thought it could not be taught in mixed ability classes at all at secondary level. In contrast 52% of mathematics teachers believed that mathematics could not be taught in mixed ability classes in any year group. Only 11% believed that mathematics could be taught in mixed ability classes in years 7, 8 and 9. The science teachers were fairly evenly divided: 25% believed that science could be taught by mixed ability methods in years 7, 8 and 9; 14% believed that it could only be taught in mixed ability classes in years 7 and 8, 34% said in year 7 only and 22% said not at all. The teachers of modern foreign languages predominantly favoured structured ability grouping: 25% indicated that modern foreign languages should not be taught in mixed ability classes, 47% said only in year 7. Of the humanities teachers, 56% said it was possible to teach humanities in mixed ability groups in years 7, 8 and 9. Only 14% said it was not possible.

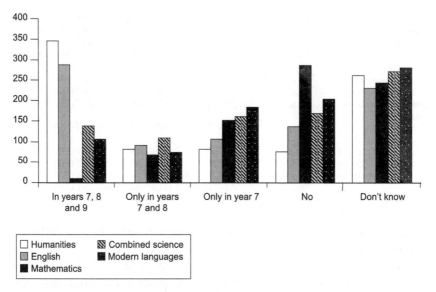

Figure 5.1: Teachers' attitudes towards the appropriateness of mixed ability for teaching different subjects

The differences in attitudes of the teachers of different subjects to the adoption of structured ability grouping in their own subject influenced their responses to other questions. For instance, 70% of English teachers agreed or strongly agreed that setting stigmatises those perceived as less able. This fell to 57% for humanities teachers, 56% for science teachers, 49% for mathematics teachers and 45% for teachers of modern foreign languages. This trend was consistent across most of the attitude statements.

The teachers gave a range of reasons for believing that particular subjects were more appropriate for mixed ability teaching than others. Some concerned the nature of the subject.

> Those subjects where progression is not linear are more suitable. (French teacher, set school)

> I'm not convinced that all subjects aren't suitable for mixed ability teaching. Where building on knowledge/skills is vital (e.g. languages) then I might be convinced. (English teacher, mixed ability school)

> Mathematics is always difficult to differentiate by outcome and range of ability widens as children get older. With some sort of grouping by ability appropriate whole class work can be followed. Even within a 'streamed' group material needs to be differentiated but there is a common language and topics. (Mathematics teacher, partially set school)

> Mathematical concepts and science concepts are very hard to teach to mixed ability due to range of knowledge pupils need to know. (Science teacher, mixed ability school)

Whether the subject was able to be taught with a common starting point and differentiated through learning outcomes was a major factor.

> It depends on whether pupils are allowed to have differentiated outcomes. In English, say, access to material should be the same but the response can be different. (German teacher, mixed ability school)

> English and humanities are suitable for mixed ability teaching because it is easier to use starting point material in some subjects which can be used as a launch point for all, being accessible to all, and then allow differentiated work to develop from it. (English teacher, set school)

> Subjects that supply neutral stimuli and assess predominantly by outcome are more suited to mixed ability teaching. (Science teacher, mixed ability school)

> It's not so much the subjects but the way that they are taught. It's harder to teach French in a find-it-out-yourself style . . . this is why I think French mixed ability classes are only suitable in year 7. (Science teacher, set school)

Some teachers felt that some subjects were simply too difficult for all students.

There is a particular challenge for language departments as to how students are offered a second language. Tackling two languages is unlikely to be viable other than for more able pupils but our all ability groups make this difficult. (Modern foreign language teacher, mixed ability school)

In modern foreign languages some content is only suitable for more able students (for example, higher grammar). (German teacher, mixed ability school)

Humanities seems more suitable for mixed ability classes as the subject matter is more diverse and therefore open to all abilities. Some subjects are not so flexible or accessible to students of low ability. (English teacher, partially set school)

Some teachers believed that all subjects could be taught in mixed ability classes providing that the teacher approached the task with a positive attitude and there were appropriate resources.

I think that the range of material covered in languages does make mixed ability teaching hard ... but it can be done if the classes are small enough and the teacher well prepared and resourced. (English teacher, mixed ability school)

Some subjects thrive on mixed ability teaching, e.g. Personal and Social Education, music, basically the arts. I do think that mixed ability teaching is possible in all subjects but the problem lies with the teachers' attitudes towards it. If they are not in favour of it they are not motivated to implement it. (Religious education teacher, set school)

Some teachers pointed out that ability in one subject may not be related to ability in others and that this could create difficulties in allocating pupils to ability groups in their subjects.

Ability in music does not always correlate with general ability in, say, core subjects. (Music teacher, mixed ability school)

Ability in drama is not necessarily related to literacy and numeracy skills ... or cognitive ability ... so what meaning of ability would be appropriate? (Drama teacher, mixed ability school)

The introduction of tiering in examinations was reported by a number of teachers as creating difficulties in teaching mixed ability classes.

Tiered SATs in mathematics makes it difficult to teach mixed ability. (Mathematics teacher, mixed ability school)

Recently we've come up against the problem of GCSE tiering and have come in certain curriculum areas to group students by tiers, particularly in maths and science. They're the two faculties at the moment that are most interested in pursuing that. (Headteacher, mixed ability school)

Across the sample there were teachers of all subjects who favoured either mixed ability teaching or setting. There was not an overall consensus. These differences were in part mediated by school type but there are clearly other influences which were not uncovered in this research.

Factors affecting attitudes to ability grouping

An overall attitude scale to setting was created by summing up the attitudinal statements which seemed best to discriminate between different views. Where necessary numerical responses were reversed so that a high score indicated a positive attitude towards setting. Using this as the dependent variable, step wise multiple regression was employed to establish which factors would best predict teachers' attitudes. Two factors were found to be important. The first was type of school, mixed ability, partially set or set (beta weight .225), the second was the subject taught (standardised beta weight .078). However, together these accounted for only 5% of the variance, leaving a great deal unexplained.

The mean attitude to setting scores for the set and partially set schools were almost identical, 93.6 (partially set) and 92.3 (set). The mean for the mixed ability schools was much lower (84.6). This difference was statistically significant ($p = .0001$). The mean scores for each subject were mathematics 99.7, modern foreign languages 96.7, science 91.8, humanities 85 and English 82.9. These differences were statistically significant ($p = .0001$). There were no significant gender or age differences in teachers' attitudes towards setting.

When multiple regression was undertaken for each type of school separately, slightly different patterns emerged. In the set schools the significant predictors were the individual school (beta weight −.128) and the subject taught (.109). In the partially set schools length of time teaching at the school was the only predictor (.175). In the mixed ability schools the subject taught (.21), the length of time teaching at the school (−.126) and whether the teacher had a higher degree (−.119) predicted attitude towards setting. The shorter the time the teacher had been teaching in a mixed ability school the more positive their attitudes towards setting. In relation to a higher level degree, e.g. masters or doctoral qualification, the higher the level of the degree the less likely the teacher was to favour setting. No significant differences were found in relation to gender or age.

Whether teachers' attitudes are influenced by the school in which they teach or whether they tend to seek out schools which share their philosophy is an open question. Certainly in one school which was committed to mixed ability teaching appointees to posts were expected to share this commitment.

> I think staff have been appointed to the school on the basis of that is how the school operates and I think they've been asked in the appointments process to prove that they're behind the all ability ethos and can actually handle it. (Headteacher, mixed ability school)

Reservations about different types of ability grouping

At secondary level teachers were asked to indicate the extent to which they supported the school's current grouping practices. Overall, 43% of the teachers had no reservations about their school's grouping practices, 43% had a few reservations, 10% had quite a lot of reservations and 2% were very opposed to the current practices. This supports the evidence that teachers' views are influenced by the grouping practices in their schools and that they share similar values with other teachers in that school. Teachers teaching in mixed ability schools had on average fewer reservations (1.45) than those teaching in partially set (1.62) or set (1.75) schools. This difference was statistically significant ($p = .001$).

The reservations which teachers had about the ability grouping practices in their school were often concerned with detail, for instance, in what years particular practices should be adopted.

> I would prefer mixed ability in year 7 as regression occurs after transfer with some pupils. Good mixed ability teaching is appropriate as children learn from more able peers and through talk. Banding and setting in year 8 is a fairer division as children are not in regression. Setting in year 9 because of SAT exams, parent pressure, and greater range of texts, so separation is needed. (English teacher, set school)

Other serious concerns raised concerned the principles involved and the benefits and costs to different groups of pupils as outlined earlier in the chapter. Teachers also raised issues about the accurate placement of pupils into ability groups particularly when this occurred very soon after they had started at secondary school.

> In year 7 pupils are often inaccurately set when entering school. This takes time to settle. I would look at setting more closely in year 7. I think mixed ability would be better. (Science teacher, set school)

> I am not sure that rigorous setting year 7 and perhaps also year 8 is essential especially with varying backgrounds students come from in terms of science experience and knowledge. (Science teacher, set school)

> I have reservations about setting. It is important to make sure it is done correctly in the first place. Sometimes a pupil works to the ability of the group and could achieve more if in a higher one. (Mathematics teacher, mixed ability school)

Another major issue which was raised by teachers was the rigidity of ability grouping structures and the difficulty of moving people between groups.

> For the setting system to work pupils need to be able to move between sets when necessary . . . not just at the end of the year. (Science teacher, set school)

> I have reservations about setting in mathematics. It is too inflexible, there is low motivation and very large class sizes in the low ability groups and discipline problems in the lower sets. (Learning support assistant, mixed ability school)

> I think one of the problems is the rigidity of set class placement . . . a child goes into a particular set and is seen as in that position for life. We want to move away from that, then people can move and it's seen as a much more fluid system . . . we don't want the children to feel that they've come in and their future is more or less mapped our for them. (Mathematics co-ordinator, primary school)

The difficulty of accurately placing pupils in sets and the problems of arranging easy movement between sets reflect the concerns raised by pupils in the previous chapter. These issues will be explored further in Chapter 7.

Summary

The research reported in this chapter demonstrates that teachers share a number of beliefs about the effects of different kinds of ability grouping. In general they believe that:

- setting benefits the more able child, ensuring that they make maximum progress;
- the able child is less inhibited by peer pressures in set classes;
- grouping practices affect pupils' self-esteem;
- setting has a damaging effect on the self-esteem of those in lower sets;
- setting stigmatises those perceived as less able;
- mixed ability grouping leads to better social adjustment for all pupils;
- the effects of different grouping policies on motivation are not clear;
- mixed ability classes provide the less able pupils with positive models of achievement;
- where classes are set there are more discipline problems in the lower ability classes.

The research demonstrates that the grouping structures adopted within a school are related to teachers' attitudes towards pupil grouping. Whether this means that teachers are influenced by their environment or whether they search out an environment which is conducive to their philosophy of education cannot be established from the current analysis. It is likely that there are complex interactions between the two. There are also differences in attitude related to the subject domain of the teacher. These depend on teachers' perceptions of the suitability of their subject for mixed ability teaching, which is related to the extent to which learning in the subject is linear and differentiation can occur through outcome.

6

Teachers' Classroom Practices

In this chapter we will explore teachers' pedagogic practices with mixed ability classes and classes grouped by ability. Mixed ability teaching is generally considered to be more demanding for teachers, requiring greater differentiation of work in the classroom. When pupils are grouped by ability teachers seem to underestimate the differences between them and tend to abandon the differentiated and varied methods they use with mixed ability classes. Teaching methods also differ in high and low ability groups, leading to a more stimulating environment, faster pace and more pressure for more able pupils and a reduction in the opportunity to learn for the lower ability groups. These differences have serious implications for pupils' learning, particularly when considered alongside the lack of movement between groups (discussed in Chapter 7). We will argue that a cycle of disincentive is frequently set up in the lowest groups, leading to a lowering of expectations which is very difficult to counteract.

School and classroom practice

Historically, high ability groups in streamed systems have tended to be taught by those teachers who were perceived as the 'best', usually the more experienced and better qualified. Low streams have tended to be allocated the less experienced and less well qualified teachers (Jackson, 1964; Barker Lunn, 1970; Ball, 1981; Hargreaves, 1967; Lacey, 1970; Rosenbaum, 1976; Burgess, 1983, Oakes, 1985; Boaler, 1997a, 1997b). Teachers working with high ability groups have reported putting more time and energy into their teaching, spending more time preparing (Rosenbaum, 1976) and being more enthusiastic (Oakes, 1985). Other scarce resources have also been channelled towards high achievers. This contrasts with the current situation in the United Kingdom where additional resources are available for pupils with statements of Special Educational Need.

Where streaming, setting or tracking occurs the activities under-taken in the classrooms of high, middle and low ability pupils differ considerably. There is often differential access to the curriculum, the top groups benefiting from enhanced opportunities (Ball, 1981; Oakes, 1985; Gamoran, 1990; Boaler, 1997a, 1997b). An informal syllabus may also operate, where for the lower streams topics are omitted and there are different expectations (Ball, 1981; Oakes, 1985). For them the knowledge on offer is generally low status and not suitable for gain-ing access to higher education (Burgess, 1983, 1984; Keddie, 1971; Oakes, 1985).

In an in-depth study of 25 schools in the USA, Oakes (1985) identi-fied differences in the kinds of knowledge available to low and high streams. For instance, high track English classes were exposed to the high status knowledge required for college entrance. Students were expected to write essays and reports and were taught to write in dif-ferent styles using a wide vocabulary. In contrast pupils in lower tracks were given young adult fiction to read and the teaching of read-ing skills was prominent using workbooks, kits and reading schemes. Writing tasks consisted of simple short narrative paragraphs, the acquisition of standard English usage, and functional literary skills. Teachers in high track classes demanded critical thinking, problem-solving, the drawing of conclusions, making generalisations, evaluat-ing, and the exercising of knowledge. In contrast low track pupils were required to undertake simple memory or comprehension tasks. They were sometimes expected to apply learning to new situations, but not often. Similar differences were found in mathematics classes. Studies examining the effects of different types of grouping on gifted pupils have found that it is the use of curriculum materials tailored to their needs which produces the greatest change in attainment (Kulik and Kulik, 1982a, 1987; Feldusen, 1989; Askew and Wiliam, 1995).

A substantial literature now indicates the tendency for instruction in lower ability groups to have a different quality from that provided for high ability groups (Evertson, 1982; Oakes, 1985; Gamoran, 1989). Observers have noted that instruction is conceptually simplified and proceeds more slowly. There is more structured written work, which leaves work fragmented (Hargreaves, 1967; Metz 1978; Schwartz, 1981; Burgess, 1983; Page, 1984; Oakes, 1985). Higher ability classes tend to be set more analytic, critical thinking tasks (Hargreaves, 1967; Oakes, 1985; Hacker *et al.*, 1991). Pupils in high ability groups are also allowed more independence and choice, opportunities are provided for discussion, and pupils are allowed to take responsibility for their own work. Low streams tend to undertake work which is more tightly structured. There is a concentration on basic skills, work sheets and repetition with fewer opportunities for independent learning, discussion and activities which promote critique, analysis and creativity (Hargreaves, 1967; Burgess, 1983; Oakes, 1985; Page, 1992). Schwartz (1981) also found that when high track students gave incorrect answers, teachers coaxed them to develop correct answers, while low track students who were incorrect were ignored.

Page (1984) suggests that streaming or tracking sets in motion a vicious cycle. Based on stereotypes and past experience, teachers hold low expectations for low ability students. Perceiving these views, students lower expectations for themselves, confirming and further reducing expectations. Boaler (1997a, 1997b, 1997c) confirms that teachers have high expectations of pupils in top sets which leads to teaching characterised by a fast pace, a sense of urgency and competition. Some pupils, particularly girls, found this anxiety-provoking, which led to a subsequent decline in achievement.

Oakes (1985) also identified what she described as a hidden agenda, high ability pupils being encouraged to work independently and be self-regulating, while for low ability students the agenda was concerned with conformity, getting along with others, working quietly, improving study habits, punctuality, co-operation, and conforming to rules and expectations.

Teachers, themselves, believe that they are matching instruction to the level of the student's ability (Rosenbaum, 1976; Wilson and Schmidts, 1978), but some researchers have suggested that differences in instruction may be a means of classroom control (Metz, 1978), lower ability groups being perceived as more difficult to manage (Findlay and Bryan, 1975). A number of projects have identified differing classroom climates in high and low ability streams (Ball, 1981; Vanfossen, Jones and Spade, 1987). These differences mean that pupils experience different physical and intellectual environments.

In the next sections we will examine the findings from the primary and secondary school research projects to establish the extent to which the evidence described above applies in the current UK educational context.

Pedagogy at primary level

In the six primary case study schools teachers were interviewed about their classroom practice. They raised issues relating to different types of ability grouping which concerned curriculum differentiation, pace, teaching strategies and attention to particular children.

The curriculum

In the primary schools where structured ability grouping was adopted, different streams and sets worked towards different National Curriculum levels (see Table 6.1). Ability grouping practices were integral to the differentiated 'delivery of the curriculum'. This was perceived to make the teacher's work easier and more manageable, as teaching could be focused at an appropriate level for pupils' needs. The pace of work was also seen to be different, with the more able pupils working at higher National Curriculum levels, at a faster pace and with more extension activities.

Teachers acknowledged that the curriculum on offer to different ability groups varied. There was also considerable pressure to raise standards.

> The curriculum that they're being offered is essentially different. (Deputy head and mathematics co-ordinator)

> The A stream get a much higher level curriculum but also because at the end of Key Stage 1 we're trying to achieve as many level 3s as possible, the time scale is very, very short so by the end of year 1, hopefully they'll have achieved level 1 so that I'm really trying to teach to level 3 more or less in a year. So not only is it a higher level, it's also much quicker as well. (Key Stage 1 teacher)

The different pace of work was stressed repeatedly.

> The top sets work at a higher level and a faster pace . . . (Deputy head mathematics co-ordinator)

> The streaming definitely helps . . . you can work at a fast pace.

Structured ability grouping was also seen as facilitating much more tightly focused teaching.

> All the differentiation has been taken away because you can go in and with my top set science, for example, I know that they're all working at level 5/6 and so I don't have to have level 3 work ready for certain children. (Key Stage 2 teacher)

> The streaming definitely helps . . . your teaching can be so much more focused and the children all understand. I think that's got a lot to do with it. (Key Stage 1 teacher)

Table 6.1:   Teaching curriculum issues

School	Teaching styles, differentiation, planning, schemes of work, national curriculum levels
School 1 Streaming at KS1 and in year 3, setting for core curriculum for rest of KS2	The KS1 'A' stream work at higher NC levels and a faster pace. The teacher adopts a more formal teaching style. The KS2 sets cover the same areas of work but at different NC curriculum levels. The top sets work at a faster rate while the lower sets undertake more practical activities, repetition and consolidation. More whole class teaching and more sophisticated language tends to be used with the higher sets. The teaching style depends on the individual teacher and the subject area.
School 2 Mixed ability/within class ability grouping in KS1, streaming for the whole of the curriculum in KS2	At KS1, within class ability grouping tends to encourage more practical activities for the lower groups. Teaching styles vary according to individual teachers. In the KS2 streams a higher level of language and questioning is adopted with the more able groups. More repetition, consolidation, and visual cues with the lower groups. Schemes of work are delivered at the appropriate level according to the needs of the group.
School 3 Setting for mathematics and English from year 1. Mixed ability/within class ability grouping for the rest of the curriculum	The curriculum is adapted according to the needs of groups based on NC levels. Lessons are generally more focused in the sets. The higher achievers work at a faster pace. The lower achievers are allowed more time and given more practical activities to meet their needs. NLS objectives have been adapted for SEN children. Teaching styles vary according to individual teachers.
School 4 Setting for mathematics from year 4. Mixed ability/within class groupings for the rest of the curriculum	Ability sets tend to foster a more formal teaching style. Lessons are more focused. Children work at NC levels according to their needs. More able work at a faster pace with more demanding questioning and more extension activities. Teaching styles vary according to individual teachers.
School 5 Cross age setting for mathematics and English	Pupils cover the same curriculum areas but at different NC levels according to age and ability. There is more problem-solving investigative work in the higher groups. The lower ability groups receive more teacher attention and have more practical activities with greater use of visual apparatus.
School 6 No setting. Mixed ability/within class grouping	Teaching styles vary according to individual teachers. More able pupils receive extension activities and are expected to work at a faster pace. Lower achievers receive more reinforcement activities. The teaching and learning policy and grouping and teaching strategies are currently under review.

It's easier in the set than when we're in the mixed ability class . . . when they're in a set, you know that all the children can do the work. Generally they're better behaved in sets than they are in their mixed ability classes, so it's easier . . . I suppose that work is more focused, and at their level really. (Key Stage 2 teacher)

Teaching strategies

Setting and streaming led to more whole class teaching. While teaching styles were generally considered to be related to the preferences, judgement and subject areas of individual teachers, a more formal approach tended to be adopted with the higher ability groups.

I'm quite formal. The children sit in rows most of the time. I group them sometimes but it's a lot of whole class teaching rather than group teaching because they are all of a similar ability by the nature of the streaming system, so they can all more or less cope with the same input although I do differentiate at times. (Key Stage 1 teacher)

We're much more directed and focused, and I do a lot more whole class teaching whereas when you've got your mixed ability classes, you have to obviously differentiate and work at all the different levels that different groups are working at so that's a lot more difficult to organise . . . I suppose my teaching style is quite formal . . . whole class teaching with the class looking at the board or computer screen and that's how it is . . . In the lower sets not so much because you've only got a few children so we tend to do more practical things and work in that way, but for the higher groups, I mean we do experiments and all that but it is much more teacher-led. (Key Stage 2 teacher)

More able pupils were reported to be given work at a higher level, at a faster pace, with more extension activities and more independent problem-solving. Pupils in less able groups were given more time to complete tasks, received more consolidation or repetitive revision activities, undertook more practical activities with less emphasis on recording, and were posed less demanding questions. There was also a reported difference in the language used with different groups of pupils.

Teaching style is very much an individual thing according to teacher. All groups do practical work but the lower ability groups tend to do more consolidation work and perhaps less written recording, less formal recording. The top groups won't be given work sheets or things to fill in. They'd be expected to record it independently, possibly even for homework. The lower ability groups will do less recording because even in the SATs testing it's not the recording that's actually being tested ... it's actual scientific knowledge and understanding. So, although they are still expected to do a certain amount of recording, there's less of an emphasis. The lower streams might do less written work. (Science co-ordinator)

There is a difference in the amount of instructions, not quality, but the language used by the teacher differs ... I'll say things once and expect them to listen to it, whereas with the lower ability streams, you might say things three or four times and then you have picture cues and then it just goes on, on those sort of terms, again and again and again, because they are low ability. (Deputy head)

In the infants, it's that the top ability group do a lot more reading and writing ... it's quite intensive, the amount of work they do ... there's a lot of talking about their ideas to me. Then the differentiation between them and the lower end is a more pictorial response with me scribing the words for them using words banks, using IT to support learning with them so they can have access to a programme that they can use so then that frees me to work with someone else. It takes a bit of sorting through in the reception year, as I said, I do a separate block for and within that, my classroom assistants feed back to me which children are racing ahead, which children aren't and in their home-work that they take home I try and address that problem ... as well as in school, they take home homework sheets so that parents can encour-age them forward. (Key Stage 1 teacher)

In maths, again, it's a similar sort of thing, there are games that they can play, they've got workbooks although I don't let them do the work-books until we've covered the work in a practical way ... and then they just race through them. I mean, very often they'll get through a workbook in a week you know, because they've done the work. The top ones ... it's much more problem-solving and investigative work that I give them to do. It's the same in the juniors. Usually the teacher sits with the lower ones at their table very often with maths because the high flyers, once it's been explained to them, they're capable of going away and doing it themselves and they might have a hiccup but then they'll just come and ask. Those children that need help really need you there, so that's the way we tend to work. M will sit with his group and S's high flyers will just come if they need you, having had the problem set. (Headteacher)

In schools where setting or streaming was in place, the effect of being taught in a smaller group, with more teacher attention, was seen to be instrumental in raising the achievement of the less able. However, concern was expressed in School 2 about the potentially negative effect of the less able not having access to successful peer role models or support from more able pupils. This was seen to be a vital feature of successful practice in School 6 where working in mixed ability groups was valued by most of the respondents, both children and adults.

All of the schools, with the exception of School 6, felt that some form of setting or streaming for at least part of the curriculum was vital if the diverse needs of pupils were to be met. School 6, which had a strong commitment to a mixed ability ethos, was reviewing its teaching and learning policy and the formation of some within class ability groups was seen as being unavoidable in the future.

Teacher expectations

Teachers expressed mixed views about the effect of ability grouping on their expectations of pupils and pupils' expectations of themselves. Some felt that expectations of the lower ability pupils were not negatively affected.

> Since we moved from streaming to mixed ability and setting it has brought on the whole year group tremendously and it has pushed our results on. The children with special needs have all moved through . . . there's no case of children sitting back and thinking 'We're in this stream'. (Headteacher, primary school).

Some were very aware of the possible consequences of structured ability grouping on expectations.

> My fears, although I've not had evidence of it, is the case of a child saying 'Well, this is all I'm able to do because I'm in this class or that class' . . . that's my concern about having it across the board. I don't really think as yet that we have an ethos that tells all children that they can succeed. We need to overcome that. (Headteacher, primary school)

The difficulty of moving pupils between groups, which will be explored fully in Chapter 7, led to an awareness that expectations about pupils could become self-fulfilling because once placed in an ability group movement out of it was unlikely.

> I think one of the problems is the rigidity of set class placement . . . a child goes into a particular set and is seen as in that position for life. We

want to move away from that, then people can move and it's seen as a much more fluid system ... we don't want the children to feel that they've come in and their future is more or less mapped our for them. (Mathematics co-ordinator, primary school).

Attention given to particular children

At primary level two main issues arose with regard to the demands on teachers. Teachers spent more time with the less able pupils.

> Some groups do get more attention ... the slower learners I suppose because when they're in a class of 34, they do need the extra attention and you differentiate with worksheets and things like this, so, for example, for the slower learners there might be less writing and more pictures and things like that, but they definitely get more attention. (KS1 mathematics co-ordinator)

> You always tend to spend more time with the lower achievers who perhaps need that bit of extra help to get started with their work or to make sure that they're doing it right, or marking it to give them the confidence to see that they are doing it right. You tend then to go the top end to see how they're getting on with the work they've been set, whether they need anything else. It is the children in the middle, as always, who tend to get left to their own devices. (KS2 mathematics co-ordinator)

Teachers also spent more time with pupils whose behaviour was disruptive or difficult.

> I'm more likely to be with the children with behaviour problems or the children with special needs who need more help with their work. I do try to ensure that I get around everyone, but in reality, I am quite aware that some children do tend to dominate. (KS1 teacher)

> The obvious attention factor is behaviour. I try to draw attention to the positive behaviour as opposed to the negative. I try to deal with things on a one-to-one basis but, inevitably, some pupils do take up more of my time. As well as that, there's also the group of those that need the help, maybe with a particular concept ... I might spend more time with those. That's where I find that ability grouping for maths by subject and by objectives useful because you've got all the ones who need that help together at once, whereas if you notice the whole class ... maybe they've not covered something and they all need help and you

could address the whole class, and then also do that 'micro' atmosphere with your groups. (KS2 teacher)

As the examples above illustrate, ability grouping was seen to reduce the level of complexity which teachers had to cope with in the primary classroom.

Pedagogy at secondary level

The issues arising at secondary level in relation to pedagogy and ability grouping were very similar to those raised at primary level. They included matching teaching to learners' needs, effects on expectations, curriculum differentiation, teaching methods, homework, behaviour management, classroom organisation and resources.

Matching teaching to learners' needs

In addition to being asked the extent of their agreement to a series of questions about pedagogy and ability grouping, the secondary school teachers offered their views as to why different types of teaching were more appropriate for particular types of pupil grouping. Most responses reflected the perceptions of the pupils outlined in Chapter 4, that is, that ability grouping enabled work to be matched to pupil needs.

Setting enables pupils' needs to be catered for more effectively and aids the placement of SEN support. (English teacher, set school)

Setting is best to enable students to progress at a rate appropriate to their needs. (French teacher, partially set school)

I would increase setting so that class teaching from the board can be more effectively geared towards the majority and extension work can be covered by more pupils. Schemes of work may be designed and carried out to suit needs of progress. (Mathematics teacher, partially set school)

I prefer setting in order to allow different students the opportunity to work at their own pace according to their ability. (German teacher, partially set school)

All pupils make more progress when set, I find. Pupils become very frustrated when they are in mixed ability groups. The more able pupils need to be stretched and the less able need specific attention. It is impossible to do this effectively in a mixed ability group. (English teacher, partially set school)

There was an appreciation that to teach mixed ability classes well was extremely difficult.

I think you've got to be a hell of a good teacher to handle mixed ability teaching and handle all the differentiating that goes with it . . . the extension material, the catch up material, group work. (Headteacher, set school)

It is easier to ensure that the lesson is aimed at the correct level if the pupils are in ability sets. Easier to modify the lesson if all the pupils are at the same level. (Science teacher, partially set school)

Some suggested that it offered challenge and stopped teachers becoming rigid in their teaching methods.

Teaching mixed ability groups keeps teachers on their toes. It forces them to be more creative and to maintain and develop a better range of teaching styles. (Science teacher, set school)

The teachers also indicated their level of agreement to several statements on the questionnaire regarding pedagogy. The detailed frequency counts related to perceptions of the effects of different kinds of ability grouping on teaching are given in Table 6.2. There was no consensus that setting leads to teachers ignoring the fact that a class always contains a range of abilities. Responses to this statement tended to reflect the ability grouping procedures adopted in the school where the teacher was working. Teachers in mixed ability schools were more likely to agree with the statement. There was also no consensus that only very good teachers can teach mixed ability classes successfully. The response was mixed and there were no differences in relation to school type. In contrast there was strong agreement that teaching is easier for the teacher when classes are set. This response went across the whole sample regardless of type of school. There was general agreement that in mixed ability classes teachers tend to teach to the average child and strong agreement that setting makes classroom management easier. This view was held particularly strongly by those who taught in partially set schools. There was strong agreement from all the teachers that developing the appropriate teaching skills necessary to teach a mixed ability class benefited all pupils.

When asked about the curriculum, most teachers expressed strong views that setting enabled pupils' curriculum needs to be better matched, although the support was stronger from those teaching in set and partially set schools. There was also strong agreement that teaching the less able pupils required a different approach from teaching the more able.

Table 6.2:　Percentage (and number) of responses to statements relating to teaching in different ability grouping structures

Statements	Type of ability grouping	Strongly agree	Agree	Neutral	Disagree	Strongly disagree
Setting leads to teachers ignoring the fact that a class always contains a range of abilities	MA school	7.1 (36)	34.6 (175)	19.6 (99)	29.1 (147)	8.9 (45)
	PS school	4 (20)	24.2 (122)	15 (76)	40.8 (206)	14.9 (75)
	Set school	2 (12)	24.8 (151)	14.1 (86)	42.1 (256)	16 (97)
p = .0001	Total	4.2 (68)	27.7 (448)	16.1 (261)	37.6 (609)	13.4 (217)
Only very good teachers can teach mixed ability classes successfully	MA school	9.5 (48)	29.2 (148)	24.7 (125)	28.1 (142)	7.3 (37)
	PS school	10.7 (54)	29.3 (148)	23 (116)	26.7 (135)	8.7 (44)
	Set school	8.1 (49)	31.9 (194)	24.7 (150)	27.3 (166)	6.7 (41)
ns	Total	9.3 (151)	30.3 (490)	24.2 (391)	27.4 (443)	7.5 (122)
Teaching is easier for the teacher when classes are set	MA school	10.9 (55)	42.9 (217)	19.2 (97)	21.9 (111)	4.7 (24)
	PS school	15.8 (80)	46.3 (234)	17.4 (88)	15.4 (78)	3.8 (19)
	Set school	11.3 (69)	47.7 (290)	18.6 (113)	18.6 (113)	3.3 (20)
p = .046	Total	12.6 (204)	45.8 (741)	18.4 (298)	18.7 (302)	3.9 (63)
In mixed ability classes teachers tend to teach to the average child	MA school	3 (15)	42.5 (215)	14.6 (74)	34.2 (173)	5.5 (28)
	PS school	4.8 (24)	51.3 (259)	16 (81)	22.8 (115)	3.4 (17)
	Set school	2.6 (16)	51.2 (311)	18.9 (115)	23.5 (143)	2.8 (17)
p = .0001	Total	3.4 (55)	48.5 (785)	16.7 (270)	26.6 (431)	3.8 (62)
Setting makes classroom management easier	MA school	6.9 (35)	48.4 (245)	22.1 (112)	18.2 (92)	3.6 (18)
	PS school	13.9 (70)	52.1 (263)	15.4 (78)	14.9 (75)	2.2 (11)
	Set school	12 (73)	51.2 (311)	14.6 (89)	18.9 (115)	2.3 (14)
p = .0001	Total	11 (178)	50.6 (819)	17.2 (279)	17.4 (282)	2.7 (43)
Developing the appropriate teaching skills necessary to teach a mixed ability class benefits all pupils	MA school	33.6 (170)	50.8 (257)	10.5 (53)	3.8 (19)	.4 (2)
	PS school	25.1 (127)	49.1 (248)	17.6 (89)	5.1 (26)	.8 (4)
	Set school	18.3 (111)	54.3 (330)	17.4 (106)	7.1 (43)	2 (12)
p = .0001	Total	25.2 (408)	51.6 (835)	15.3 (248)	5.4 (88)	1.1 (18)
Setting enables pupils' curriculum needs to be better matched	MA school	15.2 (77)	41.1 (208)	15.8 (80)	23.3 (118)	4 (20)
	PS school	25.1 (127)	47.3 (239)	14.9 (75)	8.7 (44)	2.4 (12)
	Set school	22 (134)	53.5 (325)	16.3 (99)	6.6 (40)	1.3 (8)
p = .0001	Total	20.9 (338)	47.7 (772)	15.7 (254)	12.5 (202)	2.5 (40)
Teaching the lower sets requires a different approach to teaching the higher sets	MA school	30 (152)	54.3 (275)	6.1 (31)	6.3 (32)	1.6 (8)
	PS school	42.6 (215)	49.1 (248)	3.4 (17)	2.6 (13)	1 (5)
	Set school	45.6 (277)	48.4 (294)	2.6 (16)	1.8 (11)	.8 (5)
p = .0001	Total	39.8 (644)	50.5 (817)	4 (64)	3.5 (56)	1.1 (18)

Teacher expectations

At secondary level teachers' expectations of pupils in different classes were assessed systematically through their responses to statements in the questionnaire. Table 6.3 sets out the extent to which secondary school teachers' expectations of their pupils differed depending on whether they were in set or mixed ability classes. The great majority of teachers teaching sets expected a faster rate of work from the more able pupils (89%). In mixed ability classes there was less expectation that able pupils would work at a faster rate (69%). Whether pupils were in mixed ability or set classes, the majority of teachers expected greater depth of work from the more able pupils (86%). In mixed ability classes teachers expected more independent thought from the higher ability pupils (84%) than in set classes (76%). Most teachers expected the more able children to take greater responsibility for their own written work whether they were in mixed ability (71%) or sets (76%). A higher level of analytic thinking was expected of high ability pupils whatever type of group they were taught in, mixed ability (85%) or set (88%).

To make a more sensitive comparison of differences in teaching approach engendered by the different grouping systems, paired t-tests were undertaken between the responses made by those teachers who responded to questions about teaching in mixed ability and set classes because they were involved in teaching both. The differences were small but statistically significant. Table 6.3 gives the details. Each response was given a score from 1 to 5, with 'always' scored 1 and 'never' given a score of 5. The largest differences were in relation to the pace of work. The mean for mixed ability classes was 2.03 as opposed to 1.69 ($t = -8.85$, df = 502, p = .0001). The higher score indicates that teachers had a lower expectation of the pupils working more quickly. When differences between teachers are controlled for, pace remains a major difference in expectation within different types of pupil grouping. The differences in expectations for the other aspects of teaching were small. In relation to working in depth, a mean of 1.89 for mixed ability teaching and 1.67 for ability grouped classes, for independent thought 1.9 as opposed to 2.06, for written work 2.18 as opposed to 2.08, and for analytic thought 1.74 as opposed to 1.88. What these differences signify is the power of grouping structures to influence teachers' expectations and teaching. The strongest difference is that teachers expect pupils in higher ability groups to work faster.

Table 6.3: Teacher expectations: percentages (and number) of responses

Statement	Always	Nearly always	Sometimes	Not often	Never
Teacher expectations in mixed ability classes					
I expect the more able students to work at a faster rate	23 (270)	46 (547)	27 (313)	3.2 (38)	.9 (11)
I expect the more able pupils to cover the work in more depth than the less able pupils	36 (426)	50 (588)	13 (151)	1 (14)	.3 (4)
I expect more independent thought from higher ability pupils	34 (400)	50 (595)	13 (156)	1.7 (20)	.8 (9)
I expect the more able pupils to take more responsibility for their written work	23 (243)	48 (519)	20 (211)	6 (66)	4 (40)
I expect more analytical thought from more able pupils in a class	32 (366)	53 (613)	14 (162)	2 (17)	.4 (5)
Teacher expectations in classes grouped by ability					
I expect students to work at a faster rate in the more able groups	47 (425)	42 (384)	10 (89)	1 (9)	.1 (1)
I cover topics in more depth with the more able groups	52 (471)	36 (324)	11.4 (104)	.8 (7)	.3 (3)
I expect more independent thought from pupils in the higher ability groups	25 (226)	51 (463)	19 (176)	3 (27)	2 (15)
I expect pupils in the higher ability groups to take more responsibility for their written work	30 (264)	45 (394)	16 (140)	6 (51)	4 (35)
I expect more analytical thought from pupils in the higher ability groups	39 (349)	4 (442)	11 (98)	.8 (7)	.2 (2)

When the mean scores of teachers in different types of school were compared there were significant differences in relation to a number of variables. In structured grouping there were differences in the expectations relating to pace of work expected from more able students. They were the highest in partially set schools (1.57) followed by the set schools (1.68) with the mixed ability schools having the least expectations of working at a faster pace (1.74) ($F_{905,2}$ = 3.72, p = .025). With regard to the extent to which the more able pupils were expected to cover the work in more depth, teachers in mixed ability schools (1.74) and partially set schools (1.79) had a greater expectation of this in relation to mixed ability classes as compared with set schools (1.91) (p=.004). There were also significant differences in relation to the depth with which work was covered in structured ability classes. Here teachers in partially set schools (1.55) expected to cover topics in more depth than those in set schools (1.62) and mixed ability schools (1.78) (p = .01).

When teachers in different subjects were compared there were marked differences. In classes grouped by ability the teachers of modern foreign languages markedly expected their pupils to work at a faster pace (1.48), this was followed by mathematics (1.57), science (1.61), English (1.75) and humanities (1.84). These differences were statistically significant (p = .0001). In mixed ability classes modern foreign languages and mathematics shared the same mean of 1.91, with science 2.01, humanities 2.12 and English 2.3. This suggests that in all subjects pace is affected by the type of grouping but that there are significant differences between each subject.

The responses to the other questions reflected differences in the nature of knowledge in each of the subjects and the differences in classes. In ability grouped classes there was a tendency for all subjects to cover topics in more depth although there were significant subject differences, the major difference being in relation to English. There were no significant differences in relation to the mixed ability groups. The only other significant difference in relation to mixed ability teaching was in relation to expectations about taking responsibility for written work. In the ability grouped classes there were significant differences between the subjects for all the questions except in relation to analytic thought. Table 6.4 gives the means for each subject in relation to teacher expectations.

Differentiation of the curriculum

Questions regarding the curriculum and the teaching strategies adopted indicated that in mixed ability classes over three-quarters of teachers reported that pupils tended to work on the same topic at the same time (78%) whereas in set classes a quarter of teachers indicated that they consistently covered different topics with pupils of different ability, while 38% did so sometimes.

Overall, teachers reported that the less able pupils did not cover fewer topics although this applied less to mixed ability classes (11%) than ability grouped classes (21%). In mixed ability classes differentiation was often by outcome (52%). Teachers of ability grouped classes gave strong support to the statement that different resources were used for pupils of different abilities (65%) whereas in the mixed ability classes there was a normal distribution of responses with the majority being in the 'sometimes' category. Resources were used to

Ability Grouping in Education

differentiate work in the class by most teachers 'sometimes' (62% in mixed ability classes, 52% in set classes). Teachers rejected the statement that they spent more time preparing to teach the able set groups (see Table 6.5).

Table 6.4: Mean teacher expectations by subject

Statement	Mathematics	Modern foreign languages	Science	Humanities	English
Teacher expectations in mixed ability classes					
I expect the more able students to work at a faster rate (p = .0001)	1.91	1.91	2.01	2.12	2.3
I expect the more able pupils to cover the work in more depth than the less able pupils (ns)	1.85	1.76	1.8	1.7	1.77
I expect more independent thought from higher ability pupils (ns)	1.87	1.77	1.86	1.9	1.92
I expect the more able pupils to take more responsibility for their written work (p = .0001)	2.22	1.99	2.1	2.25	2.52
I expect more analytical thought from the more able pupils in a class (ns)	1.89	1.77	1.85	1.86	1.88
Teacher expectations in classes grouped by ability					
I expect students to work at a faster rate in the more able groups (p = .001)	1.57	1.48	1.61	1.84	1.75
I cover topics in more depth with the more able groups (p = .0001)	1.54	1.49	1.5	1.57	1.82
I expect more independent thought from pupils in the higher ability groups (p = .009)	1.97	1.89	2.07	2.06	2.24
I expect pupils in the higher ability groups to take more responsibility for their written work (p = .044)	2.12	1.89	1.99	2.18	2.22
I expect more analytical thought from pupils in the higher ability groups (ns)	1.75	1.72	1.68	1.66	1.73

Table 6.5: Differentiation of the curriculum: percentages (and number) of responses

Statement	Always	Nearly always	Sometimes	Not often	Never
Mixed ability classes					
All pupils in the class work on the same topic at the same time	32 (377)	46 (543)	19 (221)	3 (36)	1 (15)
Less able pupils cover fewer topics than the more able pupils	2 (19)	9 (110)	30 (346)	30 (355)	29 (337)
I give different activities to pupils of differing ability	4 (41)	17 (203)	58 (690)	16 (195)	5 (58)
I use different resources with pupils of differing ability within the class	5 (56)	20 (237)	58 (681)	13 (156)	4 (52)
I use different resources within the class in order to differentiate work	5 (58)	21 (248)	62 (720)	10 (118)	2 (26)
All pupils work on the same task and the work is differentiated by outcome	11 (131)	41 (490)	41 (483)	6 (75)	1 (6)
Structured ability groups					
I cover different topics with groups of differing ability	11 (96)	14 (123)	38 (338)	24 (216)	14 (126)
I cover fewer topics with less able groups	6 (57)	15 (132)	36 (327)	26 (238)	17 (158)
There are some activities I wouldn't do with pupils in the less able groups	23 (216)	18 (168)	46 (427)	11 (99)	2 (19)
I use different resources for groups of differing ability	22 (200)	43 (396)	32 (294)	3 (29)	1 (11)
I use different resources within the class in order to differentiate work	6 (55)	23 (215)	52 (485)	16 (151)	3 (24)
I spend more time preparing for the more able groups	2 (19)	8 (75)	39 (343)	35 (311)	16 (142)

Paired t-tests were carried out on matching questions to compare the responses of the same teachers to questions about different types of grouping. In all cases there were statistically significant differences reflecting the differences outlined in Table 6.6. When these were compared by type of school only one difference emerged in relation to structured ability grouping. This was in relation to using different resources within the class in order to differentiate work. This was more commonly reported by teachers in mixed ability schools (2.72) than those in set (2.86) or partially set schools (2.94). The practices adopted on a more regular basis in relation to mixed ability teaching seem to be applied in this case in structured groupings. There were far more differences in relation to mixed ability teaching. In the set schools (3.65) teachers agreed more that less able pupils cover fewer topics than the more able pupils in comparison with the partially set (3.85) and mixed ability schools (3.74) ($F_{1164,2} = 3.33$, p = .036). The teachers in the mixed ability schools were more likely:

- to give different activities to pupils of differing ability (2.93) than the teachers in the set schools (3.04) and partially set schools (3.11);
- to use different resources with pupils of differing ability within the class (mixed ability 2.83, partially set 2.99, set 2.99);
- to use different resources to differentiate work (mixed ability 2.77, partially set 2.9, set 2.84).

In contrast teachers in partially set (2.35) and set schools (2.35) were more likely than those working in mixed ability schools (2.57) to allow pupils to work on the same task and differentiate by outcome. These different responses suggest that the practices that teachers adopt in their mixed ability classes are influenced by the main form of teaching adopted in the school.

There were significant differences in relation to subjects taught in relation to almost all of the above. Mathematics and English teachers were most likely to cover different topics, and fewer topics with pupils of different ability in structured ability groups, science and humanities least likely ($F_{746,4} = 24.0$, p = .0001). In structured ability groups teachers of modern foreign languages and mathematics were more likely to use different resources for groups of differing ability, use different resources within the class to differentiate work and to deliberately not undertake some activities with pupils in the less able groups. In mixed ability classes mathematics and modern foreign language teachers were more likely to give different activities to pupils of differing ability and use different resources within the class in order to differentiate work. Science and modern foreign language teachers were more likely and mathematics teachers least likely to agree that all pupils in the class work on the same topic at the same time. English and science teachers were most likely to agree that pupils worked on the same task and the work was differentiated by outcome. Mathematics and modern foreign languages were least likely to be differentiated by outcome.

Teaching methods

The learning opportunities provided for pupils of different abilities in different types of class varied considerably (see Table 6.6). Teachers provided:

- more opportunities for rehearsal and repetition for the less able (34% mixed ability classes, 57% set classes);
- more structured work for the less able (39% mixed ability classes, 68% set classes);
- more opportunities for discussion for the able (24% mixed ability classes, 32% set classes).
- more practical work for the less able (15% mixed ability classes, 21% set classes);
- more structured comprehension question and answer work for the less able (19% mixed ability classes, 34% set classes).

Table 6.6: Differentiation of teaching strategies: percentages (and number) of responses

Statement	Always	Nearly always	Sometimes	Not often	Never
Mixed ability classes					
I provide more opportunities for rehearsal/repetition of information for the less able pupils in the class	5 (54)	29 (333)	49 (559)	16 (183)	2 (22)
I set more structured work for the less able pupils in the class	5 (53)	34 (399)	50 (585)	10 (113)	2 (20)
I encourage/allow more discussion of work by more able pupils	5 (54)	19 (210)	43 (472)	25 (278)	8 (93)
I am more likely to use practical activities with less able pupils	3 (30)	12 (117)	43 (415)	31 (299)	12 (116)
I use more structured comprehension/ 'question and answer' activities with the less able pupils	2 (21)	17 (176)	54 (552)	21 (211)	6 (58)
Structured ability groups					
I provide more opportunities for rehearsal/repetition of information for pupils in the less able groups	9 (84)	48 (438)	37 (356)	6 (52)	1 (9)
I set more structured work for pupils in the less able groups	13 (122)	55 (513)	25 (231)	5 (49)	1 (11)
I encourage/allow more discussion of work in the more able groups	7 (58)	25 (213)	46 (401)	18 (156)	5 (39)
I am more likely to use practical activities with students in the less able groups	2 (17)	19 (163)	46 (401)	26 (227)	8 (67)
I use more strctured comprehension/ 'question and answer' activities with the lower ability groups	4 (32)	30 (264)	47 (413)	16 (136)	4 (34)
I use different teaching methods with different ability groups	16 (150)	45 (415)	35 (326)	3 (27)	1 (8)

Teachers reported offering a more restricted range of activities for the less able in set classes (51%). They adopted different teaching methods for different ability groups (61% set classes) while different activities were prepared for pupils of different ability within mixed ability classes (20%).

There were few differences between the teachers' responses in relation to type of school. Such differences as there were occurred in relation to teaching pupils in mixed ability classes. Teachers in set schools (3.04) and partially set schools (3.1) were more likely to encourage or allow more discussion of work by more able pupils than those in mixed ability schools ($F_{1104,2} = 3.22$, p = .04). Similarly they were more likely to use practical activities with less able pupils (set 3.19, partially set 3.43, mixed ability 3.4) and use more structured comprehension question and answer activities with the less able pupils (set 2.98, partially set 3.17, mixed ability 3.13).

Teachers of modern foreign languages and mathematics were more likely to provide opportunities for rehearsal and repetition of information for pupils in the less able groups, to provide them with more opportunities for structured question and answer sessions and to provide them with more opportunities for practical work. Teachers of modern foreign languages and English were more likely to set more structured work for pupils in the less able groups while teachers of modern foreign languages and science were more likely to encourage discussion among the more able and use different teaching methods with different ability groups.

Homework

Forty per cent of teachers in set classes reported setting shorter homework for the lower ability groups. This contrasted with mixed ability classes where the homework set varied with ability in only 18% of classes. Slightly more detailed written feedback on homework was reported as being provided for the able pupils in set classes, 18% as opposed to 12% in mixed ability classes. Table 6.7 sets out the details.

Teachers commented in the questionnaire that it was more difficult to differentiate homework in the mixed ability classes.

> It becomes more difficult to set appropriate homework for pupils in mixed ability and to ensure that these are properly marked and discussed in class and corrected. (Mathematic teacher, set school)

Table 6.7:   Differentiation of homework for different types of classes: percentages (and number) of responses

Statement	Always	Nearly always	Sometimes	Not often	Never
Mixed ability classes					
The homework I set pupils varies according to their ability	3 (37)	15 (161)	42 (457)	27 (296)	12 (135)
I provide more detailed written feedback on homework from the more able groups	3 (28)	9 (96)	287 (303)	29 (310)	31 (331)
Structured ability groups					
I set shorter homework for the less able groups	12 (108)	28 (255)	38 (344)	14 (127)	7 (65)
I provide more detailed written feedback on homework from the more able groups	5 (41)	13 (113)	31 (271)	28 (239)	24 (205)

Teachers working in mixed ability schools were more likely to set homework which varied according to ability for pupils in mixed ability classes (3.19) than teachers in partially set (3.38) or set schools (3.4). Teachers of mathematics and modern foreign languages were more likely to set homework varied according to ability, and also to set shorter homework for the less able groups. Modern foreign language teachers were more likely to give more detailed feedback on the homework of the more able pupils regardless of how they were being taught.

Behaviour management

Whether teaching in mixed ability or set classes, teachers agreed that sometimes they had to spend more time getting lower ability children to behave (42% in mixed ability, 41% in set classes). Teachers in the set classes supported this statement more (32%) than those in mixed ability classes (20%). Generally, teachers did not agree that they were stricter with pupils in the lower ability sets (51%). Thirty-six per cent said that they were sometimes (see Table 6.8).

Teachers in set schools were more likely to agree that they had to spend more time getting the children in the lower ability groups to behave (2.84) than teachers in partially set (2.99) or mixed ability schools (3.61). They were also more likely to agree that they were more strict with the pupils in the lower ability groups (3.46) than those in partially set (3.57) or mixed ability schools (3.82). Teachers of modern foreign languages reported spending more time controlling the lower ability pupils' behaviour regardless of the method of grouping.

Table 6.8: Behaviour management: percentages (and number) of responses

Statement	Always	Nearly always	Sometimes	Not often	Never
Mixed ability classes I have to spend more time getting lower ability children to behave than higher ability children	4 (44)	16 (188)	42 (491)	29 (341)	9 (107)
Structured ability classes I have to spend more time getting children to behave in the lower ability groups	9 (78)	23 (210)	41 (379)	22 (206)	5 (46)
I am more strict with the pupils in the lower ability groups	2 (17)	11 (99)	36 (319)	31 (273)	20 (174)

Organisation of the class

Teachers in all types of class agreed that they sometimes determined the seating arrangements in their classes (39% mixed ability, 38% structured grouping). Almost none of the teachers adopted within class ability grouping procedures (4% in the mixed ability classes and 2% in the structured ability grouped classes). Twenty-three per cent of the mixed ability teachers reported doing so sometimes as opposed to 20% in the set classes. A small proportion of teachers of mixed ability classes (24%) adopted mixed ability grouping practices within the class on a regular basis, 39% did so sometimes. A slightly lower proportion, 18%, of teachers working with set classes adopted mixed ability grouping practices in their classroom on a regular basis, 34% did so sometimes. In mixed ability classes, 15% of teachers grouped pupils according to the topic being covered on a regular basis, 38% did so sometimes. When teaching set classes, 12% of teachers grouped pupils according to the topic on a regular basis, while 31% did so sometimes. Overall, teachers in mixed ability classes adopt more within class grouping procedures but these are rarely based on ability. Table 6.9 provides the details.

There were significant differences between teachers in different types of school in relation to the extent to which they grouped pupils by ability within the class, whether it was a mixed ability or set class, and also the extent to which pupils were grouped within mixed ability groups. Teachers in set schools were more likely to group pupils by ability within the class than their colleagues in either partially set or mixed ability schools ($F_{1167,2} = 5.91$, p = .003; p = .034). Teachers working in mixed ability schools were more likely to form mixed ability groups in class than their colleagues in set or partially set schools when the classes were mixed ability ($F_{1112,2}$ = 4.69, p = .009) and as likely to do so as their colleagues in set schools when classes were of structured ability grouping ($F_{832,2}$ = 6.66, p = .001). Teachers in partially set schools were less likely to adopt mixed ability groups within ability grouped classes.

Table 6.9: Classroom organisation: percentages (and number) of responses

Statement	Always	Nearly always	Sometimes	Not often	Never
Mixed ability classes					
I determine the seating arrangements in my classes	22 (249)	18 (198)	39 (443)	14 (163)	7 (76)
I group pupils by ability within the class	1 (6)	3 (33)	23 (273)	25 (292)	48 (566)
I group pupils so that they are in mixed ability groups within the class	6 (61)	18 (202)	39 (437)	14 (158)	23 (256)
I group pupils in my classes according to the nature of the topic I am teaching	4 (41)	11 (126)	38 (426)	18 (205)	30 (334)
Structured ability groups					
I determine the seating arrangements in my classes	24 (220)	18 (169)	38 (355)	16 (143)	4 (34)
I group pupils by ability within the class	1 (8)	1 (12)	20 (178)	27 (239)	52 (467)
I group pupils so that they are in mixed ability groups within the class	6 (51)	12 (96)	34 (283)	17 (144)	31 (261)
I group pupils in my classes according to the nature of the topic I am teaching	3 (23)	9 (75)	31 (267)	21 (184)	36 (309)

When paired t-tests were undertaken comparing the responses of teachers teaching set and mixed ability classes, there were no significant differences relating to determining the seating arrangements in the class, grouping of pupils in mixed ability groups in the class or grouping pupils according to the nature of the topic. The only significant difference related to the grouping of pupils by ability within the class, which occurred more frequently in mixed ability classes.

English teachers made more positive responses to all the questions in this section. Clearly, group work of various kinds which is in part determined by the nature of the task is important in the teaching of English. A similar trend was observed in humanities although it was not so strong.

Shared teaching materials and resources

Overall, teachers were agreed that successful mixed ability teaching depended not only on the skills of the teacher, as outlined above, but also on the availability of appropriate resources.

> Mixed ability teaching benefits all but it does require good resourcing. (Science teacher, partially set school)

> I believe that all subjects can be taught in mixed ability as long as resources and support are available. (Science teacher, mixed ability school)

Fifty-three per cent of teachers working in mixed ability classes and 51% in set classes agreed that the teachers in their department worked together to develop resources. Whatever the nature of the teaching, in the region of 37% of teachers agreed that they had to produce a lot of their own resources in order either to teach mixed ability classes or to differentiate between classes. The great majority of teachers were nearly always happy with the resources available within their department (48% teaching mixed ability classes, 44% teaching set classes). The majority of those teaching mixed ability classes felt there were sufficient extension materials to stretch the able children (64%) while 51% felt there were sufficient resources to support the least able (see Table 6.10).

Teachers working in mixed ability schools (2.25) were more likely to agree that teachers worked together in their department to develop resources for teaching structured ability groups than those in partially set (2.44) or set (2.48) schools (p = .035). Teachers in set schools were more likely to agree that they were happy with the resources available for teaching mixed ability classes (2.52) as opposed to those working in partially set (2.73) or mixed ability schools (2.7) ($F_{1167,2}$ = 5.09, p = .006). Teachers in set schools were also more likely to agree that there were sufficient extension materials to stretch the most able (set 2.16, partially set 2.4, mixed ability 2.27) and resources to support the least able when teaching mixed ability classes (set 2.43, partially set 2.65, mixed ability 2.54). Some general subject difference trends emerged in relation to resources. Mathematics teachers were more likely to agree that they worked together to produce resources and that there were sufficient resources. Modern foreign language teachers were the least likely to agree.

Table 6.10: Teaching resources: percentages (and number) of responses

Statement	Always	Nearly always	Sometimes	Not often	Never
Mixed ability classes					
Teachers work together in my department to develop resources	24 (280)	29 (339)	36 (415)	9 (100)	3 (34)
I have to produce a lot of my own resources in order to teach a mixed ability group effectively	10 (116)	26 (301)	45 (516)	17 (192)	3 (30)
I am happy with the resources available in the department for teaching mixed ability classes	7 (85)	41 (478)	33 (391)	15 (176)	3 (40)
There are sufficient extension materials to stretch the most able pupils	18 (208)	46 (535)	27 (312)	10 (111)	.4 (5)
There are sufficient resources to support the least able pupils	10 (113)	41 (477)	36 (424)	13 (158)	1 (7)
Structured ability grouping					
Teachers work together in my department to develop resources	20 (186)	31 (289)	38 (352)	9 (87)	2 (21)
I have to produce a lot of my own resources in order to teach the different ability groups effectively	10 (96)	27 (249)	46 (426)	16 (144)	1 (12)
I am happy with the resources available in the department for teaching classes of differing ability	6 (55)	38 (349)	36 (329)	16 (152)	4 (41)

Summary

The findings reported in this chapter demonstrate that the issues relating to pedagogy and ability grouping apply equally to primary and secondary schools. They also lend support to much previous research on streaming and tracking. In general teachers believe that:

- setting enables pupils' curriculum needs to be better met;
- teaching the lower sets requires a different approach from teaching the higher sets;
- teaching is easier for the teacher when classes are set;
- setting makes classroom management easier;
- developing the appropriate teaching skills necessary to teach a mixed ability class benefits all pupils.

The evidence suggests that ability grouping restricts some pupils' opportunities. Access to the curriculum differs when pupils are put into ability groups. This extends beyond curriculum content to opportunities to develop transferable skills. The curriculum is differentiated more in set classes by content, depth, the activities undertaken and the resources used. The less able are given more opportunities for rehearsal and repetition, more structured work, more practical work, and less opportunities for discussion. They may be set less homework and the feedback they receive on that homework may be given in less detail. The expectations of teachers about the pace of work differ for mixed ability and set classes. High ability pupils are expected to work at a faster pace in set classes. In all types of classes they are expected to work at greater depth, exhibit higher levels of analytic thinking and take more responsibility for their written work. Only in mixed ability classes are they expected to demonstrate greater levels of independent thought. The less able, in contrast, have less opportunities, a slower pace and work which while it is believed to be more suited to their abilities, may be perceived by them as 'boring'. The evidence indicates that these differences exist even when the same teachers are teaching both mixed ability and set classes. This suggests that it is the structures themselves which lead teachers to change their teaching rather than their own personal teaching styles.

The data presented in this and the previous two chapters on teachers' attitudes to and pupils' experiences of ability grouping mirrors that found in earlier studies in the UK relating to streaming. Setting has been considered by some to be a middle road between streaming and mixed ability teaching. What is clear is that the negative effects which streaming had on some pupils' opportunities to learn and social and personal development apply equally to setting. In practice, where schools adopt rigid banding and setting for the majority of curriculum subjects, the same negative effects will occur. If schools wish to adopt setting procedures for some subjects, which the majority of pupils and staff seem to favour, they need to be proactive in minimising the disadvantages. How they might go about this is discussed in Chapter 8.

7

Principles, Pressures and Practicalities

The research discussed in Chapter 4 demonstrates that many pupils are unhappy with their placement in sets and do not think that the work they are doing is at an appropriate level. In this chapter we turn to organisational issues concerned with grouping pupils in schools. We consider the principles underpinning the adoption of ability grouping and mixed ability grouping practices. The strength of the debate about ability grouping, discussed in Chapter 1, suggests that opinions are underpinned by fundamental and conflicting educational values. Those who are strongly in favour of mixed ability grouping generally argue on the grounds of equity, that an educational system must value all individuals equally. Those who are strongly in favour of ability grouping tend to argue on the grounds of diversity, that ability grouping is necessary to accommodate the diverse needs of individual pupils. We ask whether these principles are reflected in the aims and values espoused by the schools and how they translate into practical arrangements within our schools. We consider whether these values, which are part of the school ethos, influence decisions about ability grouping. We draw on recent research in primary and secondary schools, which demonstrates that a variety of factors may influence grouping arrangements, the placement of pupils into groups, movement between groups and the resources allocated to different groups. Some schools do place great importance on the issue of ability grouping and decisions about grouping structures are based on strong educational values. In many schools, however, ability grouping is seen as a matter for each curriculum subject department to determine. Schools are currently under pressure to increase the amount of ability grouping. We present evidence for the prevalence of setting in primary and secondary schools. Structured ability grouping brings with it a number of problems such as the frequency with which

153

pupils can move between sets and the extent to which pupil behaviour is allowed to influence this movement.

School aims and ethos

The ethos of a school is somewhat elusive and hard to define, but is reflected in the educational aims and values of a school. Aims are made explicit through statements in the school prospectus or other documentation. Values are often more implicit and less tangible, becoming evident in the quality of relationships between teachers, between teachers and pupils and between pupils. They may also influence the way the school is organised. Values may be particularly evident through the school's provision for pupils experiencing difficulties in learning. From research on the curriculum for such pupils in ten primary and ten secondary schools, Ireson *et al.* (1992) found different philosophical orientations in schools that provided special help through withdrawal and in schools providing support in class. Those offering classroom support appeared to be more idealistic whereas those offering withdrawal were more pragmatic in their orientation.

Given the difficulties in defining school ethos, researchers have adopted a variety of interpretations and developed different measures in their work. For example, handbooks produced for the Scottish Education Department Inspectors of Schools provide indicators for use in primary and secondary schools (Scottish Education Department, 1992a, 1992b). These consist of questionnaire scales for teachers, pupils and parents to complete. The scales include indicators of teacher morale and job satisfaction, pupil morale and their perceptions of the learning context, teacher-pupil relationships, school policies and practice on equality and justice, extra-curricular activities, school leadership, discipline and communication with parents.

Researchers exploring the relationships between ethos and pupil learning have tended to focus on aspects of the classroom climate. In his research on secondary school pupils' approaches to learning, Ramsden (1991) demonstrated links between ethos and pupil attainment. His measure of ethos was a combination of the extent to which pupils felt supported by their teachers, the extent to which they were encouraged to learn independently, the clarity of goals and the extent to which students felt they and the staff shared similar aims. His analysis shows that students in high ethos schools achieve higher grades in the school leaving examination. In addition, ethos affects students' approaches to learning, with more students in high ethos schools adopting deep approaches, seeking to understand rather than simply reproduce curriculum subject matter. They are more intrinsically interested in studying. His findings are consistent with other research on classroom environments, which has found higher achievement in environments that are perceived to be cohesive, satisfying and organized (Fraser, 1989).

In Chapter 3 we presented some of our findings concerning the pupils' feelings about school, which may be viewed as their perceptions of school ethos. We also presented information on pupils' views about and preferences for different types of grouping in Chapter 4. In this chapter we turn to information we collected from head teachers and senior staff about the aims and ethos of the school and how they saw ability grouping in relation to these. We also provide information from heads of department and curriculum managers on the practical aspects of ability grouping.

In our research, we interviewed head teachers and other members of staff in both primary and secondary schools. In the 45 secondary schools participating in the secondary school project, we interviewed the head teacher and the teacher with responsibility for the timetable, henceforth referred to as the curriculum manager. We also collected information from heads of department via questionnaires, which included both closed and open questions. In the six primary schools we interviewed the head teacher, the deputy head teacher, the subject co-ordinator for each of the core curriculum subjects, two class teachers (one from Key Stage 1 and one from Key Stage 2), the Chair of Governors and a parent governor. In the sections that follow, MA is used to denote a Mixed Ability school, Partially Set denotes schools with small amounts of setting and Set refers to schools with higher levels of setting (see Chapter 2 for details).

Aims, ethos and pupil grouping

When asked to describe the aims of the school, head teachers in both primary and secondary school usually referred to their written mission statements. In all six primary schools and a third of the secondary schools (4 MA, 6 Partially Set, 5 Set) head teachers stated their main aim as providing the opportunity for individual students to achieve their full potential.

The interpretation of the aims in relation to the schools' grouping policy revealed the differing ethos of schools. This link was clearest in the schools with the strongest beliefs in either mixed ability grouping or in setting and streaming. In the schools with less strongly held beliefs about ability grouping, a more pragmatic approach was evident.

For example, a head teacher in a school that grouped pupils by ability in every subject was quite clear about the link between the school's aims and ability grouping policy.

> Well if you look at the aims . . . 'To prepare pupils for their future lives' . . . that's the first aim of the school . . . so I could argue . . . if I wanted to be ideological . . . that in real life people tend to get put together in ability groupings according to task . . . therefore, the school reflects that . . . I think that's a pure debating point . . . more realistically though one of the things is that we're trying to get the maximum out of each child . . . and I don't believe you can do that . . . I do not believe you can do it in mixed ability. (Set)

The head of one of the mixed ability schools was equally clear.

> The aims of the school start off by saying that we will demonstrate that all members of the school community are of equal value . . . I think all ability is vital to this . . . we can't demonstrate that people are of equal value if we start to separate them out and say you are better than somebody else or you are worse . . . and no matter how schools try and disguise this, the message is very, very clear to youngsters . . . they know they are in a bright group, they know they are in a 'thick' group and I use the word 'thick' advisedly in that's what kids often say 'we can't do this because we're thick' . . . that is our first aim . . . it's our primary aim . . . if we don't do that we won't get other things right. (MA)

Four schools in the sample had religious affiliations, three being Catholic and one Church of England. In two of these schools, head teachers explained how religious beliefs directly affected the grouping policy.

> Essentially you know . . . if you take the image of Christ . . . the apostles I would imagine were a very mixed ability grouping and I don't think He went out of his way to choose very bright people in society . . . and we really do believe that with mixed ability teaching . . . mixed ability grouping . . . you can help the brighter ones when they help their classmates . . . they do the immediate teaching and educational research shows that that's the best way of developing in themselves whatever they've been learning. (MA)

The school is a Church of England School . . . so the message that we send out to our community is one of inclusion and one of every child having every opportunity to succeed . . . not just academically either . . . so the real push or impetus in the school has always been towards inclusion and towards building community learning for which no child is excluded from any particular group. (Partially Set)

A third of the secondary head teachers described a 'mixed philosophy' approach to grouping in their schools, with a variety of grouping practices in different subject departments. This approach to grouping was a deliberate strategy in these schools and it was seen as part of the wider school ethos.

I don't impose an orthodoxy on various subject departments . . . we take a pragmatic view according to the individual groups of students and the predelictions and beliefs of the teaching staff within a faculty. (Partially Set)

We're not governed by a sort of rigid view or dogmatic view . . . that there has to be one fixed policy . . . so that we actually look at each area of the curriculum and decide what works best for that area and keep it under review . . . so we operate an arrangement of mixed ability, wide ability and then setting in certain curriculum areas. (Partially Set)

I haven't come in with a philosophy as a head teacher and said that either setting or mixed ability is right . . . I still think probably the mixed philosophy is best for the school. (Partially Set)

It is clear from these statements from head teachers that educational values play a large part in ability grouping policy and practice. A clear demarcation exists between those who see mixed ability grouping as an essential means of demonstrating the equal value of all individuals and those who see ability grouping as an essential means of preparing pupils for a society structured on the basis of ability. In between these two extremes are those who have a mixed philosophy and adopt a combination of grouping systems. Their approach to ability grouping is more pragmatic and allows them to accommodate a variety of practices in different subject departments.

Pressures to group by ability

Head teachers and staff in the schools are subject to a number of pressures to adopt setting. In the current education market, schools are in competition to attract pupils. The competition is fiercer in certain areas and head teachers are well aware of the preferences of parents. In our 45 secondary schools, one third of head teachers mentioned that parents were in favour of setting (4 MA, 5 Partially Set , 7 Set). As one head teacher in a set school said:

> It has enormous parental support in fact . . . I mean when you sell it to parents . . . when I talk to them about it . . . there is no doubt in their mind that it is a good thing . . . whether it is a good thing it doesn't seem to matter but nobody has ever come and said 'I'd much prefer my child to be taught in a mixed ability mathematics, English group or anything' . . . it's just never raised . . . as soon as you say 'setting' they're satisfied. (Set)

> Parental expectation I would say definitely is a key factor . . . it's not people coming up knocking on our door saying 'I want my child to be in a set' . . . the community here doesn't articulate its views necessarily in that way . . . they are in some ways quite reticent to approach the school on what they see as professional issues . . . but they have quite clear ideas about what they wanted for their children . . . so we found we were losing our most able children to other schools who did operate on those sorts of principles. (Partially Set)

For some schools, the pressure was specifically connected to the question of provision for more able children. This had prompted a reconsideration of grouping policy.

> We became aware of parents of able children going elsewhere because they didn't like mixed ability teaching and so we responded to that pressure. (Set)

> I have used the setting to attract parents to think about the school for bright kids . . . I think that's been part of the policy really if I were being honest about it . . . it was increasingly a question that came up . . . what are you doing about able children? Do you have setting in this school? To answer 'No we don't' and then to justify your exam results actually puts you in a very difficult position . . . you had to have been saying 'We don't have setting in this school and of course we don't need it because how could we do better than we've done' and we couldn't say that. (MA)

The second head teacher's comment about the school's overall performance makes reference to a recommendation in the 1997 government

White Paper, which states 'Unless a school can demonstrate that it is getting better than expected results through a different approach, we make the presumption that setting should be the norm in secondary schools.' (DfEE 1997, p.38). The school managers clearly felt that they would have some difficulty demonstrating that their results were 'better than expected' and were considering setting as a means of raising attainment.

Some schools felt under pressure even though their examination results were good. One school with partial setting was located in a middle class area, where it was in competition with schools making greater use of ability grouping. Although the examination performance of pupils was comparable, parental desire for setting remained.

> There are huge pressures on the school to move towards setting in terms of recruitment and I have a feeling that relatively soon I'm going to issue guidance to heads of subject to group the children . . . set the children by ability wherever it is practicable and possible because to be very frank our neighbouring schools are winning our children at the beginning of Key Stage 3 on that plank . . . the parents will tell us quite clearly that they want their bright children to be taught with bright children and they don't want them sitting next to others . . . it's against the ethos of the school but I'm afraid . . . it's no use having an ethos and no children to teach it to . . . it is a real absolute moral dilemma. (Partially Set)

Head teachers in our six primary case study schools also mentioned external pressures of performance league tables. All justified the grouping patterns, from the most highly set to mixed ability, in terms of raising attainment. In four schools, the implementation of the National Literacy Strategy had influenced grouping practices by increasing the amount of ability grouping within the classroom.

The examination system was seen as an additional pressure to group by ability in the secondary schools. Head teachers in a quarter of the schools in our sample mentioned tiered examination papers at GCSE having an influence on their decisions to move toward setting, particularly in mathematics and science. Tiered papers restrict the grades that can be attained by pupils who are entered for the lower tiers. In mathematics for example, there are currently three tiers and the top grade for the intermediate tier is C. It was seen as problematic to teach a class of students who would be taking different level examination papers.

It is clear that for many schools the demand from parents for setting has played an important part in the decision to increase the amount of ability grouping. Schools can ill afford to become unpopular with parents, as this has an immediate impact on the school budget. A school that loses popularity with parents of more able children can also face difficulties as the intake becomes more skewed to the lower range. In some cases, senior staff felt they were faced with a moral dilemma, experiencing a conflict between the values of the market and their educational values. Given that research throughout the 20th century has demonstrated little impact of ability grouping on attainment, its popularity with parents is somewhat surprising. Two head teachers, one in a primary school and one in a secondary school suggested that the majority of parents imagine that their children will be in the top set. This may be one reason why there is a preference for setting, but there are probably many other factors to do with the cultural traditions and value systems in this country, which will be considered in the final chapter of this book.

Grouping patterns

Both primary and secondary schools adopt a wide variety of grouping arrangements. Grouping arrangements differ from school to school and within a school there are different arrangements as pupils move up the school from one year to another. Overall, the amount of ability grouping increases as children grow older and setting is more common in secondary than in primary schools. Even in the primary schools, however, there is considerable variation in the extent to which ability grouping is adopted.

The scope for setting and streaming in primary schools is limited by the size of the intake. Our case study sample of six primary schools included one school that used streaming up to year 3, followed by setting in years 4 to 6. This was an unusually large school with excellent resources. Setting in primary schools is only possible in larger schools with two or more classes in each year group. Smaller primary schools have little scope for setting as they may have only one class per year group and some have even less. Sometimes children from more than one year group are combined to form sets. This 'cross age grouping' is sometimes used as a solution when the intake in a particular year is too large for one class and too small for two. Another form of ability grouping utilised in primary schools is within class grouping. Children are grouped according to ability within the classroom. It is common practice in English primary classrooms to seat the children around tables, rather than in rows. Seating arrangements may be changed during the day, with children moving from mixed ability groupings to ability groups for certain parts of the curriculum. The use of ability groups is now a common practice, following the introduction of the literacy and numeracy hours, which require children to work in ability groups for part of the time.

We completed a survey of ability grouping practices in primary schools during the 1998-99 school year (Hallam *et al.*, 1999). We sent a questionnaire to a representative random sample of 2000 primary, junior, JMI and infant schools in England and Wales. The questionnaire requested information about the local education authority, whether the school was grant maintained, the type of school and the number of pupils on roll. We provided two versions of the questionnaire, one for completion by schools with all pupils in same-age classes and one for schools with some or all mixed-age classes. ('Mixed age' classes refers not to teaching groups which may be cross-age, but to pupils from different year groups who are registered together as a class.) Schools were asked for information about their grouping practices in each year group, for all curriculum subjects. In all, 765 schools returned questionnaires, a response rate of 38%. This survey revealed that in the majority of primary schools pupils are in mixed ability classes. Just under half the schools in the sample had some or all mixed age classes. The vast majority of these (91%) were small schools, with less than 100 pupils. In the core subjects of mathematics and English, the most prevalent arrangement was ability groups within mixed ability classes. In all other subjects the most common arrangement was mixed ability groups within mixed ability classes. The incidence of setting was low and streaming was negligible. Setting was most common for mathematics and English in years 5 and 6, but occurred infrequently for other subjects. Overall, there was more ability grouping in mathematics than in any other subject. By year 6, the vast majority of pupils (96%) were in ability groups for mathematics, either within class ability groups or sets. This survey broadly confirms the findings of Ofsted (1998) and demonstrates that the majority of English primary schools children are in mixed ability classes for much of the day.

In secondary schools in England and Wales, setting is used extensively. Overall, the use of setting increases as pupils move up the school. Some schools retain mixed ability classes in year 7 and introduce setting in year 8. This allows time for pupils to settle in and for teachers to make their own assessments of pupils' attainment. In some schools setting is introduced later, or not at all. The year in which setting is introduced varies from one curriculum subject to another. As reported in Chapter 5, some subjects, such as English and humanities, are considered more suitable for mixed ability teaching than others such as mathematics and modern foreign languages.

Setting itself is not a uniform practice and may be organised in a variety of ways. The patterns in secondary schools include the following:

- rigorous setting, taking the whole year group and placing the highest attaining pupils in set 1, the next in set 2 and so on
- broader setting, for example two set 1s, two set 2s, two set 3s
- accelerated set, with the remainder of the year group in parallel sets
- parallel lower sets, e.g. one set 1, one set 2 and two sets 3s
- time-table halves, with each half year group being taught a particular subject at a different time; set patterns may be the same in both halves or they may differ in the two halves
- gender setting, with some or all sets composed of only boys or only girls.

In addition, mixed ability grouping practices vary, with some classes composed on a random basis, while others may be balanced to achieve a particular mix, for example on the basis of gender or ethnicity.

Resources may influence the decision to adopt a particular grouping pattern, such as timetable halves. Some decisions to adopt broader groupings are also influenced by awareness of behavioural problems that may occur in lower sets with rigorous grouping.

Forming groups

The allocation of pupils to groups is carried out on the basis of a variety of types of information. In both primary and secondary schools, a variety of assessments are used, including Key Stage tests, standardised tests, internal assessments and examinations and teacher judgement. In our primary case study research deputy head teachers, curriculum co-ordinators and class teachers were asked about the formation of groups and classes. Those in the schools using more setting used more standardised, external assessments, such as NFER tests, in addition to the statutory and optional Key Stage tests. In the primary schools with less ability grouping, there was less emphasis on testing, standardised tests were used less and teachers relied more on their own assessments of progress through the curriculum. Most staff reported that data from tests was supplemented by other information, such as end of year reports from previous teachers and discussions with pupils and parents where appropriate. Where children are grouped within their classes, decisions on grouping are generally made by the class teacher and the consistency of grouping practices varies from school to school. Social factors are taken into account in the formation of groups, especially in areas of curriculum in which there is less ability grouping but also when a particular mix of children would make a difficult teaching group. Pupils' behaviour also influences decisions about group placement and even the number of ability groups. Efforts are made to avoid grouping children with behavioural difficulties together. The school with the highest level of setting and streaming was able to create parallel ability groups in order to separate children with behavioural difficulties. Not all schools have a sufficient level of staffing to achieve this.

In the secondary schools, heads of department completed a questionnaire, which asked about information used when forming pupil groups. Responses to these questions were received from 41 heads of English and mathematics departments and 42 science departments in the 45 schools. The majority of departments used the pupils' performance in internal assessments and examinations as the basis for grouping, but this varied from one curriculum subject to another. As there was less setting in English, it is not surprising to find less reliance on assessments for grouping. Over half the mathematics and science departments used internal assessment (24), against only 7 of the English departments. Internal assessments included end of year examinations, module tests and end of term tests. After internal assessments, the Key Stage 2 test results were the most frequently used. Just under half the mathematics and science departments made use of this information but only five English departments, all of which were in set schools. Only 18 departments used other information, such as reports, from primary feeder schools. External tests were sometimes used, with eight departments using unspecified NFER tests and nine using Cognitive Ability Tests (CATs). Four English and three mathematics departments in Set schools used the NFER tests whereas five science, two English and two mathematics departments used the Cognitive Ability Tests. Fewer tests were used in the mixed ability schools. Teachers' opinions about a child's potential, their 'feel' for the child or staff recommendation were also factors in deciding group placement in about a third of mathematics and science departments and seven English departments. Overall, mathematics and science departments make greater use of assessments, both Key Stage 2 tests and their own internal assessments. English departments use less assessment, but this increases in the schools where there is more setting in English.

Pupils' behaviour and motivation was also taken into account in the formation of groups. This included attitudes, effort and self-esteem. More English (8) and mathematics (9) departments than science (3) took these factors into account. Some departments stressed that they did not allow such factors to influence group placement.   Social factors, such as friendship groups or disruptive combinations of pupils, also influence groupings. This was more frequently considered in science (11) and least in English (2). The concern with social factors in science may be to do with practical group work in the science curriculum.

Gender was also a factor in the formation of classes, particularly in English in Set schools. Heads of ten English departments, including seven in Set schools, took gender into consideration. Some schools arranged a gender balance in classes, while others arranged some single sex groups. A few departments also considered the placement of pupils with special needs in the formation of groups. When learning support teachers provide support in class, rather than through withdrawal, it is a more effective use of resources to place pupils receiving support in a small number of classes. The heads of all three departments referred to this in one mixed ability school.

When pupils are regrouped, schools have the opportunity to form groups of differing sizes. In our sample of secondary schools, there was considerable variation in the class sizes within subjects that grouped by ability. All except one of those that mentioned differences in class sizes across the curriculum stated that the less able groups had fewer pupils, so that support could be provided for lower ability groups and pupils with special educational needs. When specific subjects were mentioned in terms of differential class sizes, mathematics was always the subject used as an example, although sometimes alongside one or both of English and science. Most bottom sets were said to be roughly half the size of top sets. The largest differential was found in one school with four times as many pupils in the top set than the bottom set (8 in the bottom group and 32 in the top group). The one exception in our sample was a set school where there was a policy of having a smaller group for the more able. The largest number of pupils in a top set thought to be feasible was 35.

The size of the year group is a factor influencing the number of classes and their size. Half the curriculum managers in our sample mentioned intake as a factor determining the size of classes. Most tutor groups were between 27 and 30, but the range extended from 23 to 32. Fluctuations in year groups meant that members of staff were faced with hard economic choices. One head teacher summed up the situation as follows.

> What is the issue here is just what your intake is. If you've got 150 children say and you've got five classes of 30 you really need six to allow the movement in the setting . . . but the six could also do you for 165 children . . . and the problem is that if you've got 165 you get funded for the extra 15 but if you've got the 150 you've got the same number of teaching groups very uneconomically used . . . but the problem is . . . the argument would go is that you should have five classes of 30 and you're just being extravagant . . . but if you want setting to work and not every time you move a child up move one down you can't operate in multiples of 30. (MA, Head Teacher)

Here the issue of intake is linked with economic factors, the ideal solution of having six classes being considered in terms of the additional cost of an extra teacher. This cost is weighed against the need to enable movement between groups, which becomes problematic when classes are already full. The issue of movement between groups will be considered more fully later in the next section.

Movement between groups

In many secondary schools pupils are placed in a class or tutor group for registration and some other activities. In mixed ability schools pupils remain in this class for lessons in all subjects. In schools with setting pupils are regrouped for some lessons and the extent of regrouping depends on the amount of setting. When pupils are taught in mixed ability classes they remain in their tutor group, so any movement between groups for a particular subject is essentially a movement of tutor group. There is relatively little movement between groups in the schools using mainly mixed ability grouping. Three schools in our sample made use of non-tutor group mixed ability groups. One mixed ability school regrouped pupils thoroughly in year 9. The movement of pupils between mixed ability groups was mainly to do with social relationships, such as friendship groups or occasionally clashes between particular teachers and pupils. Some schools cited the school house system operating as a constraint in moving pupils between groups since pastoral systems and the timetable were affected.

In neither our primary nor our secondary school projects have we been able to collect quantitative information on the number of pupils moving between ability groups. In both projects, however, we collected some information from interviews about movement between groups. Staff in primary schools using ability grouping emphasised that their grouping systems were fluid and that children could move. This could be done half-termly or at the end of term or end of year and was normally carried out following an assessment.

In secondary schools, pupils are usually able to move between sets, although schools tend not to keep records of the frequency of such movements. Curriculum managers reported that movement occurred 'fairly frequently', although they were not specific as to exactly how often and what number of pupils this involved. Four curriculum managers commented that movement occurred most frequently in Years 7 and 8 but had settled down by Year 9.

Movement generally occurs after internal assessments. However, schools vary in the frequency in which these are carried out, some completing assessments each half term, while others are completed only once a year through end of year exams. The level of monitoring of movement between groups is also very variable. Some schools keep a very close eye on pupils. For example in one of the partially set schools, the members of the mathematics department met once a fortnight to identify anybody who should be moved up or down. Similarly in another partially set school, the heads of department were allocated three hours over two weeks to undertake classroom observations. In other schools it was acknowledged that movement between groups in different subjects was rather 'ad hoc' and that this was a cause for concern. Some curriculum managers saw the need for implementation of a more formal, common and accountable grouping policy framework.

Constraints on movement

The size of classes can limit the scope for pupils to move between sets. When pupils are moved up the sets, the top set can become too large, preventing further upward movement.

> . . . in particular, there's an upward movement and there's almost no downward movement in most subjects . . . so you start off with a top

set the beginning of the year of 33 and by the end of the year it's 36 and there isn't room in the classroom for 36 people. (Partially Set)

. . . it doesn't just go down to the relative merits or de-merits of an individual pupil, there has to be space in the next group for a child to move. (Set)

. . . every time you put somebody up chances are somebody else has got to come down so actually both kids have to be . . . one has to be an A and the other one has to be an E because otherwise you get a bit of a problem . . . well one of them has got to be held . . . somebody will often say 'Well somebody's ready to come up okay I'll take him and have one extra and we'll see what happens' . . . or else sometimes if they've already got 32 then somebody has to wait for promotion. (Set)

Another factor that was mentioned as making movement between groups problematic was the curriculum, especially in science because of the tendency to do topic work relating to biology, chemistry and physics on a rotational 'carousel' basis.

If you move a student they're instantly in the wrong place on the carousel and will repeat some work and miss others. (Partially Set)

Within science for example we have to wait until we've gone through a series of modules because if you switch from one group to another they may not have covered a particular module or have covered it twice . . . so there are times within the year when swaps can take place but it's a fairly informal. We don't like to change too much and actually the pupils don't like to change too much because you're running a different curriculum. (Partially Set)

Some curriculum managers commented that they saw it as vital that pupils were aware of the capacity to move between sets, for motivational reasons.

They do understand that things are not static and that if you work hard you will be moved up . . . even if I have to create a large group I will do that . . . rather than leave you where you are . . . or I'll bring people down for a while and they know that they then have to work hard to get themselves back up again. (Set)

Obviously you try and minimise the disruption and it might only be a handful of students throughout the year but there are opportunities for movement and students know that at the beginning. (MA)

Behavioural and motivational factors

There was a concern amongst some curriculum managers that pupils were not moved solely on the basis of their attainment or ability. Decisions to move pupils down a set are sometimes based on behavioural factors.

> We do tend to move them about yes and they [departments] do it on . . . they do a test and they shunt people around . . . I think they do it more often than they should . . . and they don't always do it for the right reasons in my opinion . . . they tend to do it for people who aren't working say put them down a set . . . well I would say make them work . . . but I mean, that's the school policy and they manage it and from time to time I do intervene and say 'Well why are you doing this? Why is this pupil who I know is very bright sitting in a middle set when they clearly can do the work in half the time that anybody else can do it in?' But those are the kind of issues you always get when you have ability setting. (MA)

> I would say that the rationale that's given to most students is that . . . if they are going from a higher set to a lower set . . . the rationale given to them is to do with their performance . . . their academic or intellectual performance . . . whereas I suspect the reason may be that their motivation is not high either because I think that there's a confusion for teachers in assessing attainment and assessing motivation . . . and I think we confuse them sometimes . . . I mean I think that's partly to do with the way that we look at attainment and ability and so on . . . we do sometimes move pupils because we think it's to do with their attainment and so on but actually it isn't . . . it's to do with some other contributory factor. (MA)

One such contributory factor is a pupil's behaviour. Many curriculum managers expressed dissatisfaction with the placement of pupils in a set lower than their potential on account of their behaviour. This appears to occur most frequently with boys. One set school tackled this by moving such pupils up a set, rather than down, as a means of managing their behaviour.

> I think we have an acceptance that . . . pupils should not be dumped because they are not behaving very well and in fact in some subjects we actually do the opposite . . . where kids aren't behaving very well we push them up . . . a number of cases where real troublesome kids have been mucking around and sort of being 'daft' have gone up a set or two sets even sometimes to work . . . and everybody's working and they

sort of get down to it and it's helped them a lot to manage their own behaviour . . . so they see the bad behaviour doesn't get them into a situation where they can intellectually coast which is often the sort of problem with kids that move down the sets . . . that they're much brighter than they ought to be there and they get bored. (Set)

But there are some boys in top sets who have not exhibited the kind of attitude and behaviour of the rest of the group and they have been moved . . . now I personally have a problem with this because if we're setting by academic ability then we should say 'Right they deserve a place in the top set they should maintain that' and we should provide whatever support and contact in order for them to achieve their potential. (Set)

Ability or attainment?

In addition to the difficulty of clarifying whether motivational factors were at the root of a pupil's poor performance, schools are confronting the problem of clarifying the distinction between ability and attainment. The difference between grouping by performance and grouping by ability was highlighted. Various curriculum managers spoke of the difficulties inherent in ability grouping in terms of recognising *potential* achievement in contrast to actual achievement. They were concerned that pupils with potential should not be moved down even if their performance dropped. Senior managers in some schools were making concerted efforts to tackle this issue through reassessing their grouping policies.

. . . although we're not yet convinced that it's being fully implemented because of people understanding the process and the need to get the right kind of data to make sure it works . . . the idea is to move towards groupings which are established on the basis of potential rather than performance . . . so that we're not looking to set up groups where you have if you like children who aren't behaving properly and therefore not doing their work . . . all ending up in one group . . . that's precisely what we're trying to avoid. (Partially Set)

For five curriculum managers (3 Partially Set and 2 Set) the 'right kind of data' was that provided by cognitive ability tests (CATs). These were seen as being able to measure a pupil's ability or potential, in contrast to their actual attainment as indicated by scores gained in other assessments. Senior managers anticipated that members of the school staff were unlikely to share their enthusiasm for these tests.

They realised that subject departments would be reluctant to implement new grouping policies based on standardised data.

> Some departments will move down just purely and simply on performance. We're trying to get around this by . . . making more use of standardised tests . . . CAT tests YELIS tests . . . and my personal belief is if students have the ability I feel they should be kept in top sets and pushed rather than allowed to slide . . . but some departments work purely and simply on the fact that if they want to slide they'll slide and . . . we're trying to get around that we're trying to make it a policy within the school that well next year with target setting it's going to be even more so . . . people have to look at these standardised tests and have to basically take them into account when setting. (Set)

> Now we do know the child's true ability because we do cognitive ability testing here . . . and what I would like is to test them for that and then put them into ability sets . . . now that will be interesting because teachers will still have kids that they would not have put in a top set but they are in a top set because they've actually got the potential ability and then we really are addressing expectation properly and underachievement . . . so that's something I'd like to introduce but I'm approaching it carefully because I think it will be a bit of a shock to the teacher system. (Partially Set)

It seems that the decision to put pupils into ability groups introduces a new set of problems associated with finding fair and accurate ways of deciding who should be in which group. Some schools are grappling with the problem of whether motivational and attitudinal factors should be allowed to influence these decisions, while others are concerned with the problem of teasing out ability and attainment. In their different ways, schools are acknowledging that ability is an elusive construct, which is difficult to measure. Its relationship with attainment is not a perfect one. Motivation, attitudes and behaviour are also important factors, which need to be put into the equation.

As with all tests of general ability, the use of Cognitive Ability Test scores to determine ability groups within subjects should be viewed with caution since such standardised tests measure general rather then subject specific ability. Although there are separate verbal and non verbal Cognitive Ability Tests, and these may be reasonably good predictors of performance in English and mathematics, they are less reliable predictors of attainment in other subjects. Perhaps more importantly, no standardised test provides a perfect prediction of attainment in any subject, and some pupils will always achieve far more or less than indicated by test scores. This is partly because of limitations in the predictive power of such tests, none of which should be relied on alone. It is also because cognitive ability is only one of several personal attributes that influence attainment. Other factors, such as pupils' personal circumstances and their motivation also influence attainment. There is always a danger of overemphasising the influence of ability and underestimating motivational factors, especially effort. Too great a reliance on standardised test scores could also lead to a situation in which pupils are streamed on the basis of their general ability rather than grouped according to their attainment in each curriculum subject.

To summarise, movement between groups, while seen as desirable, appears to be fraught with practical difficulties. In secondary schools, movement generally takes place following assessments, which may be carried out infrequently. Even movement between ability groups in the primary classroom may be problematic because of working relationships and friendships between the children. Such difficulties may result in pupils being moved rather infrequently. When pupils are in sets, the size of the year group and decisions to create smaller lower groups often limits the scope for movement, particularly into higher groups. The structure of the curriculum also makes changing groups problematic as the groups move at different paces through the curriculum. This makes it easier to move pupils down a set than up. Those who do move up may find that they have missed certain aspects of the curriculum.

Senior managers in some schools were unhappy with the school's practices in assigning pupils to groups and recognised the need for change. They were concerned with developing ways of clarifying ability, attainment and behaviour. Some schools were attempting to deal with this through the production and analysis of more assessment statistics and others were turning to target setting on an individual basis.

Resources and grouping

In both primary and secondary schools, resources can influence grouping practices. The organisation of the school timetable imposes certain constraints on grouping. In primary schools with mixed ability classes, constructing the timetable is relatively straightforward. Each class teacher spends the majority of the day with the class and therefore it is only the use of specialist areas, such the use of the hall for physical education, or specialist resources such as computers, that must be organised. When pupils are regrouped for particular subjects, constructing the timetable becomes more complex.

In secondary schools, constructing the timetable is an intricate and lengthy process with many factors having to be taken into consideration. Schools have particular local factors to take into account, each of which may limit the scope for setting. These include the number and size of specialist teaching rooms available for certain subjects, time for travelling between split sites, the need to accommodate part-time staff and co-ordinating the sixth-form timetable with other schools in a consortium. Staffing is a major consideration for ability grouping, as all sets are taught at the same time. The simultaneous teaching of a subject is referred to as 'blocking' and it may be carried out either across the year group or 'parallel blocked' across half the year group if a school has insufficient staff to teach all sets simultaneously. In this case, half the year group will be scheduled for a subject at one time and half at another, thus halving the number of specialist staff needed. Managers in the majority of the 45 secondary schools in our sample reported that the school faced difficulties in providing enough staff in particular curriculum subjects to enable all pupils to be taught at the same time. Several schools indicated that this restriction on the timetable was one of the reasons why mixed ability teaching was adhered to earlier on in the school.

Earlier research indicates that, in streamed systems, resources are distributed unevenly with the higher ability groups benefiting at the expense of the lower groups. This research suggests that there is a tendency for the more highly qualified and experienced teachers to teach the top streams. In our primary school case studies we found no evidence that this was the case. All classes had access to the full range of school resources.

In the secondary schools, heads of department are primarily responsible for deciding which teachers will teach each year group and class. There was evidence that in some schools the more experienced and highly qualified members of staff taught the top sets and older pupils.

> ... there are one or two people who by tradition teach in the upper school rather than the lower school ... I'd say there's a status involved in the different year groups ... but I think that again is not a stated thing ... no-one says that. (MA)

Others were firmly of the opinion that teachers should be able to teach at all levels and should be given the opportunity to do so.

I expect everybody in the department to be able to teach that subject to all levels . . . if they (head of department) say I've got somebody who cannot teach it to a high level I want to know why . . . are we employing them . . . because basically that's a restriction. (Set)

. . . the heads in my last school thought that the best teachers go with the best kids . . . you know I don't agree with that . . . it's done on a purely equitable basis . . . so if you had say in mathematics a top set in year 9 you'd have set 2 in year 8 and set 3 in year 10 . . . so everyone takes their turn. (MA)

Many curriculum managers acknowledged that for teachers a balance of age groups and ability groups was desirable, but there were a number of factors to be taken into consideration. Several indicated that less experienced teachers would not teach examination years (year 11 or A level). In some cases certain individuals were thought to be better suited to teaching particular ability or year groups.

. . . there are one or two people who prefer and have an expertise in a particular area with a particular ability range and they would tend to be given that group year on year . . . because it best fits the needs of the department . . . the teacher is happy with it the head of department is happy with it and the children are best served that way. (MA)

. . . there are some staff who we feel are better equipped to teaching lower ability sets or middle ability sets rather than higher sets . . . you've got a moral obligation to be very careful about how you match classes and staff. (Partially Set)

There are also teachers who are just simply better at teaching particular age groups . . . there are teachers who are better with 6th form . . . if someone doesn't have 'A' level in a particular subject . . . it may be that the rigours of an 'A' level are just too much and I'm not prepared to experiment on the pupils. (Partially Set)

In addition to academic qualifications, the ability of the teacher to control a class was taken into account by the heads of department. It was acknowledged that teachers whose classroom control skills were good might be given the more difficult classes while other members of staff might be more protected.

The pressure of performance in league tables sometimes affects the allocation of teachers. This was mentioned by two curriculum managers in our sample, one of whom said:

... the pressure to raise exam results means that you put onto your top sets the people who've got proven records rather than because it's their turn basically to have the top set ... it is more directed than it was even three years ago ... directed by the heads of faculty because of external pressures basically. (Set)

A number of factors influence the scope of schools to operate ability grouping effectively. Although there were differences between the schools, common themes included staffing, room, curriculum and economic constraints. Initial pupil intake affected class sizes and therefore grouping practices. Carousel arrangements in the curriculum of subjects such as science and craft, design and technology reduced flexibility of movement between groups. There seems to be a growing concern about ability grouping and behaviour.

Summary

Educational values underpin grouping arrangements in schools. In some schools, the link is very clear and explicitly stated in documentation such as the school prospectus. This is particularly true in schools with a strong adherence to mixed ability or to setting. Head teachers in some of these schools were very clear about the link between the aims of the school and their ability grouping policy. A more pragmatic approach is taken in schools with a combination of setting and mixed ability grouping. This approach may be purely on pragmatic grounds, or may be part of a deliberate style of management in which responsibility for grouping arrangements is delegated to the subject departments. It is significant, however, that in both primary and secondary schools, each of the many different types of grouping arrangements are justified on the grounds of their effectiveness in raising attainment.

School ethos encompasses far more than the statement of the aims of the school and its ability grouping arrangements. Schools with religious affiliations are very clear about their ethos in relation to religious beliefs and values. A particularly important issue is the value placed on individual pupils, with concerns that ability grouping runs counter to an inclusive philosophy and is associated with valuing certain pupils over others. In particular there is concern that with increased ability grouping, too much weight might be placed on academic attainment, with other important qualities being undervalued.

Ability grouping brings with it a number of practical issues, including the fair and accurate placement of pupils into groups, movement between groups and the allocation of teachers to groups. Schools use a variety of assessments to place pupils into groups and factors other than attainment may be taken into consideration. Movement between groups may occur infrequently and upward movement may be difficult, with large top sets preventing movement. Higher ability groups tend to be larger than lower groups but here again there is considerable variation between schools. This is generally justified as a way of providing support for the less able pupils. In primary schools, movement between ability groups within the classroom is more practicable, but not always easy as teachers take social and working relationships into account when forming groups. For many small primary schools, setting is not an option unless children in different year groups are combined.

Once ability grouping is in place in a school, teachers are confronted with the problems of how pupils' behaviour, motivation and potential affect placement and movement between sets. Decisions about movement may be influenced by pupils' behaviour, the amount of effort they put into their work and teachers' judgements about their potential. The consequence of these judgements may have profound effects on individual pupils.

The organisational difficulties that accompany ability grouping in schools indicate that groups will always contain a mix of abilities and that a significant proportion of pupils will be placed in a group that is too high or low in terms of the academic work covered. There is ample evidence that teachers' expectations of pupils are influenced by ability grouping and that they alter their classroom pedagogy in line with these expectations. This means that ability grouping does not solve the problem of providing teaching that is well matched to pupils' needs. Mixed ability teaching can work well, but is perceived by teachers to be more difficult to implement in the classroom. In the next chapter, we will consider some alternatives to structured ability grouping and mixed ability teaching.

8

Alternative Ways of Grouping
Pupils in School

The evidence presented in this book suggests that increasing the extent of setting and banding in our schools will not provide an effective solution to the problem of underachievement and may lead to the increased alienation of some pupils exacerbating current social problems. Equally, mixed ability teaching, as it has recently been practised in many schools, has not provided an appropriate learning environment for all pupils to reach their full potential. In this chapter we will consider how some of the difficulties with setting and mixed ability teaching might be ameliorated and suggest alternative ways of grouping pupils between and within classes.

As we have seen in Chapter 6, when considering how to group pupils, schools have to take account of a range of factors relating to their current circumstances. These relate to practical matters of timetabling and staffing and the school's reflections on its strengths and weaknesses in relation to its current pupils' academic, personal and social development. In selecting appropriate grouping practices, schools may need to prioritise the needs of particular groups of pupils at any one time, while also taking account of the evidence that individual pupils respond to ability grouping in different ways (Boaler, 1997a, 1997b, 1997c). If the needs of each cohort of pupils are to be met, grouping practices will need to be flexible and responsive to changing pupil needs. The concerns of staff, parents and the wider school community will also play a part in determining the practices adopted. Once determined, their success will depend on how they are implemented. If major changes are to be made, staff will need to be persuaded of their necessity and provided with training and appropriate resources to implement them. Without their commitment, particularly where there is active dissent, any changes are doomed to failure.

176

In the next sections we will outline a range of alternative grouping strategies. These are not mutually exclusive. They may be implemented in various complementary combinations to enhance the academic, personal and social development of different groups of pupils. The first section will consider how schools can structure grouping between classes. This will include discussion of the strengths and weaknesses of each type of grouping including setting, mixed ability teaching, vertical grouping, structured gender groupings, modularisation of the curriculum and special activity groups. The second section will consider ways in which teachers can organise learning within the classroom. This will consider within class grouping of various types and individualised instruction.

Between class groupings

In this section we consider a variety of between class groupings. These include setting, mixed ability, vertical grouping, gender grouping, modularisation and special activity groups.

Setting

The earlier chapters in this book have set out the research evidence and highlighted some of the problems of adopting structured ability grouping through setting or ability banding. One option for schools to consider is maintaining such grouping structures but attempting to minimise their negative effects. In practice this would mean that:

- students should remain in mixed ability classes for the greater part of the time, their main point of identification being with a mixed ability class;
- to achieve this, structured ability grouping should be adopted only where teaching and learning in the subject domain depended on pupils having shared prior knowledge and levels of attainment;
- procedures for assigning pupils to sets should be based on attainment in that particular subject, not general achievement or other factors, for example, behaviour;
- there should be frequent assessment of progress followed by reassignment to different groups where appropriate;
- where necessary 'bridging' groups should be set up to enable pupils to cover work needed for moving to a higher group;
- within groups teachers must vary their pace and level of instruction

to correspond to students' needs, adopting a range of methods and resources;
- some differentiation of work should occur within the class;
- high status teachers should be allocated to teach the lower sets;
- teachers should have high expectations of pupils in the lower sets;
- pupils should not be denied access to the curriculum or opportunity to take examinations because of their group placement;
- the school should provide those pupils who are less academically able with opportunities to excel in other areas;
- the school should demonstrate that it values all of its pupils.

The particular benefits of setting and to a lesser extent ability banding are that they allow work to be set at an appropriate level for the pupil and make the management of learning easier for the teacher. If the drawbacks can be minimised as outlined above then it may be an effective grouping practice. The danger for schools is the development of an ethos which stresses academic achievement to the exclusion of all else; an environment where high ability is reified leaving the majority of pupils feeling unvalued with a subsequent loss to their self-esteem, confidence and academic attainment.

Mixed ability teaching

Mixed ability teaching means literally teaching a class which includes children with a full range of abilities. When there was a shift in educational values in the 1960s towards equal opportunities, streaming declined and mixed ability teaching became the most common form of grouping in primary schools (Lee and Croll, 1995). It also became more popular in the lower years of secondary education. Its advocacy in the Plowden Report (DES/CACE, 1967) and concerns about disaffection and alienation at secondary level (Hargreaves, 1967) assured its increasing implementation through the 1970s. The Plowden Report indicated that mixed ability teaching would provide all pupils with equal access to a common curriculum and would promote the matching of individual learning programmes to the needs of individual pupils (DES, 1978). In these terms, the success of mixed ability teaching depended on the teacher moving away from whole class teaching to being able to cater for the whole ability range of the class through individualised learning programmes (Gregory, 1986). The Plowden Report recognised that it would be difficult to translate this ideal into practice.

In fact, in most cases, the ideal was not translated into practice (HMI, 1978; Kerry and Sands, 1984). Observation of teachers in the classroom has shown that teachers tend to teach at a whole class level to an 'imaginary average' child even though the range of abilities necessitates differentiation within the class (HMI, 1978; Wragg, 1984; Hacker and Rowe, 1993). The style of teaching adopted has been similar to that adopted in set or streamed classes (Boaler, 1997a, 1997b; Rowan and Miracle, 1983; Rosenbaum, 1976; Barr and Dreeben, 1977). Whole class teaching has predominated and there has been little evidence of genuine mixed ability group work. Teachers at primary level have often seated pupils by ability but pupils have worked individually. Able pupils have sometimes acted as teachers' aides to help the slower learners. Group work has tended to be used as an organisational device (Galton, Simon and Croll, 1980). Group composition has often been based on decisions about classroom management (see Chapters 4 and 5). Much group work has been described as limited and impoverished, time being spent undertaking trivial tasks (HMI, 1978, 1979; Sands, 1981a, 1981b; Reid *et al.*, 1982). The cognitive demands made on students have tended to be low, as has the quality of the verbal interactions between pupils (Kerry, 1982b, 1982c; Sands and Kerry, 1982; Kerry and Sands, 1984). Few group tasks have made sufficient cognitive demands on the more able and in many cases have not stretched average pupils. Few teachers have adopted individualised learning programmes to satisfy the needs of their pupils (Kerry, 1982a; Kerry and Sands, 1984), except where work cards or textbooks are used, often in mathematics, or where reading schemes are used.

Overall, little differentiation has occurred. This has led to higher ability children being insufficiently stretched (HMI, 1978; Wragg, 1984; DES, 1992) and some lower ability children being unable to cope with the work. The evidence indicates that this also applies to streamed and set classes (DES, 1992). Generally, pupils' needs have not been met by mixed ability teaching, as it has been practised, at either primary or secondary levels (DES 1991, Ofsted, 1993, 1994, 1995). Even teachers considered as effective in teaching mixed ability classes have experienced problems providing instruction at appropriate levels for high and low ability pupils (DES, 1991, 1992; Ofsted, 1994). Both groups tend to become bored, although for different reasons. In the case of low ability pupils this frequently leads to disruption (Kerry, 1982a). Teachers have tended to make inadequate use of assessment information and often lack detailed knowledge of the range of ability in their classes. Some are insufficiently skilled in recognising the particular needs of boys and girls, of children from ethnic minority groups or more able pupils. There has also been a tendency for teachers to have too low expectations of pupils, particularly in inner city schools (Ofsted, 1993).

Successful mixed ability teaching relies heavily on teacher skills (Reid *et al.*, 1982). Successful mixed ability teachers are flexible, use a variety of teaching modes in one lesson, vary the pace and style of approach, use a range of audio-visual media and encourage a variety of pupil activities. They have informal relationships with their pupils, involve pupils in decision-making and engage them in learning activities (Kerry and Sands, 1984). To successfully teach mixed ability classes teachers need access to appropriate resources and facilities (Schools Council, 1977; Ingleson, 1982). One of the difficulties for teachers is that they have often had to spend a great deal of time developing differentiated materials for teaching in mixed ability classes. There are also strong arguments that mixed ability teaching may be better suited to some curriculum areas than others (Kerry, 1980; Reid *et al.*, 1982).

Despite the difficulties outlined above there are advantages in adopting mixed ability teaching. It:

- provides a means of offering equal opportunities;
- addresses the negative social consequences of structured ability grouping by encouraging co-operative behaviour and social integration;
- can provide positive role models for the less able pupils;
- can promote good relations between pupils;
- can enhance pupil/teacher interactions;
- can reduce some of the competition engendered by structured grouping;
- can allow pupils to work at their own pace;
- can provide a sense of continuity and security for primary pupils when they transfer to secondary school;
- forces teachers to acknowledge that the pupils in their class are not a homogeneous group;
- encourages teachers to identify pupils' needs and match learning tasks to them.

For mixed ability teaching to be successful teachers need to be highly skilled and supported by a wide range of resources differentiated to satisfy pupil needs across the ability range. To reduce the time spent managing classroom activities some within class grouping may need to be adopted. These will be discussed later in the chapter.

Vertical grouping

As our primary survey and others have shown (Bouri and Barker Lunn, 1969; Arrowsmith, 1989; Draisey, 1985; Veenman, 1995; Hallam *et al.*, 1999) a large proportion of small primary schools, of necessity, have to adopt vertical grouping structures, that is putting children in classes which include more than one year group. Vertical grouping has also been adopted by some schools because of its perceived educational benefits (Veenman, 1995). The reasons given for its voluntary adoption relate to the social and family-like structure of classes where pupils, at least one year apart in age, are taught by the same teacher, staying together for several years. The purported benefits are not dissimilar to those made for mixed ability teaching (Veenman, 1995):

- students have the opportunity to form relationships with a wider variety of children;
- teaching such a wide diversity of students demands that teaching is individualised;
- the complex and changing social environment in such classes encourages the development of a balanced personality;
- the self-concepts of the less able older children are enhanced when they are asked to help younger students;
- the student stays with the same teacher for several years allowing closer and more secure relationships to develop;
- fewer anxieties about learning develop because the atmosphere is conducive to academic and social growth;
- younger students can benefit from the opportunity to observe, emulate and imitate a wide range of behaviours exhibited by older students, while older students have the opportunity to take responsibility for younger students;
- vertical grouping promotes co-operation and other forms of pro-social behaviours, and minimises competition and the need for discipline;
- the use of different learning materials provides opportunities for younger students to benefit from exposure to more advanced curricula while providing older students with the opportunity to benefit from reviewing earlier work;
- students at different levels of cognitive development can provide intellectual stimulation for each other;

- vertical grouping enables a relaxation of the rigid curriculum with its age-graded expectations, which are not appropriate for all pupils.

Reviews of the effects of vertical grouping (Pratt, 1986; Miller, 1990; Veenman, 1995) have concluded that there are no significant differences between cross age and single age groupings on pupils' academic achievement or social and personal development. Teachers' feelings are generally negative. They find that it increases their workload; that the management of the class is more difficult because they perceive that they are trying to teach two classes simultaneously; there is less opportunity for oral instruction because teaching one group may disrupt the other; there are more interruptions in the learning process; pupils receive less individual attention; and it is harder for pupils to concentrate on their work. Teachers also comment that they have not received training for vertical grouping (Veenman, 1995). A major difficulty currently for the teachers in the United Kingdom, and one which has led to alternative grouping arrangements being made in some cases, is the need to prepare pupils in some year groups for national examinations.

At secondary level vertical grouping has been relatively rare, although there are cases in United Kingdom schools where individual pupils have been moved to a higher year group because of their perceived need to be undertaking work at a more advanced level. In some schooling systems, pupils have to pass end-of-year examinations in order to move on to the next grade. Failure to do so means that the year has to be repeated. This practice has not been adopted systematically in the United Kingdom. Evidence relating to the effectiveness of such a strategy has indicated that students may be no more successful having retaken the year and that there can be high drop-out rates (Soutter, 1993).

Cross age or vertical grouping practices have been developed in the USA targeted at particular areas of learning. These can be very specific, for example the Joplin plan for literacy, or may be broader in conception, for example relating to mathematics. The principles underlying these programmes are identical to setting but the children are drawn from different year groups. Some have been very successful in raising attainment. Key features for success include flexibility, frequent assessment of attainment, increased teaching time for the set groups, organisation of the subject areas by attainment levels and the use of texts and materials at an appropriate level (Gutierrez and

Slavin, 1992). The successful programmes share all the features of successful setting.

Vertical grouping shares many common characteristics with mixed ability grouping. The difficulties that the teacher faces in relation to the differentiation of the curriculum and the management of learning are very similar. In common with mixed ability teaching there seem to be no detrimental effects to overall academic attainment and there is some evidence of positive personal and social outcomes (Veenman, 1995). Where cross age groups are set up, matching pupils for prior knowledge and skill to receive tuition together supported by appropriate learning materials with clear targets to achieve in relation to a specific learning outcome, they share similar characteristics to setting. The evidence demonstrates that they can increase academic attainment.

Structured gender groupings

In the recent past policy-makers and educators alike have been concerned about the nature and causes of gender differences in attainment. While girls' achievement overall has increased at GCSE and A level there are still marked differences between preferences, take-up and attainment in different subjects (Elwood, 1998). Some schools, in attempting to optimise their pupils' performance, have explored whether teaching girls and boys separately might be beneficial in some curriculum areas. The rationale underlying this is that boys and girls learn differently and in mixed sex classrooms may inhibit each others' learning. Research suggests that in general, girls prefer 'connected' ways of knowing which rely on intuition, creativity and experience; boys prefer 'separate' ways of knowing emphasising logic, rigour and abstraction (Gilligan, 1982). These ways of knowing may be better facilitated in different learning environments. Connected knowing is fostered in a more open learning environment where pupils can explore work together and develop understanding. Boys seem to prefer competitive, fast paced learning environments which demand factual knowledge and little reflection (Boaler, 1997c). They also tend to dominate classroom interactions with teachers (Kelly, 1988; Howe, 1997).

Personal development also differs. Boys seem to need to be accepted into a masculine peer culture which adopts a laid back approach to academic work (Phillips, 1998). This applies even to high achieving boys (Power *et al.*, 1998). Consistent with this, boys tend to attribute failure to lack of effort whereas girls attribute it to lack of ability (Dweck *et al.*, 1978). Girls rate hard work as being important in contributing to academic success whereas boys rate cleverness, talent and luck. Girls are more conscientious than boys in doing their homework (Cowan and Hallam, 1999). Boys seem to be achievement motivated, playing the academic game, while girls want to understand what they are learning (Boaler, 1997c).

Because of these perceived differences there has been considerable debate about whether single-sex teaching may have benefits. The evidence at school level is inconclusive mainly because of methodological difficulties. Within schools, small-scale projects have reported benefits. Such a case study is reported by Ireson (1999). An Ofsted inspection highlighted the need to raise boys' standards of literacy. Mixed and single gender groups were set up in year 9 for the teaching of English. In the classes for the boys the learning environment was competitive and they wanted and were able to see progress to the next level. The pace was quick, the delivery punchy, activities were set and undertaken in short bursts, instructions contained specific information about what was required and when, feedback was specific and related to national examination levels, much work was oral, and there was little written work. The teacher stressed short- and long-term goals and focused on concrete learning outcomes; there was much praise and encouragement. The boys reported that they weren't distracted by the girls, didn't have to show off for them or worry about feeling silly in front of them, and felt more able to ask the teacher for help. They spent more time on task, were better able to think about their learning, developed considerable metacognitive skills, were better motivated and had improved self-esteem, and a team spirit developed within the class. In the girls' class, the teacher reported difficulties in getting the girls to contribute to discussions, although they enjoyed undertaking written work, which was of a very high standard. The pace of the lessons was faster than previously with no interruptions, no risk of indiscipline and work which was very focused. Overall, the teacher felt that there was little guidance on how to teach girls. In this particular instance, the boys appeared to have derived more benefit from the single gender tuition than the girls. No evidence about attainment was available.

Overall, there has been insufficient large-scale research to demonstrate whether separate teaching of boys and girls is beneficial to either in the short or long term. As the case study demonstrated, it may contribute to enabling schools to focus on the different needs of boys and girls in the classroom, enabling teachers to acquire a deeper understanding of the issues and what strategies may be most success-ful with each group. This may then be applied to teaching throughout the school.

Modularisation of the curriculum

Groups can be structured through the modularisation of the curricu-lum. This allows students greater choice and control over the way in which they progress through school. Such a system fully adopted at secondary level could facilitate the broadening of access to learning throughout the community. Long-term developments might include classes taking place in the evenings and at weekends in addition to 'normal' school times. Timetabling would become more flexible and there would be more stress on independent study with an increase in library and computer facilities to make this possible. Schools would become centres of learning for the whole community with classes including adults and school-aged children. Such a scenario would enable schools to play a central role in the development of a learning society. Such developments are likely in the long term as educational structures change in response to changing patterns of employment.

At the moment, in the United Kingdom, all-embracing modular sys-tems have not been implemented within the compulsory phases of education, although beyond it they have flourished for many years. However, some schools have developed systems which are semi-mod-ular and operate alongside the National Curriculum. In one such school a modular curriculum is introduced alongside the core cur-riculum in year 9 for 16% of the time, increasing to 28% of the time, in years 10 and 11 (for details see Ireson, 1999). The rationale was to increase student motivation by promoting personal ownership of learning, offering as wide a range of subjects as possible and allowing students to decide how much time they wanted to commit to particu-lar subjects and giving them the opportunity for specialisation in cer-tain areas. The overall aim was to raise attainment. Modules are short with catchy titles. Examples are given in Table 7.1. Work completed in them can lead to success in 7 to 11 GCSE subjects. They can be taken for interest or to extend studies in areas where pupils are having dif-ficulty or want to learn more. There are four nine-week modules in year 9, five modules of 12 weeks in year 10 and two 16-week modules in year 11. As modules begin at different times of the year, choices can be staggered and pupils can rethink their academic progress at any time. Some modules are offered as part of the core curriculum and as part of the optional system.

Overall, the modular system has very positive benefits. It operates in a market so staff have to make the modules attractive to students and they are constantly challenged to make the modules interesting and develop new ideas. Because they may be teaching pupils taking core and optional modules, in groups of different sizes, mixed ability and mixed age, teachers have to adopt a range of teaching methods and be flexible. Students make choices and can be architects of their own learning. They evaluate each module, which empowers them. The ethos is positive. Pupils attend module classes because they want to. Disaffection and truancy have been reduced, motivation has been improved and pupils have more positive self-esteem. As the modules go across normal class groups there are opportunities for increased social mixing. The flexibility of the modular system enables a range of examination choices to be made, it enables pupils to consolidate work that they are unsure of by taking modules which support their core areas, and the school has raised achievement. There are some disadvantages of the system. Administratively it is complex and there are problems monitoring pupils' routes through the modules. Each module has to be self-contained and in the current system modules are at only one level. It is expensive in staffing terms and pupils tend to make choices which are stereotypical. Nevertheless it has had a major positive impact on academic achievement and the social and personal development of the pupils. Some of its difficulties arise because it is attempting to operate a modular system simultaneously with a compulsory core curriculum.

Table 7.1:   Examples of modules and their descriptions

Science: Forensic science III – the continuing adventures in analysis land! Find out how scientific methods are used to analyse and identify samples of various materials. Is the accused guilty?

IT Business 2000 – Spreadsheets – this module will provide you with the opportunity to develop and extend your knowledge in using spreadsheets. You will design and model a series of spreadsheets to monitor the accounts for a business of your choice. You will learn to present these figures in different formats and go on to use them to forecast future budgeting.

Food technology: Hot and Spicy – an investigation of some exotic places, people and foods. Find out how herbs and spices are used to enhance your food.

The main benefits of modular systems lie in the way that they can empower learners and increase motivation and self-determination. They also offer flexibility. Learners can select modules which will satisfy their needs and the curriculum can be differentiated through the need for successful completion of some modules being prerequisite to the taking of others. Modularisation can facilitate the integration of academic and vocational pathways and may be the simplest way to reduce disaffection and improve attendance at school.

Special activity groups

Withdrawing children for special activities has traditionally been used in the United Kingdom to provide additional support for children experiencing difficulties in specific areas, often literacy. However, the principle of providing 'special activities' can be applied to groups formed across or within year groups or within classes for a very wide range of purposes. Activity groups can be set up to satisfy particular short-term needs for particular groups of pupils; for example, intensive literacy courses. Facilities might be available on a permanent basis with pupils slotting in and out as required; for instance, in units to support pupils at risk of exclusion. Alternatively, time could be allocated each week within the timetable to offer a range of special activities; for example, study skills classes, extension or catch up work, social skills classes. There are many possibilities. Specific groups can be run alongside normal curriculum classes to offer integrated provision for pupils with moderate to severe learning difficulties (Ireson, 1999). What special activity groups offer to the school is flexibility to arrange groups to satisfy particular needs. In some cases schools may wish to offer pupils an element of choice.

Intensive literacy and numeracy classes

Some secondary schools have set up intensive classes in literacy or numeracy where there has been a need to help a particular group of new pupils to catch up. Such intensive classes can provide an alternative or an addition to structured ability grouping in English. The purpose is to increase pupils' literacy skills so that they are able to take part fully in mainstream lessons. Typically, the child's needs will be identified and an individual learning plan will be devised, implemented and progress monitored. Children receive detailed feedback and individual help. As soon as the child has made sufficient progress they return to mainstream lessons. Pupils approach such programmes with different perspectives. Some see them as a vehicle to help them move on quickly, others as a safe place to be able to learn (Ireson, 1999). Programmes may also involve support from parents, other older pupils or mentors. The effectiveness of such programmes seems to depend on small group sizes, the opportunities for one-to-one tuition and the continuity, commitment and support of teachers. Where older pupils are involved in mentoring or as part of a paired reading scheme, the 'helping' ethos of the school is supported. Such programmes can be very effective in improving reading ages in a relatively short time and enabling pupils to go on and succeed academically. They reduce the pressure on mainstream teachers, leaving them to focus on the other children. The difficulties of such programmes are their expense and the lack of suitable learning materials.

Study skills, metacognition and thinking skills

There has been increasing interest over the last 30 years in the possibility of teaching students transferable skills concerned with understanding their own learning, thinking and studying. Research on metacognition grew out of Flavell's (1971) early work on the development of memorisation strategies in young children. Metacognition refers to an individual's awareness of their own learning and thinking processes and how to use them effectively. Metacognition can be explicit or implicit (Brown, 1987). Explicit metacognition refers to conscious knowledge which we have about our own learning and thinking. Implicit metacognition refers to knowledge that is not in our conscious awareness and which operates in a fairly automatic way; for instance, slowing the pace of reading when a passage is difficult.

Most research attempting to develop metacognitive learning skills in students has been undertaken in higher education. Initially, two different approaches to learning were identified, deep and surface, to which a third, achieving, was added (Marton and Saljo, 1976; Entwistle, 1981). Schmeck (1983) identified different levels of processing which related closely to the already identified approaches to learning. This research changed thinking about student learning suggesting that it was possible for individuals to influence the outcome of their learning by improving their learning strategies. Programmes were developed to this end (Dansereau, 1978). Typically, courses teach students strategies for enhancing their learning. These may be cognitive, for example thinking skills, or support strategies, for example ensuring the learning environment is optimal. Early evaluations suggested that some of these programmes were inducing students to adopt surface approaches to learning rather than the desired deep approaches (Ramsden, Beswick and Bowden, 1986), which led to a change of emphasis and an attempt to encourage students to be more reflective about their learning (Gibbs, 1981). There has also been an acknowledgement that the development of learning and problem-solving skills is inextricably intertwined with domain knowledge (Glaser, 1984) and that learning to learn programmes can only be beneficial if students learn to integrate skills within a domain. Although much of the early work on encouraging students to learn how to learn developed in higher education, there have been attempts to apply the ideas at school level. Selmes (1987) explored students' approaches to learning in secondary school and recommended programmes to encourage students to adopt more effective studying strategies.

Various initiatives have recently been set up within and outside of school hours to support students in their learning (Ireson, 1999; Sharp, Osgood and Flanagan, 1999). They draw on a wide range of ideas and early evaluations suggest that they are beneficial in encouraging pupils to take more responsibility for their own learning and enhancing their learning skills, motivation, self-esteem and confidence. Depending on the nature of the particular programme and the way that it is implemented, they may also encourage teachers to reflect on the learning process and change their teaching methods to better support it and develop greater coherence and co-operation between school departments.

In addition to learning skills there are now a number of programmes which teach thinking skills (McGuiness, 1999). These fall into three main categories, those which are taught independently of the curriculum, those which are embedded in the curriculum and those which are infused into the curriculum, across all curriculum subjects. Those which are taught independently of the curriculum include Feuerstein's Instrumental Enrichment (Feuerstein *et al.*, 1980), the Somerset Thinking Schools Course (Blagg, 1991) and Lipman's Philosophy for Children (Lipman, Sharp and Oscanyan, 1980). Thinking skills taught within the curriculum developed from the work of Adey and Shayer (1994) in their Cognitive Acceleration through Science Education (CASE). Similar programmes have now been developed in mathematics. In geography a programme promoting thinking skills based on a list of key geographical concepts is available (Leat, 1998). The infusion method is illustrated by the ACTS project (Activating Children's Thinking Skills). This is designed for pupils at the upper primary level (McGuiness *et al.*, 1997). What all these projects have in common is a belief that children can be taught to think and that these skills can have an impact on the child's cognitive functioning across a range of activities. Early evaluations have been very positive (McGuiness, 1999) and there is much ongoing work in this field.

Groups to reduce disaffection and improve attendance and behaviour
Although there has been a tendency to separate out disaffection and behaviour problems from academic issues, they are irrevocably intertwined. As we have seen, some schools adopt particular grouping structures as a means of dealing with difficult behaviour and the allocation of pupils to particular groups may be based on decisions relating to behaviour rather than academic attainment. While some incidents of poor behaviour result from an inappropriate curriculum poorly delivered, in some cases difficult behaviour has as its cause circumstances outside of the school. In these cases pupils may need additional support to assist them in overcoming their difficulties. Schools have successfully set up groups to support attendance; provide opportunities for the development of social skills and anger management; and promote better behaviour (Hallam, 1996; Hallam and Castle, 1999). Such groups can be created to deal with specific problems in particular groups of children for a limited period or might operate as part of a unit to support pupils at risk of exclusion from school. Whichever approach is adopted the aim should be the reintegration of the pupil into mainstream education as soon as they are ready and able to cope.

The main advantage of groups set up for special activities is their flexibility. Whether they are set up to withdraw pupils from curriculum subjects or tutor group time, are on offer in the lunch hour or after school or are timetabled as special activities, they offer flexibility which other methods of structuring groupings do not. They can be offered for short periods of time to satisfy particular needs without disruption to the whole school timetable.

Within class grouping procedures

Within class grouping of various types has been adopted in primary schools in the United Kingdom over a number of years (Harlen and Malcolm, 1997) but it has usually been on a rather informal basis (Hallam and Toutounji, 1996). At secondary level, as we saw in Chapter 5, it is used rarely (Harlen and Malcolm, 1997). International research reviews of within class grouping procedures suggest that there are positive academic effects for all pupils when within class grouping procedures are implemented appropriately (Bossert, 1988; Topping, 1992; Johnson and Johnson, 1990; Slavin, 1990b; Cohen, 1994; Creemers, 1994).

In the United Kingdom, the need for a greater emphasis on group work within the classroom has been stressed frequently. This may be in ability groups to assist in the acquisition of basic skills through increasing interaction between teachers and pupils (DES, 1978; Barker Lunn, 1984; Mortimore *et al.*, 1988) or in mixed ability groups to facilitate particular tasks. Reviews which consider United Kingdom research have been undertaken by Yeomans (1983), Bennett (1985), Galton and Williamson (1992) and Harwood (1995).

The largest United Kingdom project (Galton, Simon and Croll, 1980) identified several different kinds of group work: joint group work, where pupils engage in specific tasks which contribute to an overall theme; seated group work, where children sit together but work individually, albeit undertaking the same work; and co-operative group work, where ideas are pooled as part of a joint piece of work. Observation revealed that 80% of group work was seated group work (Galton, Simon and Croll, 1980; Galton *et al.*, 1987). Joint group work could be found in most classrooms (Galton, 1981) and was generally used in art, craft and general studies but not in relation to basic skills. Little collaborative work was observed. Other United Kingdom research has explored the kinds of interactions which occur between pupils when they are working on particular tasks in groups. Taken together the evidence from this and some international research suggests that:

- When pupils work in groups on specific tasks, self-esteem and motivation can be enhanced (Galton and Williamson, 1992; Slavin, 1990b).
- Groups function best when they are mixed ability including the most and least able. High ability pupils make a key contribution to group functioning and also enhance their own skills (Bennett and Cass, 1989; Swing and Peterson, 1982; Webb, 1991).
- Groups should, where possible, be representative in terms of gender and ethnic groupings (Slavin, 1990b).
- Teachers need to encourage groups to work independently and intervene rarely so that decisions are reached by the group (Harwood, 1989; Cohen, 1994; Slavin, 1990b).

- Group work is valuable for the development of exploratory talk (Barnes, Britton and Rosen, 1969; Barnes and Todd, 1977; Tough, 1977).
- Success in group tasks depends on pupils' ability to raise questions, to listen attentively to each other, and to manage disputes whenever they arise (Tann, 1981).
- Group processes and performance differ depending on the nature of the task (Tann, 1981; Biott, 1987; Bennett and Dunne, 1989; Cohen, 1994).
- Levels of interaction are higher when the task is practical (Bennett, 1985).
- When the task involves discussion of abstract ideas, the level of interaction may be low but of a high quality. Teachers should not be discouraged by this (Dunne and Bennett, 1990; Galton and Williamson, 1992).
- Problem-solving tasks with a clear measurable outcome tend to generate a higher level of collaboration than open-ended tasks (Crozier and Kleinberg, 1987).
- Pupils need to be taught how to collaborate. This involves the teacher setting clear goals and giving immediate feedback on progress through discussion (Biott, 1987; Webb, 1983, 1985; Burden, Emsley and Constable, 1988; Glaye, 1986).

In the United Kingdom, most within class grouping practices are carried out by teachers working to their own rationale. They have received little guidance as to the most effective ways to group pupils. As we have seen in Chapters 4 and 5, grouping may be based on the need for pupils to work well together. In the USA more formal approaches to grouping pupils have been developed. These are known as co-operative grouping practices.

Co-operative learning

Co-operative learning can be applied in several ways. All the methods have in common that pupils work together to learn and are responsible for one another's learning as well as their own. There are three fundamental principles: rewards are given to teams; each individual is accountable for their own contribution; each team member must have an equal opportunity of being successful. For example, in Student Teams–Achievement Divisions pupils are assigned to four-member learning teams mixed in prior levels of knowledge, gender and ethnicity. The teacher presents the material to be learned. The pupils then work in teams to ensure that they have all mastered the lesson. Pupils are then tested on the material to be learned. At this point they must work independently. Scores are compared to past team averages and points are awarded on the degree to which past performance is matched or exceeded. The points are totalled to derive team scores and from this teams meeting certain criteria may earn further rewards. The whole process is undertaken over a number of lessons. Such techniques have been adopted with learners of all ages from seven to college entrance. They are most appropriate for areas with well-defined learning objectives. A variant replaces the tests with competitions that provide an added incentive for the children.

Another alternative is called Team Assisted Individualisation. This combines co-operative learning with individualised instruction and was designed to be used in mathematics lessons. The teams are set up with four members of different prior knowledge and ability. The pupils enter an individualised sequence of work based on a test of their prior knowledge on that topic. They then proceed to work at their own pace. Team members check each other's work and help each other with problems. Final unit tests are taken without help and are marked by pupil monitors. Each week the teacher totals the units acquired by each team. Rewards are then given for team performance. The teacher's time in class is spent on explaining new topics to small groups of children drawn from the various teams who are working on the same topic or level, so although the teams are mixed ability, the teacher works with pupils of the same ability.

If the procedures are undertaken appropriately, co-operative grouping can be a very effective way of supporting academic learning and can also have positive social effects (Slavin, 1990b). Learning outcomes vary according to the quality of the method used and how well it is implemented. Two things are important for success: group goals and individual accountability. When these are both present, the results are consistently positive. In addition, co-operative learning rarely has negative effects and does not hold back able pupils. Where co-operative learning is adopted, children express greater liking for their classmates. It promotes ethnic mixing and inter-ability friendships and improves attitudes to school. It also increases self-esteem, has positive effects on achievement for all children, and improves the integration of children with special educational needs (Slavin, 1990b). However, a British literature review by Bennett (1985) outlined methodological difficulties in the research. Nevertheless, implementation of co-operative grouping procedures in Holland, where there are certain cultural similarities with the United Kingdom (Roeders, 1989), showed positive academic and social outcomes. Where it is unsuccessful it is often because the procedures have been inappropriately applied, with teachers failing to carry out the necessary testing, recording of progress and feedback procedures. In the USA teachers have found the methods easy to use and pupils seem to like them. They would seem to provide an appropriate means of structuring and managing within class groups particularly in primary schools and the lower secondary years. Such groupings provide pupils with structured opportunities to learn from each other while being able to demonstrate a degree of independence from the teacher. At all levels where they have been deployed they have been demonstrated to be effective (Creemers, 1994; Cohen, 1994). In the USA co-operative learning techniques are often adopted in conjunction with mastery learning.

Mastery learning

Mastery learning was initially developed by Bloom from a model of learning proposed by Carroll (1963). The model suggested that learning outcomes depended on time spent learning in relation to time needed for learning. Time spent learning depended on opportunity and motivation. Time needed for learning depended on specific abilities or prior knowledge, the capability of the learner to understand instructions and the quality of the teaching. The underlying assumption of the model is that anyone can learn anything providing that they are prepared to expend the necessary amount of time. From this Bloom (1976) developed what has come to be known as mastery learning. In Group Based Mastery Learning or Learning for Mastery the teacher introduces the topic, the pupils spend time learning and working on the materials, then the pupils are tested. Their performance is assessed against set criteria, usually 80% to 90% accuracy. Those students who do not achieve mastery initially are given feedback and corrective activities by the teacher or pupils who were successful on the test and the topic is explained again using alternative methods and materials. Those pupils who initially failed the test retake it. When a specified number of pupils have mastered the topic (usually 80%) the class moves on to another topic. In some cases this cycle may be repeated more than once to ensure a higher level of mastery.

There have been a number of reviews of mastery learning (Lysakowski and Walberg, 1982; Walberg, 1984; Bloom, 1984a, 1984b;

Guskey and Gates, 1985; Kulik and Kulik, 1986; Kulik and Kulik, 1990), which are consistent in showing that mastery learning groups in no case perform worse than controls and often do better. Where mastery learning procedures have been adopted in the United Kingdom they have had promising results (for example, Parkinson, Mitchell and Johnstone, 1983; Arblaster *et al.*, 1991). Slavin (1987c), while criticising aspects of mastery learning, believes that it has considerable potential, although its structure has tended to restrict its use to tasks that have very clear and measurable learning outcomes. Although there are practical difficulties for the teacher in the management of the time when some pupils have completed the work and others have not, it can be an extremely useful technique to ensure that everyone has grasped the essentials of a particular topic. Lai and Biggs (1994) have suggested that mastery learning in its current form might lead to a surface approach to learning. It is certainly successful for those adopting surface approaches. However, they believe that it could be adapted to encourage learning at higher levels of abstraction.

There are also personalised systems of mastery learning. The most common of these is the Personalised System of Instruction or the Keller Plan (Keller, 1968). This has been used mainly in higher education. It involves establishing unit objectives for a course of study and developing tests for each unit. Students choose when to take a test and may resit it as often as they wish until they achieve a passing score. Students typically work on self-instructional materials and/or with peers to master the course content. Lectures are given to supplement rather than guide the learning process. The system is extremely effective in raising standards with a very high proportion of students achieving the highest grades.

Within class ability grouping

United Kingdom research on group work has indicated that collaborative group work is more effective when it is carried out with mixed ability groups. However, there may be circumstances where teachers wish to group pupils within the class by ability for instructional purposes and the setting of work. When they do this they need to take decisions about the size of the groups. This will inevitably influence their homogeneity. The size of groups may depend on a range of factors that are out of the teacher's control, for example, classroom size, and the arrangement of the furniture (Harlen and Malcolm, 1997). The evidence suggests that within class ability grouping is most effective when it occurs with pupils in groups of three or four (Lou *et al.*, 1996). Groupings of such small numbers will inevitably reduce the amount of time that a teacher can spend with any particular group. The evidence also indicates that such groups are most productive when they work together over a number of weeks (Lou *et al.*, 1996).

An alternative to grouping pupils by ability within the class to enable differentiated instruction to take place is to develop a tiered curriculum which enables whole class exposition but differentiates the work which follows. A United Kingdom school that has adopted such a system applies a four-tier system in all subjects in years 7–13 (Ireson, 1999). The levels are:

- Basic – the minimum acceptable for a student of a particular age to achieve;
- Standard – the average performance expected for a student of a particular age;
- Extended – above average performance for a student of a particular age;
- Advanced – at least one year in advance of an average student of a particular age.

All departments use the differentiated structure. All pupils learn the same topic or skill. Differentiation is through the level of difficulty. Students select for themselves the level of work that they will attempt even if the teacher initially thinks it is inappropriate. The teacher's task is to negotiate change with the student should the aim prove unrealistic. Pupils' choices of level tend to be either realistic or aspirational. They do not adopt the easy option. In year 9 pupils select the set that they will go in. The sets formalise the levels that the pupils have been working at in years 7 and 8. Pupils usually make realistic choices but whatever their choice they are allocated to that set unless they negotiate a move. 'Sink' sets are avoided by all sets operating with at least two levels. If a pupil consistently gets good marks at one level, the teacher will suggest that they try a higher level. Teaching strategies vary. In some lessons it is identical for all tiers, in others it may be differentiated in parts. Sometimes pupils work independently using computers and other research resources for investigative work or engage in practical or experimental work.

There are a great many advantages to this system:

- pupils are at the centre of learning;
- although child centred the system is structured and tightly controlled;

- there is a common language of achievement which can be used by pupils, parents and teachers, which is clear and simple to understand;
- the shared language provides a framework for planning, reporting and recording;
- the system facilitates cross-subject comparisons;
- the different levels of task are explained at the start of each lesson so students can make an informed choice and are motivated throughout the lesson;
- teachers have accurate perceptions of what pupils can actually do;
- students take responsibility for their own work and acquire considerable metacognitive skills;
- the system encourages students to work independently;
- students become well motivated;
- students develop a clear understanding of their own capabilities (there was a correlation of .9 between students' predictions and their GCSE results in comparison to a correlation of .7 for staff predictions);
- because students select the levels that they will work at there is no stigmatisation of the lower ability levels;
- self-esteem is improved in the lower ability pupils;
- SEN pupils work within the same system;
- pupil behaviour is better;
- achievement has been raised.

The main drawback of the system relates to the heavy workload for the staff in preparing differentiated materials. However, if the system was adopted more widely materials could be made available commercially. Because the system places more responsibility on the pupils, it is not always easily accepted by outsiders. The school has to cover teacher absences from within, although these are rare, because of the difficulties of inducting supply teachers.

Overall advantages of within class groupings

Evidence from the international literature suggests that there can be positive academic and social effects for all pupils when within class grouping procedures are implemented appropriately (Creemers, 1994). Within class grouping provides teachers with the opportunity to meet the needs of pupils of different abilities while reducing the problems inherent in managing individualised learning. Pupils can learn to support each other working in groups, which reduces the pressure on the teacher, and working co-operatively may increase pupil motivation. Pupils also have the opportunity to develop their social and communication skills. Within class grouping can be based on a range of different pupil attributes, of which ability may be one.

The main advantage of adopting grouping structures within as opposed to between classes is their flexibility. Pupils can be moved between groups easily and teachers can restructure groupings regularly based on their knowledge of pupil progress, levels of achievement, behaviour and rates of work. Different groupings can be adopted for different purposes. The evidence, particularly from the primary case studies, suggests that teachers already do this. What seems to be lacking in the United Kingdom is the formulation of this practice into clear guidance on when and how to group pupils for what purposes which can be used in the training of teachers. What has also emerged clearly from the research is the lack of commercially available materials which teachers can draw on to assist them in differentiating work. Our evidence suggests that within schools teachers tend to pool resources. If this sharing of ideas and materials was extended between schools it would considerably reduce the burden on teachers.

Individualised instruction

While there has been considerable criticism of mixed ability teaching because of its failure to individualise instruction in the classroom, some systems of individualised instruction have been developed which do operate successfully particularly with older students. As we saw earlier, in the USA, the Personalised System of Instruction, an individualised mastery learning programme, has proved effective for older students in a range of environments. Successful individualised programmes are based on instruction tailored to the assessed abilities of each student; students working at their own pace, receiving periodic reports on their mastery, and planning and evaluating their own learning; and the provision of alternative materials and activities. Where these criteria are satisfied, individualised programmes have been shown to be more effective than whole class instruction in relation to cognitive and affective outcomes (Waxman *et al.*, 1985).

Learning programmes based on rigid learning objectives have not been popular in the United Kingdom. However, an individualised programme known as school based flexible learning has shown considerable promise in geography teaching (Hughes, 1993). Pupils learn through independent study supervised through tutorials which are regular planned meetings between the teacher and a small group of four to six pupils. The tutorials are used for planning, clarifying, explaining subject-specific matters, monitoring general progress and assessment. The key principles underlying the system are that pupils should take increasing responsibility for their learning; teaching and learning take place at an individual level; pupils should be made aware of how they learn and how specific learning activities contribute (or otherwise) to their progress. For the system to operate effectively pupils need to receive close support and guidance on a regular, planned basis and teachers need to have appropriate resources including study guides for the topics to be covered. The students are gradually shaped into working in this way over the period of their secondary education beginning with small steps in year 7 to much greater independence of working in year 11.

The system has proved very successful academically and in relation to the personal development of the students. A comparison was undertaken with parallel classes being taught geography by more traditional methods. Over a four-year period, the percentage of pupils gaining a grade A to C in geography using flexible learning rose from 41% to 85% and using traditional methods from 16% to 59%. The flexible learning system had consistently better results in geography and pupils taught in this way achieved better results in geography than in their other GCSEs. Pupils and their parents reported increased motivation, greater effort and increased work. The students explained this in relation to being given greater responsibility, independence and choice; being able to work at their own pace; not having to go over things they already knew; and having access to individual help when they needed it.

For pupils in the later stages of their schooling such individualised teaching methods may be appropriate for some subjects in their entirety and for aspects of others. The ways of working that students develop not only prepare them for further study at AS, A level and beyond but also increase motivation and performance. This seems largely because they have a much greater degree of control over their own learning.

Whatever type of grouping is adopted to ensure that all pupils' needs are being met, schools need to develop ways of monitoring the academic, social and personal development of each pupil. While national systems of testing have provided transparent means of monitoring progress in some subject areas they do not apply across the curriculum, neither do they take account of students' all-round development. Pupils have consistently reported that they would like to feel supported by teachers but that this is not always the case (Chaplain, 1996). Appropriate tutorial systems in school can be very important. They enable pupils to develop positive relationships with a member of staff throughout their school career, through which they receive academic guidance and pastoral support can be very important (Hallam, 1996).

Summary

In this chapter we have set out a range of alternative grouping structures. These can operate at the level of the school or within classes. They are not mutually exclusive and schools often operate more than one system simultaneously. The evidence suggests that the major factor in groupings being effective in raising attainment and promoting positive personal and social development is that they offer *sufficient flexibility* to meet changing demands at school, class, group and individual levels. Highly structured school-based systems tend to lack this flexibility.

The most appropriate ways for individual schools to develop flexibility in grouping will depend on their size, resources and pupil intake. There is no simple 'off the shelf' recipe for success. Pupil needs are likely to change over time and schools must be able to respond to them. In addition, where there is a perceived need for change, its implementation must take account of existing staff attitudes and allow time for discussion of different options so that staff have ownership of new systems.

A major consideration is the age of the pupils and how the grouping system can not only ensure their attainment academically but also promote positive social and personal development. In primary school, systems which require a large measure of independent, unsupervised work giving pupils a high degree of choice may be inappropriate, but as pupils progress through secondary school, where there are currently high levels of disaffection, motivation can be increased by offering pupils choice and giving them much greater responsibility for their own learning. This also offers preparation for lifelong learning in that it enhances the development of transferable learning skills.

Whatever systems are adopted, they should be carefully considered before implementation and their effectiveness monitored over time taking account of the wide range of factors identified earlier. This information can be used to refine policy and practice or if necessary provide the impetus for major change. Efforts to make grouping practices more effective need to be regarded as an ongoing long-term commitment. There are no quick fix solutions.

9

Conclusions

Ability grouping has been the subject of research for most of the twentieth century since Whipple carried out a study of the effects of special class placement on a group of high-aptitude 5th and 6th graders in the USA in 1919. Since then hundreds of studies have been undertaken and there have been many literature reviews and syntheses of research findings. Despite this, the field has been characterised by controversy and polemic. There are several reasons for this. Firstly, there has been no clear definition of what has been meant by 'effective' in relation to educational outcomes. Different systems of grouping can advantage and disadvantage different groups of children and provide for different kinds of effectiveness, academic, social and personal. Contrasting types of grouping therefore can be judged as effective by the adoption of different criteria of effectiveness. Those favouring structured grouping have tended to stress its effectiveness in terms of pupil achievement whereas those against have stressed the inequity of the system and its social and personal consequences. Secondly, the research undertaken has rarely been able to consider the academic, social and personal consequences of different types of grouping together. Conclusions about the consequences of different grouping types have therefore had to be drawn across studies adopting different methodologies which has made definitive comparisons difficult. Thirdly, and perhaps most importantly, different types of grouping benefit different groups of pupils. Streaming and setting tend to benefit the more able, whereas mixed ability structures tend to benefit the less able. The type of pupil grouping which is adopted is therefore underpinned by different philosophical values which are inevitably linked to political ideology. Because of this, policy decisions about pupil grouping have often been based on ideological principles rather than educational ones. If we wish to develop ways of grouping pupils which will benefit the academic, personal and social development of *all* pupils we have to leave behind outdated ways of thinking about grouping structures and move towards systems which are sufficiently flexible to respond to the ever changing needs of pupils.

Conceptions of intelligence

Underlying the whole question of selective education, streaming, banding and setting are questions relating to the nature of intelligence. Historically, intelligence has been viewed by many as a single entity which can be measured quantitively by IQ tests. This conception of the nature of intelligence is clearly compatible with systems of selective education and the institutionalised grouping of pupils by ability. Many of the schools in our research used some form of intelligence test to inform the placement of pupils into groups or to establish whether pupils were underachieving. Underlying these practices are assumptions about the nature of intelligence: that it can be measured by simple tests, that it is relatively fixed and that scores on intelligence tests relate to pupils' capacity to learn.

Recent conceptualisations of intelligence suggest a more complex picture. Gardner (1993, 1999) proposes a theory of multiple intelligences, including linguistic, logico-mathematical, spatial, musical, bodily-kinaesthetic, interpersonal, intrapersonal, naturalist and spiritual/existential. Sternberg (1984) has developed a triarchic theory that considers intelligence in three ways: firstly, intelligence and the internal world of the individual, or the mental mechanisms that underlie intelligent behaviour; secondly, intelligence and the external world of the individual, or the use of these mental mechanisms in everyday life in order to attain an intelligent fit to the environment; and thirdly, intelligence and experience, or the mediating role of one's passage through life between the internal and external worlds of the individual. Ceci (1990) proposes a bio-ecological theory, which like Gardner's is based on multiple potentials. The theory stresses the importance of context including motivational forces, the social and physical aspects of a particular learning environment or task and the knowledge domain in which the task is embedded. Knowledge and aptitude are viewed as fundamentally inseparable; learning therefore acquires a crucial role in the development of intelligence. Other researchers have further suggested that even within single subject domains, individuals attaining similar overall levels of expertise can exhibit differing patterns of attainment which may be achieved by differing processing styles (Sloboda, Davidson and Howe, 1994; Hallam, 1998). This research not only raises issues regarding the notion of a single unitary intelligence but questions assumptions about the unitary nature of 'ability' even within single subject domains.

Historically, the IQ view of intelligence has tended to be related to an assumption that intelligence is both genetically determined and immutable (Ceci, 1990). However, recent research indicates that the genetic basis of intelligence is complex depending on the contribution of many rather than a single gene (Plomin, 1986). Further, geneticists now view behaviour as reflecting the functioning of the whole organism, being dynamic and changing in response to the environment (Plomin and Thompson, 1993). Even research using traditional techniques acknowledges an important role for the environment, heritability estimates for general intelligence being in the region of 50%. Existing evidence also indicates large discrepancies between heritability estimates for specific cognitive abilities and school achievement, implying that other factors are implicated in school performance. Taken together these studies acknowledge a crucial role for the environment in the development of intelligence. This is further supported by evidence that IQ scores can be improved by training (Feuerstein *et al.*, 1980; Sternberg and Weil, 1980) and are influenced by the length of time in school (Ceci, 1990).

The unitary view of intelligence proposes that IQ scores predict learning outcomes in school and subsequent success in employment. Correlations of IQ with school grades vary a great deal but are usually within the range of 0.4 to 0.6 (Block and Dworkin, 1976; Brody, 1985). This represents 36% of the variance, leaving much unexplained. There is also an increasing body of research indicating mismatches between IQ scores and performance on tasks requiring complex cognitive skills (Ceci, 1990). Job status, because of its relationship with academic attainment, is related to IQ scores but the relationship with actual work performance is very low (Jenson, 1970; Ceci, 1990). Researchers now acknowledge that learning outcomes depend on the complex interactions of many factors including the characteristics of the learning situation, motivation, effort, belief in the possibility of success, opportunity, knowledge of learning strategies, self-awareness and prior knowledge in addition to ability (Carroll, 1963; Entwistle, 1981; Biggs and Moore, 1993; Hallam and Ireson, 1999). Recently, Goleman (1996) has suggested that what he describes as emotional intelligence is more important than measures of cognitive ability in predicting success in life. Intelligence or ability, then, as traditionally conceived, is now believed to play a much smaller part in an individual's success than was once believed.

Cross-cultural studies comparing the educational systems in Japan and Taiwan with those in the USA suggest that the Western stress on ability grouping minimises the importance of student, teacher and parental effort. The concept of differential ability sets a ceiling on what can be expected from a child. In Japan and Taiwan, pupils, with support from parents and teachers, are expected to put in additional effort if they are not successful (George, 1989; Stevenson and Lee, 1990). No one expects pupils to be removed from the classroom for special interventions or to make it easier to move ahead. There is no ability grouping in state schools prior to 10th grade in Japanese schools. The school day is longer and people are encouraged to work hard. The Western emphasis on ability may serve to lower our expectations of what pupils can achieve. Increased attainment at primary level in literacy and numeracy in recent years where the majority of pupils have attained levels initially seen as 'average' supports this.

Clarity of educational aims

For schools to optimise their grouping arrangements they need to be clear about the aims of education. The National Curriculum (DfEE/QCA, 1999) sets out clearly the values and purposes underpinning the school curriculum:

> Education influences and reflects the values of society, and the kind of society we want to be. It is important, therefore, to recognise a broad set of common values and purposes that underpin the school curriculum and the work of schools. Foremost is a belief in education, at home and at school, as a route to the spiritual, moral, social, cultural, physical and mental development, and thus the well-being, of the individual. Education is also a route to equality of opportunity for all, a healthy and just democracy, a productive economy, and sustainable development. Education should reflect the enduring values that contribute to these ends. These include valuing ourselves, our families and other relationships, the wider groups to which we belong, the diversity in our society and the environment in which we live. Education should also re-affirm our commitment to the virtues of truth, justice, honesty, trust and a sense of duty.
>
> At the same time, education must enable us to respond positively to the opportunities and challenges of the rapidly changing world in which we live and work. In particular, we need to be prepared to engage as individuals, parents, workers and citizens with economic, social and cultural change, including the continued globalisation of the

economy and society, with new work and leisure patterns and with the rapid expansion of communication technologies.

From this are derived two very specific aims:

- to provide opportunities for all pupils to learn and achieve;
- to promote pupils' spiritual, moral, social and cultural development and prepare all pupils for the opportunities, responsibilities and experiences of life.

The inclusive nature of these aims indicates that pupil groupings should not knowingly be adopted by schools so as to benefit one group of pupils at the expense of another. The evidence presented in this book indicates that some forms of grouping traditionally adopted in the United Kingdom, particularly when taken to extremes, tend to do this. What is needed, as outlined in Chapter 7, are flexible systems which can adapt to changing needs and which work to motivate and sustain interest in learning in all pupils through and beyond compulsory schooling.

The long-term effects of different forms of grouping

Most research has examined the effects of pupil grouping in the short term, although there has been some follow up of career paths through further/higher education and work. Postlethwaite and Denton (1978) showed that mixed ability and streamed systems showed few differences in connection with the number and quality of pupils who opted to stay on at school, go on to further education or work. Tests of career aspiration were also similar. Essen, Fogelman and Tibbenham (1978) found negligible association between school-leavers' future plans and their school's ability grouping policy, although aspirations differed according to whether pupils were in the top, middle or lowest range of ability. The proportions choosing each kind of job were broadly similar in spite of different grouping procedures.

Recent evidence from research considering motivation and training indicates that the long-term effects of negative school experiences include a reluctance to take up training opportunities (Maguire, Maguire and Felstead, 1993; McGivney, 1992). Pupils' experiences in their school years have a lasting impact on their lives. Negative attitudes to learning inculcated during the school years can impact on each individual's motivation to continue or return to education later in life. The values and aims of education espoused within the National

Curriculum suggest that attitudes to learning may be an important educational outcome in the twenty-first century. The ways that pupils are grouped within and between schools have effects which go beyond academic attainment. There was evidence in our research that where pupils do not feel valued by the school they will seek other ways of maintaining their self-esteem. This may be through sub-cultures which hold anti-education values, where it is 'cool' to be disaffected. While schools may be able to 'contain' such behaviour in the short term, in the long term the alienation of disaffected young people has substantial costs to society as a whole.

Effective schools

Every school is unique and 'has its own characteristics which are shaped by such factors as its location, pupil intake, size, resources and most important the quality of its staff' (Reid, Hopkins and Holly, 1987). The effects of the same system of pupil grouping may be different between schools and even within the same school when they are implemented differently by individual teachers. Our research has revealed differences at the school level between schools adopting similar types of grouping, although no consistent patterns have emerged. There is also considerable evidence from pupils indicating the importance they attach to teacher qualities in supporting their learning. Together these suggest that the quality of the teaching is important in mediating the academic, social and personal outcomes of different types of ability grouping.

Early research on school effectiveness suggested that schools were equally effective or ineffective for all of their pupils (Rutter *et al.*, 1979; Reynolds, 1982). It has now been demonstrated that schools can differ in their relative effectiveness for different groups of pupils (Aitken and Longford, 1986). Some work suggests that pupils from homes of high socio-economic status (Cuttance, 1992) and of high ability (Gray, Jesson and Jones, 1986) are more affected by their schools than pupils of lower socio-economic status or lower ability. However, McPherson and Willms (1987), while demonstrating that the effects of comprehensivisation in Scotland varied considerably according to the social class of pupils, found that working class pupils gained more over time than others.

Schools can also be differentially effective for high or low ability children (Willms and Cuttance, 1985). Nuttall *et al.* (1989) using multi-level modelling methodology showed large differences in relative effectiveness for different types of pupils in schools in London. Taking the experiences of able and less able children, the differences in performance outcomes could be as small as 11 Verbal Reasoning Quotients or as large as 28, even after adjusting for differences in pupils' abilities at the time of joining the schools. The study also found variation in the way in which schools impacted on boys and girls and in their effects on pupils of different ethnic groups, with some schools widening the gap and others narrowing it. Smith and Tomlinson (1989) found similar differences, although the effects were smaller. There are also different patterns of achievement in different subject domains within a school (Levine, 1992). The evidence also indicates that schools can be differentially effective in relation to different educational outcomes, academic and social (Galloway, 1983; Gray, McPherson and Raffe, 1983; Mortimore *et al.*, 1988; Steedman, 1980; Sammons, Thomas and Mortimore, 1997).

While a particular type of pupil grouping has not been identified as a key characteristic of effective schools (Sammons, Hillman and Mortimore, 1995), it seems to contribute to their differential effectiveness with regard to different groups of pupils. Our research has shown differences in pupil attainment dependent on interactions between grouping structures and prior learning in mathematics. There are clear differences in attitudes to school depending on the ability groups pupils are in. Some structures favour the more able pupils, others the less able. The differences in teacher attitudes towards setting observed in the different types of schools and between schools within types suggest that there are shared staff values in schools. These are likely to be communicated in many subtle ways to pupils. They may then feel able to identify with the values of the school or not. This will have subsequent effects on their attitudes to school.

School ethos

There were substantial differences between the secondary schools in our research in relation to pupils' attitudes, self-esteem and satisfaction with the school and its grouping practices. At primary level there were also differences in the extent to which pupils liked school and were teased by other pupils. These differences did not appear to be linked in any systematic way to the schools' grouping policies, reasons for adopting them, or teachers' satisfaction with them. Schools' rationales for adopting particular grouping practices were consistently related to issues of raising standards and doing the best to help each child achieve his or her full potential. The means schools adopted for achieving these aims were very different.

Pupils generally shared the rationale given by the school for the adoption of particular grouping practices. Their comments about grouping practices, at primary and secondary level, mirrored those of the teachers. In addition, the quantitative data at secondary level demonstrated that pupils generally preferred the kind of grouping that was on offer in their school. Differences in preferences were also related to the ability level of the pupil, with low ability pupils tending to prefer mixed ability classes, and gender, girls preferring setting to a greater extent than boys.

While there was no systematic evidence linking structured grouping practices to ethos there were indications in the qualitative data of differences between schools which shared similar grouping practices. Schools, which on paper espoused similar aims, seemed to communicate very different sets of values in their practices and in the interactions between teachers and pupils. It was in the everyday exchanges between teachers and pupils that the shared values of staff were communicated to pupils. In some cases pupils were compared unfavourably with pupils in other sets, in others teachers were not prepared to respond to questions about work, in others there were differences in the extent to which homework was set and marked. Everyday interactions of this kind implied that some pupils' work was of less value and that, from the school's perspective, the pupils themselves were of less value. Pupils' reported dislike of some teachers indicated that within any single school individual teachers behaved differently. However, our data suggest that schools exert considerable influence over the attitudes of the teachers working there. From this, we might conclude that if there is a strong shared ethos among the staff which values academic achievement above all else, this will be communicated in subtle ways to the pupils in the school, leaving some feeling alienated and others superior. The development of shared staff values, which go beyond the public presentation of school ethos, may take time and once established such values may be very difficult to change. Evidence from our research of failed trials of mixed ability teaching and resentment about changes to more structured grouping systems are clear indicators of resistance to change. In other schools changes had been made successfully. In some cases these were initiated in response to outside evaluations, e.g. Ofsted inspections. The evidence also indicated differences in teacher attitudes based on the subject that they taught.

Curriculum subjects and assessment systems

Most previous work on structured grouping has not considered the comparable effects of different types of grouping on pupil performance or self-concept in relation to different subjects. The research reported in this book shows that a high level of setting in mathematics tends to polarise attainment, improving the performance of the most able while reducing that of the less able. In science and English, setting procedures have little impact on attainment when prior knowledge is taken into account. The effects on academic self-concept are also different between curriculum subjects with self-concept in English being influenced by setting, while self-concept in mathematics and science are not. Other factors, for instance gender, also play a part.

Teachers of different subjects hold relatively consistent views about the nature of their subject and whether it is suitable for being taught in mixed ability groups. These differences are mediated by the type of school in which the teacher is working. Teachers of mathematics and modern foreign languages are most in favour of setting while teachers of English and humanities see the benefits of mixed ability teaching. Science tends to fall between the two. It may be that even within subjects some areas of the curriculum are more suited to mixed ability teaching than others. The teaching methods that teachers adopt also reflect these differences. In developing policy on grouping whether at the school, curriculum or classroom level these factors need to be taken into account.

Our research has revealed that assessment systems have a major impact on the types of pupil groupings adopted. The introduction of tiers in Key Stage tests and General Certificate of Secondary Education (GCSE) examinations have led many schools to adopt structured grouping systems to meet examination requirements. One of the principles underlying effective learning and teaching is constructive alignment (Biggs, 1996), that is, that assessment should be aligned with what is taught. Here, schools are aligning their grouping practices to match assessment procedures. This serves to deny opportunities to many pupils, often in core curriculum subjects.

The selection of grouping systems by individual schools

The most important characteristic of effective grouping is its ability to meet pupils' changing learning needs. The key to this is flexibility. How flexibility can be achieved will vary depending on the size of the school, available space, staffing and resources. Particular combinations of grouping may be more appropriate for pupils of particular ages. As pupils move through the school system, in order to maintain motivation, it may be beneficial to increase opportunities for choice, undertaking independent learning and empowerment. The nature of the groupings adopted at any particular point in time will also depend on the make-up of particular cohorts of pupils, particular classes and the expertise of teachers employed at the time.

The research revealed that change in schools is often instigated through external evaluations or changes of management. If schools are to be able to adopt flexible grouping to maximise the academic, personal and social development of their pupils they need to have ways of monitoring the effectiveness of their grouping structures so that changes can be instigated internally when there is room for improvement. This requires that schools develop ways of systematically monitoring:

- progress across *all* curriculum subjects;
- pupils' attitudes towards learning and school;
- pupils' self-esteem;
- levels of disaffection (through attendance, unauthorised absence and fixed term and permanent exclusions).

The data collected can be used to inform decisions about grouping structures between and within classes. Further information can be gained from the implementation of a properly resourced tutorial system to monitor the progress of individual pupils as they progress through school.

Different grouping procedures depend heavily for their effectiveness on the ways that they are implemented by teachers (Gamoran, 1986; Creemers, 1994). To facilitate this, teachers may need considerable training. The teachers in the secondary study were almost unanimously agreed that the strategies they acquired when being trained to teach classes of mixed ability benefited all their teaching. The evidence at primary and secondary level suggests that teachers would also benefit from guidance regarding different types of within class grouping and different approaches to teaching groups, e.g. co-operative learning, implementing different levels of differentiation.

The future

Schools in their present form were designed for the industrial age (Bayliss, 1998). They have been remarkably stable in their structure over the last hundred years and most changes made have been relatively superficial (Cuban, 1990; Sarasan, 1990). During that time society has changed. One hundred years ago it was more rigid in its structures – class, gender roles, religious identity – and working practices. Our society is now multicultural, class and religion play a smaller part in the identity formation of most people and gender roles have changed considerably. The nature of work has also changed. Manufacturing industry in the United Kingdom continues to decline while there has been an increase in the service industries and their availability to customers. As a consequence there are fewer unskilled employment opportunities and a rising demand for a better educated workforce which is literate, numerate and has information processing skills. Working practices have generally become less rigid with flexi-working hours, more choice of when to take lunch, breaks, holidays, more part-time and hourly paid work and more working from home. These changes in working patterns have not been reflected in school structures and practices. Schools are attempting to provide education for the changing needs of the twenty-first century in structures designed for the greater rigidity of the nineteenth century. More flexibility is required.

Chapter 8 outlined possible alternatives to traditional grouping structures and the ways that they have been implemented in some schools. In the long term, it seems likely that secondary education will go beyond the level of modularisation outlined there to systems which will offer more diversity in curriculum choice with greater mixing of vocational and academic options. Alongside this schools are likely to be open for longer hours with educational opportunities on offer to whole communities. For this level of flexibility to develop there will need to be changes to the way examinations are currently conceived, with systems becoming less age related and examinations being taken when students have attained the appropriate level. In addition, systems of inspection will need to be more encouraging of innovation to overcome the conservatism that seems inherent in many current school practices.

References

Abraham, J. (1989) Testing Hargreaves' and Lacey's differentation-polarisation theory in a setted comprehensive, *British Journal of Sociology, 40(1)*, pp. 46–81.

Adey, P. and Shayer, M. (1994) *Really Raising Standards: Cognitive Intervention and Academic Achievement*. London: Routledge.

Aitken, M. and Longford, N. (1986) Statistical modelling issues in school effectiveness studies, *Journal of the Royal Statistical Society, Series A, 149(1)*, pp. 1–43.

Arblaster, G. A., Butler, C., Taylor, A. L., Arnold, C. and Pitchford, M. (1991) Same-age tutoring, mastery learning and the mixed ability teaching of reading, *School Psychology International, 12*, pp. 111–18.

Arrowsmith, J. (1989) In search of the perfect vintage (primary and pre-school), *The Times Scottish Educational Supplement, 1188*, p. 4.

Askew, M. and Wiliam, D. (1995) *Recent Research in Mathematics Education 5–16* (Ofsted Reviews of Research). London: HMSO.

Askew, M. and Wiliam, D. (1998) Assessment and classroom learning, *Assessment in Education, 5*, 1, 11–73.

Ball, S. J. (1981) *Beachside Comprehensive: a Case-Study of Secondary Schooling*. Cambridge: Cambridge University Press.

Barker Lunn, J. C. (1970) *Streaming in the Primary School*. Slough: NFER.

Barker Lunn, J. C. (1984) Junior school teachers: their methods and practice, *Educational Research, 26*, pp. 178–88.

Barnes, D. and Todd, F. (1977) *Communication and Learning in Small Groups*. London: Routledge and Kegan Paul.

Barnes, D., Britton, J. and Rosen, H. (1969) *Language, the Learner and the School*. Harmondsworth: Penguin.

Barr, R. and Dreeben, R. (1977) Instruction in classrooms. In L. S. Shulman (ed.) *Review of Research in Education 5*. Itasca, IL: Peacock.

Bayliss, V. (1998) *Redefining School*. London: Royal Society for the Encouragement of Arts, Manufacturers and Commerce (RSA).

Benn, C. and Chitty, C. (1996) *Thirty Years On: Is Comprehensive Education Alive and Well or Struggling to Survive?* London: Fulton.

Bennett, N. (1985) Interaction and achievement in classroom groups. In N. Bennett and C. Desforges (eds) *Recent advances in classroom research, British Journal of Educational Psychology, Monograph Series no. 2.*

Bennett, N. and Cass, A. (1989) The effects of group composition on group interactive processes and pupil understanding, *British Educational Research Journal, 15(1)*, pp. 19–32.

Bennett, N. and Dunne, E. (1989) *Implementing Cooperative Groupwork in Classrooms*. Exeter: University of Exeter, School of Education.

Berends, M. (1995) Educational stratification and students' social bonding to school, *British Journal of Sociology of Education, 16(3)*, pp. 327–51.

Biggs, J. (1996) Enhancing teaching through constructive alignment, *Higher Education, 32(3)*, pp. 347–64.

Biggs, J. B. and Moore, P. J. (1993) *The Process of Learning.* Englewood Cliffs, NJ: Prentice Hall.

Biott, C. (1987) Cooperative groupwork: pupils' and teachers' membership and participation, *Curriculum, 8(2)*, pp. 5–14.

Blagg, N. (1991) *Can We Teach Intelligence?* Hillsdale, NJ: Lawrence Erlbaum Associates.

Blandford, J. S. (1958) Standardised tests in junior schools with special reference to the effects of streaming on the constancy of results, *British Journal of Educational Psychology, 28*, pp. 170–3.

Blatchford, P. (1997) Pupils' self-assessments of academic attainment at 7, 11 and 16 years: effects of sex and ethnic group, *Educational Psychology, 67*, pp. 169–84.

Block, N. and Dworkin, G. (eds) (1976) *The IQ Controversy.* New York: Pantheon.

Bloom, B. S. (1976) *Human Characteristics and School Learning.* New York: McGraw-Hill.

Bloom, B. S. (1984a) The 2 sigma problem: the search for methods of instruction as effective as one-to-one tutoring, *Educational Researcher, 13(6)*, pp. 4–16.

Bloom, B. S. (1984b) The search for methods of group instruction as effective as one-to-one tutoring, *Educational Leadership, 41(8)*, pp. 4–17.

Boaler, J. (1997a) Setting, social class and the survival of the quickest, *British Educational Research Journal, 23*, pp. 575–95.

Boaler, J. (1997b) When even the winners are losers: evaluating the experiences of 'top set' students, *Journal of Curriculum Studies, 29*, pp. 165–82.

Boaler, J. (1997c) *Experiencing School Mathematics: Teaching Styles, Sex and Setting.* Buckingham: Open University Press.

Boaler, J., Wiliam, D. and Brown, M. (2000) Experiences of ability grouping – disaffection, polarisation and the construction of failure, *British Educational Research Journal, 28(5)*, pp. 631–48.

Board of Education, Consultative Committee on the Primary School (1930) *The Primary School* (Hadow Report). London: HMSO.

Bossert, S. T. (1988) Cooperative activities in the classroom, *Review of Research in Education, 15*, pp. 225–50.

Bouri, J. and Barker Lunn, J. C. (1969) *Too Small to Stream: a Study of Grouping in Small Junior Schools.* Slough: NFER.

Brody, N. (1985) The validity of intelligence. In B. B. Wolman (ed.) *Handbook of Intelligence.* New York: John Wiley and Sons.

Brown, A. (1987) Metacognition, executive control, self-regulation and other more mysterious mechanisms. In F. Weinert and R. Kluwe (eds) *Metacognition, Motivation and Understanding.* Hillsdale, NJ: Lawrence Erlbaum Associates.

Burden, M., Emsley, M. and Constable, M. (1988) Encouraging progress in collaborative groupwork, *Education 3-13, 16(1)*, pp. 51–6.

Burgess, R. G. (1983) *Experiencing Comprehensive Education: a Study of Bishop McGregor School.* London: Methuen.

Burgess, R. G. (1984) It's not a proper subject: it's just Newsom. In I. Goodson and S. Ball (eds) *Defining the Curriculum.* London: Falmer.

Byrne, B. M. (1988) Adolescent self-concept, ability grouping and social comparison: re-examining academic track differences in high school, *Youth and Society, 20*, pp. 46–67.

Byrne, B. M. (1996) Academic self-concept: its structure, measurement, and relation to academic achievement. In B. A. Bracken (ed.) *Handbook of Self Concept* (pp. 287–316). Chichester: Wiley.

Byrne, B. M. and Shavelson, R. J. (1996) On the structure of social self-concept for pre-, early and late adolescents: a test of the Shavelson, Hubner and Stanton (1976) model, *Journal of Personality and Social Psychology*, 70, pp. 599–613.

Carroll, J. B. (1963) A model of school learning, *Teacher College Record*, 64, pp. 723–33.

Ceci, S. J. (1990) *On Intelligence . . . More or Less: a Biological Treatise on Intellectual Development*. Englewood Cliffs, NJ: Prentice Hall.

Chaplain, R. (1996) Pupils under pressure: coping with stress at school. In J. Rudduck, R. Chaplain and G. Wallace (eds) *School Improvement: What Can Pupils Tell Us?* London: David Fulton.

Chapman, J. W. (1988) Learning disabled children's self-concepts, *Review of Educational Research*, 58, pp. 347–71.

Clammer, R. (1985) Mixed ability teaching: meanings and motives. A study of two geography departments, *SERCH*, 7, pp. 17–19.

Cohen, E. G. (1994) Restructuring the classroom: conditions for productive small groups, *Review of Educational Research*, 64, pp. 1–35.

Cowan, R. and Hallam, S. (1999) *What Do We Know About Homework?* Viewpoint 9. London: Institute of Education, University of London.

Creemers, B. P. M. (1994) *The Effective Classroom*. London: Cassell.

Crook, D., Power, S. and Whitty, G. (1999) *The Grammar School Question*, London: Institute of Education.

Cross, D. (1988) Selection, setting and streaming in language teaching, *System*, 16, 1, pp. 13–22.

Crozier, S. and Kleinberg, S. (1987) Solving problems in a group, *Education 3–13*, 15(3), pp. 37–41.

Cuban, L. (1990) A fundamental puzzle of school reform. In A. Leiberman (ed.) *Schools as Collaborative Structures: Creating the Future Now*. New York: Falmer.

Cuttance, P. (1992) Evaluating the effectiveness of schools. In D. Reynolds and P. Cuttance (eds) *School Effectiveness: Research, Policy and Practice*. London: Cassell.

Daniels, J. C. (1961a) The effects of streaming in the primary schools: I. What teachers believe, *British Journal of Educational Psychology*, 31, pp. 69–78.

Daniels, J. C. (1961b) The effects of streaming in the primary schools: II. Comparison of streamed and unstreamed schools, *British Journal of Educational Psychology*, 31, pp. 119–26.

Dansereau, D. (1978) The development of a learning strategies curriculum. In H. F. O'Neil (ed.) *Learning Strategies*. New York: Academic Press.

Deitrich, F. R. (1964) Comparison of sixth grade pupils in two school systems; ability grouping compared to heterogeneous grouping, *Journal of Educational Research*, 57, pp. 507–12.

Department for Education and Employment and Qualifications and Curriculum Authority (1999) *The National Curriculum*. London: DfEE/QCA.

Department for Education and Science (1978) *Primary Education in England: a Survey by HM Inspectors of School*. London: HMSO.

Department for Education and Science, CACE (1967) *Children and their Primary Schools* (the Plowden Report). London: HMSO.

Department for Education and Science, HMI (1978) *Mixed Ability Work in Comprehensive Schools*. London: HMSO.

Department for Education and Science, HMI (1979) *Aspects of Secondary Education in England*. London: HMSO.

Department for Education and Science (1989) *Discipline in Schools: Report of the Committee of Enquiry Chaired by Lord Elton*. London: HMSO.

Department for Education and Science (1991) *National Curriculum and Special Needs: Preparations to Implement the National Curriculum for Pupils with Statements in Special and Ordinary Schools, 1989–90: a report by HM Inspectorate*. London: Department of Education and Science.

Department for Education and Science (1992) *The Education of Very Able Children in Maintained Schools: a Review by HMI*. London: HMSO.

Devine, D. (1993) A study of reading ability groups: primary school children's experiences and views, *Irish Educational Studies, 12*, pp. 134–42.

Douglas, J. W. B. (1964) *The Home and the School*. London: MacGibbon and Kee.

Draisey, A. G. (1985) Vertical grouping in the primary school – a positive view, *Education Development, 9(1)*, pp. 3–11.

Dunne, E. and Bennett, N. (1990) *Talking and Learning in Groups*. London: Macmillan.

Dweck, C. S., Davidson, W., Nelson, S. and Enna, B. (1978) Sex differences in learned helplessness: II. The contingencies of evaluative feedback in the classroom and III. An experimental analysis, *Developmental Psychology, 14(3)*, pp. 268–76.

Eilam, B. and Finegold, M. (1992) The heterogeneous class: a solution of just another problem? *Studies in Educational Evaluation, 18(2)*, pp. 265–78.

Elwood, J. (1998) Gender, assessment and achievement: considering the interactions and what we can learn about the underachievement of boys and girls, *Leading Edge, 2(3)*, pp. 158–66.

Entwistle, N. J. (1981) *Styles of Learning and Teaching*. New York: John Wiley and Sons.

Essen, J., Fogelman, K. and Tibbenham, A. (1978) Some non-academic developmental correlates of ability-grouping in secondary schools, *Educational Studies, 5(1)*, pp. 83–93.

Evertson, C. M. (1982) Differences in instructional activities in higher and lower achieving junior high English and math classes, *Elementary School Journal, 82*, pp. 219–32.

Feldusen, J. F. (1989) Synthesis of research on gifted youth, *Educational Leadership, 46(6)*, pp. 6–11.

Ferri, E. (1971) *Streaming Two Years Later: A Follow Up of a Group of Pupils Who Attended Streamed and Nonstreamed Junior Schools*. London: NFER.

Feurstein, R., Rand, Y., Hoffman, M. B. and Miller, R. (1980) *Instrumental Enrichment: an Intervention Program for Cognitive Modifiability*. Baltimore, MD: University Park.

Findlay, W. and Bryan, M. (1975) The pros and cons of ability grouping, *Phi Delta Kappan, 66*, p. 12.

Finley, M. K. (1984) Teachers and tracking in a comprehensive high school, *Sociology of Education, 57*, pp. 233–43.

Flavell, J. H. (1971) First discussant's comments: what is memory development the development of? *Human Development, 14*, pp. 272–8.

Fogelman, K. (1983) Ability grouping in the secondary school. In K. Fogelman (ed.) *Growing up in Great Britain, Papers from the National Child Development Study*. London: Macmillan for NCB.

Fogelman, K., Essen, J. and Tibbenham, A. (1978) Ability grouping in secondary schools and attainment, *Educational Studies, 4(3)*, pp. 201–12.

Fraser, B. J. (1989) Twenty years of classroom climate work: Progress and prospect, *Journal of curriculum studies, 21*, 307–27.

Frost, A. W. (1978) Mixed ability versus streaming in science – a controlled experiment, *School Science Review, 60*, pp. 347–50.

Galloway, D. (1983) Disruptive pupils and effective pastoral care, *School Organisation, 13*, pp. 245–54.

Galton, M. (1981) Teaching groups in the junior school, a neglected art, *Schools Organisation, 1(2)*, pp. 175–81.

Galton, M. and Williamson, J. (1992) *Groupwork in the Primary Classroom*. London: Routledge.

Galton, M., Simon, B. and Croll, P. (1980) *Inside the Primary Classroom*. London: Routledge and Kegan Paul.

Galton, M., Patrick, H., Appleyard, R., Hargreaves, L. and Bernbaum, G. (1987) *Curriculum Provision in Small Schools: the PRISMS Project, Final Report*. University of Leicester.

Gamoran, A. (1986) Instructional and institutional effects of ability grouping, *Sociology of Education, 59*, pp. 185–98.

Gamoran, A. (1989) Measuring curriculum differentiation, *American Journal of Education, 97*, pp. 129–43.

Gamoran, A. (1990) The consequences of track-related instructional differences for student achievement. Paper presented at the Annual Meeting of the American Educational Research Association, Boston.

Gamoran, A. and Berends, M. (1987) The effects of stratification in secondary schools: synthesis of survey and ethnographic research, *Review of Educational Research, 57*, pp. 415–35.

Gardner, H. (1993) *Frames of Mind: The Theory of Multiple Intelligences*. New York: Basic Books.

Gardner, H. (1999) Are there additional intelligences? The case for naturalist, spiritual and existential intelligences. In J. Kane (ed.) *Education, Information and Transformation*. Englewood Cliffs, NJ: Prentice Hall.

George, P. (1989) *The Japanese Junior High School: a View from the Inside*. Columbus, OH: National Middle School Association.

Gibbs, G. (1981) *Teaching Students to Learn: a Student Centred Approach*. Buckingham: Open University Press.

Gilligan, C. (1982) *In a Different Voice: Psychological Theory and Women's Development*. Cambridge, MA: Harvard University Press.

Glaser, R. (1984) Education and thinking: the role of knowledge, *American Psychologist, 39*, pp. 93–104.

Glaye, A. (1986) Outer appearances with inner experiences – towards a more holistic view of group-work, *Educational Review, 38(1)*, pp. 45–56.

Goleman, D. (1996) *Emotional Intelligence: Why it can Matter more than IQ*. London: Bloomsbury.

Gray, J., Jesson, D. and Jones, B. (1984) Predicting differences in examination results between local education authorities: does school organisation matter? *Oxford Review of Education, 10,1*, pp. 45–68.

Gray, J., Jesson, D. and Jones, B. (1986) The search for a fairer way of comparing schools' examination results, *Researching Papers in Education, 10(1)*, pp. 91–122.

Gray, J., McPherson, A. and Raffe, D. (1983) *Reconstructions of Secondary Education*. London: Routledge and Kegan Paul.

Gregory, R. P. (1984) Streaming, setting and mixed ability grouping in primary and secondary schools: some research findings, *Educational Studies, 10(3)*, pp. 209–26.

Gregory, R. P. (1986) Mixed ability teaching – a rod for the teacher's back? *Journal of Applied Educational Studies, 15(2)*, pp. 56–61.

Guskey, T. R. and Gates, S. L. (1985) A synthesis of research on group-based mastery learning programs. Paper presented at the annual meeting of the American Educational Research Association, Chicago.

Gutierrez, R. and Slavin, R. E. (1992) Achievement effects of the non-graded elementary school: a best evidence synthesis, *Review of Educational Research, 62*, pp. 333–76.

Guttman, Y., Gur, A., Daniel, S. and Well, D. (1972) *The Effects of Ability Grouping on Learning Achievements and Psychosocial Development.* Jerusalem: Szold Institute.

Hacker, R. G. and Rowe, M. J. (1993) A study of the effects of an organisation change from streamed to mixed-ability classes upon science classroom instruction, *Journal of Research in Science Teaching, 30(3)*, pp. 223–31.

Hacker, R. G., Rowe, M. J. and Evans, R. D. (1991) The influences of ability groupings for secondary science lessons upon classroom processes. Part 1: homogenous groupings (Science Education Notes), School Science Review, 73, 262, 125–9.

Hallam, S. (1996) *Improving School Attendance.* Oxford: Heinemann.

Hallam, S. (1998) *Instrumental Teaching: a Practical Guide to Better Teaching and Learning.* Oxford: Heinemann.

Hallam, S. and Castle, F. (1999) *Evaluation of the Behaviour and Discipline Pilot Projects (1996–99) Supported under the Standards Fund Programme.* London: DfEE.

Hallam, S. and Ireson, J. (1999) Pedagogy in the secondary school. In P. Mortimore (ed.) *Understanding Pedagogy and its Impact on Learning.* London: Paul Chapman Publishing.

Hallam, S. and Toutounji, I. (1996) *What Do We Know About the Groupings of Pupils by Ability?* London: Institute of Education, University of London.

Hallam, S., Ireson, J., Chaudury, I. A., Lister, V. and Davies, J. (1999) Ability grouping practices in the primary school: a survey of what schools are doing. Paper presented at the annual conference of the British Educational Research Association, University of Sussex, Brighton, 2–5 September.

Hallinan, M. and Sorensen, A. (1985) Ability grouping and student friendships, *American Educational Research Journal, 22*, pp. 485–99.

Hallinan, M. and Williams, R. (1989) Interracial friendship choices in secondary schools, *American Sociological Review, 54*, pp. 67–78.

Hargreaves, D. H. (1967) *Social Relations in a Secondary School.* London: Tinling.

Harlen, W. and Malcolm, H. (1997) *Setting and Streaming: A Research Review* (Using Research Series 18). Edinburgh: SCRE.

Harvey, T. J. (1981) The correlation between IQ, Science achievement and gender of secondary school students when taught in mixed ability groups, *The Australian Science Teachers Association, 27(2)*, pp. 89–94.

Harwood, D. (1989) The nature of teacher–pupil interaction in the active tutorial work approach: using interaction analysis to evaluate student-centred approaches, *British Educational Research Journal, 15*, pp. 177–94.

Harwood, D. (1995) The pedagogy of the world studies 8–13 project: the influence of the presence/absence of the teacher upon children's collaborative work, *British Educational Research Journal, 21(5)*, pp. 587–612.

HMI (1978) Department for Education and Science, Mixed ability work in Comprehensive Schools. London: HMSO.

HMI (1979) Department for Education and Science, Aspects of Secondary Education in England. London: HMSO.

Howe, C. (1997) *Gender and Classroom Interaction: a Research Review.* Edinburgh: SCRE.

Hughes, M. (1993) *Flexible Learning: Evidence Examined.* Stafford: Network Educational Press Ltd.

Husen, T. and Boalt, G. (1967) *Educational Research and Educational Change: the Case of Sweden.* Stockholm: Almquist.

Ingleson, S. (1982) Creating conditions for success with mixed ability classes. In M. K. Sands and T. Kerry (eds) *Mixed Ability Teaching.* London: Croom Helm.

Ireson, J. (1999) *Innovative Grouping Practices in Secondary Schools.* LondonL DfEE.

Ireson, J. and Hallam, S. (1999) Raising standards: is ability grouping the answer? *Oxford Review of Education, 25(3)*, pp. 343–58.

Ireson, J., Hallam, S. and Plewis, I. (2001) Ability grouping in secondary schools: effects on pupils' self-concepts, *British Journal of Educational Psychology.*

Ireson, J., Mortimore, P. and Hallam, S. (1999) The common strands of pedagogy and their implications. In P. Mortimore (ed.) *Understanding Pedagogy and Its Impact on Learning.* London: Paul Chapman Publishing.

Ireson, J., Evan, P., Redmond, P. and Wedell, K. (1992) Developing the curriculum for pupils experiencing difficulties in learning in the ordinary school: a systematic comparative analysis, *British Educational Research Journal, 18(2)*, 155–73.

Ireson, J., Hallam, S., Hack, S., Clark, H. and Plewis, I. (in press) Ability grouping in English secondary schools: effects on attainment in English, mathematics and science, *Educational Research and Evaluation.*

Ireson, J., Hallam, S. and Hurley, C. (in preparation) Pupils' relationships with school: does ability grouping make a difference? Paper presented at the BPS Education Section Conference, Worcester, September 2001.

Jackson, B. (1964) *Streaming: an Education System in Miniature.* London: Routledge and Kegan Paul.

Jenson, A. R. (1970) Another look at culture-fair testing. In J. Helmuth (ed.) *The Disadvantaged Child.* New York: Brunner-Mazel.

Jesson, D. (2000) *Further evidence on comparative GCSE performance between selective and non-selective schools and LEAs.* Paper presented at the NUT Secondary Education Conference, March.

Johannesson, I. (1962) School differentiation and social adjustment of pupils, *Educational Research, 4*, pp. 133–9.

Johnson, D. W. and Johnson, R. T. (1990) Cooperative learning and achievement. In S. Sharan (ed.) *Cooperative Learning: Theory and Research.* New York: Praeger.

Keddie, N. (1971) Classroom knowledge. In M. F. D. Young (ed.) *Knowledge and Control.* London: Collier-MacMillan.

Keller, F. S. (1968) Goodbye, teacher . . ., *Journal of Applied Behavioural Analysis, 1*, pp. 79–89.

Kelly, A. (1988) Gender differences in teacher–pupil interactions: a meta-analytic review, *Research in Education, 39*, pp. 1–23.

Kerckhoff, A. (1986) Effects of ability grouping in British secondary schools, *American Sociological Review, 51*, pp. 842–58.

Kerckhoff, A. C., Fogelman, K., Crook, D. and Reeder, D. (1996) *Going Comprehensive in England and Wales: a Study of Uneven Change.* London: Woburn Press.

Kerry, T. (1980) RE: a suitable case for mixed ability? *British Journal of Religious Education, 3(2)*, pp. 46–52.

Kerry, T. (1982a) Providing for slow learners, *Special Education: Forward Trends, 8(4)*, pp. 9–11.

Kerry, T. (1982b) The demands made by RE on pupils' thinking. In J. Hull (ed.) *New Directions in Religious Education.* Lewes, Sussex: Falmer.

Kerry, T. (1982c) Teachers' identification of exceptional pupils and their strategies for coping with them. PhD thesis, University of Nottingham.

Kerry, T. and Sands, M. K. (1984) Classroom organisation and learning. In E. C. Wragg (ed.) *Classroom Teaching Skills: the Research Findings of the Teacher Education Project.* London: Routledge.

Keys, W., Harris, S. and Fernandes, C. (1996) *Third International Mathematics and Science Study: First National Report. Part 1 and Appendices.* Slough: NFER.

Kulik, C.-L. C. and Kulik, J. A. (1982a) Effects of ability grouping on secondary school students: a meta-analysis of evaluation findings, *American Educational Research Journal, 19*, pp. 415–28.

Kulik, C.-L. C. and Kulik, J. A. (1982b) Research synthesis on ability grouping, *Educational leadership, 39*, 619–21.

Kulik, C.-L. C. and Kulik, J. A. (1990) Effectiveness of mastery learning programmes: a meta-analysis, *Review of Educational Research, 60*, pp. 265–99.

Kulik, J. A. (1991) *Ability Grouping. Research-based decision making series.* Storrs, CT: National Research Center on the Gifted and Talented, University of Connecticut.

Kulik, J. A. and Kulik, C.- L. C. (1984) Effects of accelerated instruction on students, *Review of Educational Research, 54*, 409–26.

Kulik, J. A. and Kulik, C.- L. C. (1986) Operative and interpretable effect sizes in meta-analysis. Paper presented at the annual meeting of the American Educational Research Association, San Francisco.

Kulik, J. A. and Kulik, C.- L. C. (1987) Effects of ability grouping on student achievement, *Equity and Excellence, 23 (1–2)*, pp. 22–30.

Kulik, J. A. and Kulik, C.- L. C. (1992) Meta-analytic findings on grouping programs, *Gifted Child Quarterly, 36(2)*, pp. 73–7.

Lacey, C. (1970) *Hightown Grammar.* Manchester: Manchester University Press.

Lacey, C. (1974) Destreaming in a 'pressured' academic environment. In J. Eggleston (ed.) *Contemporary Research in the Sociology of Education.* London: Methuen.

Lai, P. and Biggs, J. (1994) Who benefits from mastery learning? *Contemporary Educational Psychology, 19*, pp. 12–23.

Lawrence, F. and Munch, T. W. (1984) The effects of grouping of laboratory students on selected educational outcomes, *Journal of Research in Science Teaching, 21*, pp. 699–708.

Leat, D. (1998) Thinking through geography, Cambridge: Chris Kingston Publishing.

Lee, J. and Croll, P. (1995) Streaming and subject specialism at key stage 2: a survey in two local authorities, *Educational Studies, 21, 2*, pp. 155–65.

Levine, D. U. (1992) An interpretative review of US research and practice dealing with unusually effective schools. In D. Reynolds and P. Cuttance (eds) *School Effectiveness: Research, Policy and Practice.* London: Cassell.

Lipman, M., Sharp, A. M. and Oscanyan, F. S. (1980) *Philosophy in the Classroom.* Philadelphia: Temple University Press.

Lou, Y., Abrami, P. C., Spence, J. C., Poulsen, C., Chambers, B. and d'Apollonia, S. (1996) Within-class grouping: a meta-analysis, *Review of Educational Research, 66(4)*, pp. 423–58.

Lughart, E., Roeders, P. J. B., Bosker, R. J. and Bos, K. T. (1989) *Effective school-kenmerken in het voortgezet onderwijs. Deel 1: Literatuurstudie (Effective schools characteristics in secondary education. Part 1: Literature review.* Groningen: RION.

Lysakowski, R. and Walberg, H. (1982) Instructional effects of cues, participation, and corrective feedback: a quantitative synthesis, *American Educational Research Journal, 19*, pp. 559–78.

Maguire, M., Maguire, S. and Felstead, A. (1993) *Factors Influencing Individual Commitment to Lifetime Learning: a Literature Review.* Leicester: Centre for Labour Market Studies.

Marks, J. (1991) *Standards in Schools.* London: Social Market Foundation.

Marks, J. and Cox, C. (1984) Educational attainment in secondary schools, *Oxford Review of Education, 10, 1*, pp. 7–31.

Marks, J., Cox, C. and Pomian-Srzednicki, M. (1983) *Standards in English Schools: An Analysis of Examination Results of Secondary Schools in England for 1981.* London: National Council for Educational Standards.

Marks, J., Cox, C. and Pomian-Szrednicki, M. (1985) *Standards in English Schools, Second Report.* London: National Council for Educational Standards.

Marsh, H. W. (1987) The big-fish-little-pond effect on academic self-concept, *Journal of Educational Psychology, 79*, pp. 280–95.

Marsh, H. W. (1991) The failure of high-ability high schools to deliver academic benefits: the importance of academic self-concept and educational aspirations, *American Educational Research Journal, 28*, pp. 445–80.

Marsh, H. W. and Parker, J. (1984) Determinants of student self-concept: is it better to be a relatively large fish in a small pond even if you don't learn to swim as well? *Journal of Personality and Social Psychology, 47*, pp. 213–31.

Marsh, H. W. and Peart, N. (1988) Competitive and cooperative physical fitness training programs for girls: effects on physical fitness and on multidimensional self-concepts, *Journal of Sport and Exercise Psychology, 10*, pp. 390–407.

Marsh, H. W. and Rowe, K. J. (1996) The negative effects of school-average ability on academic self-concept: an application of multilevel modelling, *Australian Journal of Education, 40(1)*, pp. 65–87.

Marsh, H. W., Byrne, B. M. and Shavelson, R. (1988) A multifaceted academic self-concept: its hierarchical structure and its relation to academic achievement. *Journal of Educational Psychology, 80*, pp. 366–80.

Marsh, H. W., Chessor, D., Craven, R. G. and Roche, L. (1995) The effects of the gifted and talented program on academic self-concept: the big fish strikes again, *American Educational Research Journal, 32*, p. 285–319.

Marsh, H. W., Koller, O. and Baumert, J. (1999) Reunification of East and West German school systems: longitudinal multigroup study of academic self-concept, achievement and multiple frames of reference. Paper presented at the 8th European Association for Research on Learning and Instruction conference, Gothenburg, Sweden.

Marsh, H. W., Parker, J. and Barnes, J. (1985) Multidimensional adolescent self-concepts: their relationship to age, sex and academic measures, *American Educational Research Journal, 22*, pp. 422–44.

Marton, F. and Saljo, R. (1976) On qualitative differences in learning I: outcome and process, *British Journal of Educational Psychology, 46*, pp. 4–11.

Maughan, B. and Rutter, M. (1987) Pupils' progress in selective and non-selective schools, *School Organization, 7, 1*, pp. 49–68.

McDermott, J. W. (1976) The controversy over ability grouping in American education, 1916–1970. Doctoral dissertation, Temple University, Philadelphia. Xerox, University Microfilms.

McGivney, V. (1992) *Tracking Adult Learning Routes*. Leicester: NIACE.

McGuiness, C. (1999) *From Thinking Skills to Thinking Classrooms*. London: DfEE.

McGuiness, C., Curry, C., Greer, B., Daly, P. and Salters, M. (1997) *Final Report on the ACTS Project: Phase 2*. Belfast: Northern Ireland Council for Curriculum, Examinations and Assessment.

McPherson, A. and Willms, D. (1987) Equalisation and improvement: some effects of comprehensive organisation in Scotland. Paper presented to the Annual Meeting of the American Educational Research Association, May.

Metz, M. H. (1978) *Classrooms and Corridors: the Crisis of Authority in Desegregated Secondary Schools*. Berkeley: University of California Press.

Metz, M. (1983) Sources of constructive social relationship in an urban magnet middle school, *American Journal of Education, 91*, pp. 202–45.

Miller, B. A. (1990) A review of the quantitative research on multi-grade instruction, *Research in Rural education, 7(1)*, pp. 1–8.

Ministry of Education (Israel) (1965) *Survey of Grouping*. Jerusalem: The Pedagogic Secretariat (Hebrew).

Mortimore, P., Sammons, P., Stoll, L., Lewis, D. and Ecob, R. (1988) *The Junior School Project*. London: ILEA, Research and Statistics Branch.

NEA (1968) *Ability Grouping: Research Summary*. Washington: National Education Association.

Neave, G. (1975) *How They Fared: The Impact of the Comprehensive School on the University*. London: Routledge and Kegan Paul.

Newbold, D. (1977) *Ability Grouping: the Banbury Enquiry*. Slough: National Foundation for Educational Research.

Nicholls, J. G. (1989) *The Competitive Ethos and Democratic Education*. Cambridge, MA: Harvard University Press.

Nuttall, D., Goldstein, H., Prosser, R. and Rasbash, J. (1989) Differential school effectiveness, *International Journal of Educational Research, 13(7)*, pp. 769–76.

Oakes, J. (1982) The reproduction of inequity: the content of secondary school tracking, *The Urban Review, 14(2)*, pp. 107–20.

Oakes, J. (1985) *Keeping Track: How Schools Structure Inequality*. New Haven: Yale University Press.

Oakes, J., Gamoran, A. and Page, R. (1991) Curriculum differentiation: opportunities, consequences and meanings. In P. Jackson (ed.) *Handbook of Research on Curriculum*. New York: Macmillan.

Ofsted (1993) *Access and Achievement in Urban Education*. London: Office for Standards in Education.

Ofsted (1994) *Primary Matters: a discussion on Teaching and Learning in Primary Schools*. London: Office for Standards in Education.

Ofsted (1995) *Annual Report of Her Majesty's Chief Inspector of Schools, 1993/94: Part 1, Standards and Quality in Education*. London: Office for Standards in Education.

Ofsted (1998a) *Setting in Primary Schools: a Report from the Office of Her Majesty's Chief Inspector of Schools*. London: Office for Standards in Education.

Ofsted (1998b) Page, R. N. (1984) Perspectives and processes: the negotiation of educational meaning in high school classes for academically unsuccessful students. Unpublished PhD dissertation, University of Wisconsin.

Page, R. (1992) *Lower Track Classrooms: a Curricular and Cultural Perspective*. New York: Teachers College Press.

Parkinson, B. L., Mitchell, R. F. and Johnstone, R. M. (1983) Mastery learning in modern languages – a case study, *PLET, 20(1)*, pp. 43–53.

Peverett, R. (1994) teaching 9–11 year olds. In National Commission of Education, *Insights into Education and Training*. Oxford: Heinemann.

Phillips, A. (1998) It's just so unfair, *Times Educational Supplement*, 13 November.

Plewes, J. A. (1979) Mixed ability teaching: a deterioration in performance, *Journal of Research in Science Teaching, 16*, pp. 229–36.

Plomin, R. (1986) *Development, Genetics and Psychology*. Hillsdale, NJ: LEA.

Plomin, R. and Thompson, L. E. (1993) Genetics and high cognitive ability. In G. R. Bock and K. Ackrill (eds) *The Origins and Development of High Ability*. New York: John Wiley and Sons.

Postlethwaite, K. and Denton, C. (1978) *Streams for the Future: the Long-term Effects of Early Streaming and Non-streaming – the Final Report of the Banbury Enquiry*. Banbury: Pubansco Publications.

Power, S., Whitty, G., Edwards, T. and Wigfall, V. (1998) School boys and school work: gender identification and academic achievement, *International Journal of Inclusive Education, 2(2)*, pp. 135–53.

Pratt, D. (1986) On the merits of multi-age classrooms, *Research in Rural Education, 3(3)*, pp. 111–15.

Ramsden, P. (1991) Study processes in grade 12 environments. In B . J. Fraser and H. J. Walberg (eds) *Educational Environments: Evaluation, Antecedents and Consequences*. Oxford: Pergamon Press.

Ramsden, P., Beswick, D. and Bowden, J. (1986) Effects of learning skill interventions on first year university students' learning, *Human Learning, 3*, pp. 151–64.

Raundenbush, S. W., Rowan, B. and Cheong, Y. F. (1992) Contextual effects on the self-perceived efficacy of high school teachers, *Sociology of Education, 65*, pp. 150–67.

Reay, D. (1998) Setting the agenda: the growing impact of market forces on pupil grouping in British secondary schooling, *Curriculum Studies, 30,5*, pp. 545–58.

Reid, K., Hopkins, D. and Holly, P. (1987) *Towards the Effective School*. Oxford: Blackwell.

Reid, M. E., Clunies-Ross, L. R., Goacher, B. and Vile, D. (1982) *Mixed Ability Teaching: Problems and Possibilities*. Windsor: NFER-Nelson.

Reynolds, D. (1982) The search for effective schools, *School Organisation, 2(3)*, pp. 215–37.

Reynolds, D. and Farrell, S. (1996) *Worlds Apart? A Review of International Surveys of Educational Achievement Involving England*. London: HMSO.

Reynolds, D., Sullivan, M. and Murgatroyd, S. (1987) *The Comprehensive Experiment: a Comparison of the Selective and Non-selective System of School Organization*. London: Falmer.

Roeders, P. (1989) The coaching classroom: increasing school effectiveness by a child oriented, creatively based educational method. Paper given to 12th International School Psychology Association (ISPA) Conference, Ljublyana, August.

Rosenbaum, J. E. (1976) *Making Inequality: The Hidden Curriculum of High School Tracking*. New York, London: Wiley.

Rosenberg, M. (1979) *Conceiving the Self*. New York: Basic Books.

Ross, J. M., Bunton, W. J., Evison, P. and Robertson, T. S. (1972) *A Critical Appraisal of Comprehensive Education*. London: NFER.

Rowan, B. and Miracle, A. W. (1983) Systems of ability grouping and the stratification of achievement in elementary schools, *Sociology of Education, 56*, pp. 133–44.

Rudd, W. G. A. (1956) The psychological effects of streaming by attainment with special reference to a group of selected children, *British Journal of Educational Psychology, 28*, pp. 47–60.

Rutter, M., Maughan, B., Mortimore, P. and Ouston, J. (1979) *Fifteen Thousand Hours: Secondary Schools and their Effects on Children*. London: Open Books.

Sammons, P., Hillman, J. and Mortimore, P. (1995) *Key Characteristics of Effective Schools: a Review of School Effectiveness Research*. London: Office for Standards in Education.

Sammons, P., Thomas, S. and Mortimore, P. (1997) *Forging Links: Effective Schools and Effective Departments*. London: Paul Chapman Publishing.

Sands, M. K. (1981a) Group work: time for re-evaluation, *Educational Studies, 7, 2*, pp. 77–86.

Sands, M. K. (1981b) Group work in science: myth or reality?, *School Science Review, 26*, p. 221.

Sands, M. K. and Kerry, T. (eds) (1982) *Mixed Ability Teaching*, London: Croom Hill.

Sarason, S. (1990) *The Predictable Failure of Educational Reform: Can We Change Before it's Too Late?* San Francisco, CA: Jossey-Bass.

Scottish Education Department Inspectors of Schools (1992a) *Using ethos indicators in primary school self-evaluation: taking account of the views of pupils, parents and teachers*. Edinburgh: Scottish Office Education Department.

Scottish Education Department Inspectors of Schools (1992b) *Using ethos indicators in secondary school self-evaluation: taking account of the views of pupils, parents and teachers*. Edinburgh: Scottish Office Education Department.

Scheerebs, J., Nanninga, H. C. R. and Pellgrum, W. J. (1989) Generalizability of instructional and school effectiveness indicators across nations; preliminary results of a secondary analysis of the IEA second mathematics study. In B. P. M. Creemers, T. Peters and D. Reynolds (eds) *School Effectiveness and School Improvement, Proceedings of the Second International Congress, Rotterdam.* Lisse: Swets and Zeitlinger.

Schmeck, R. R. (1983) Learning styles of college students. In R. Dillon and R. R. Schmeck (eds) *Individual Difference in Cognition.* New York: Academic Press.

Schools Council (1977) *Mixed Ability Teaching in Mathematics.* London: Evans/Methuen.

Schwartz, F. (1981) Supporting or subverting learning: peer groups patterns in four tracked schools, *Anthropology and Education Quarterly, 12,* pp. 99–121.

Selmes, I. (1987) *Improving Study Skills.* London: Hodder and Stoughton.

Scottish Office (1996) *Achievement For All: a Report on Selection Within Schools.* Edinburgh: HMSO.

Sharp, C., Osgood, J. and Flanagan, N. (1999) *The Benefits of Study Support: a Review of Opinion and Research.* London: DfEE.

Shavelson, R. J., Hubner, J. J. and Stanton, G. C. (1976) Self-concept: validation of construct interpretations, *Review of Educational Research, 46,* pp. 407–41.

Slavin, R. E. (1987a) Ability grouping and student achievement in elementary schools: a best evidence synthesis, *Review of Educational Research, 57(3),* pp. 293–336.

Slavin, R. E. (1987b) Grouping for instruction, equity and effectiveness, *Equity and excellence, 23(1–2),* 31–6.

Slavin, R. E. (1987c) Mastery learning re-considered, *Review of Educational Research, 57,* pp. 175–213.

Slavin, R. E. (1990a) Achievement effects of ability grouping in secondary schools: a best evidence synthesis, *Review of Educational Research, 60,* pp. 471–90.

Slavin, R. E. (1990b) Co-operative learning. In C. Rogers and P. Kutnick (eds) *The Social Psychology of the Primary School.* London: Routledge.

Slavin, R. E. and Karweit, N. L. (1985) Effects of whole class, ability grouped and individualised instruction on mathematics achievement, *American Educational Research Journal, 22(3),* pp. 351–67.

Sloboda, J. A., Davidson, J. W. and Howe, M. J. A. (1994) Is everyone musical? *The Psychologist, 7(8),* pp. 349–54.

Smith, D. and Tomlinson, S. (1989) *The School Effect.* London: National Children's Bureau.

Sorenson, A. B. and Hallinan, M. T. (1986) Effects of ability grouping on growth in academic achievement, *American Educational Research Journal, 22, 3,* pp. 351–67.

Soutter, A. (1993) Progress at age 12 of children assessed as failures by their teachers at 5, 6 or 7. Paper presented at the annual conference of the British Psychological Society Education Section conference, 19–21 November, Easthampstead Park, Wokingham, Berks.

Steedman, J. (1980) *Progress in Secondary Schools.* London: National Children's Bureau.

Steedman, J. (1983) *Examination Results in Selective and Non-Selective Schools: Findings of the National Development Study.* London: National Children's Bureau.

Sternberg, R. J. (1984) Toward a triarchic theory of human intelligence, *Behavioural and Brain Sciences, 7,* pp. 269–315.

Sternberg, R. J. and Weil, E. M. (1980) An aptitude-strategy interaction in linear syllogistic reasoning, *Journal of Educational Psychology, 72,* pp. 226–34.

Stevenson, H. and Lee, S. (1990) Contexts of achievement: a study of American, Chinese and Japanese children, *Monographs of the Society for Research in Child Development, Vol, 221(55), Nos. 1–2*. Chicago: University of Chicago.

Stipek, D. and Daniels, D. H. (1988) Declining perceptions of competence: a consequence of changes in the child or in the educational environment, *Journal of Experimental Psychology, 80, 3.* pp. 352–6.

Sukhnanden, L. and Lee, B. (1998) *Streaming, setting and grouping by ability: a review of the literature.* Slough: National Foundation for Educational Research.

Swing, S. and Peterson, P. (1982) The relationships of student ability and small-group interaction to student achievement, *American Educational Research Journal, 19,* pp. 259–74.

Tann, S. (1981) Grouping and groupwork. In B. Simon and J. Willcocks (eds) *Research and Practice in the Primary Classroom.* London: Routledge and Kegan Paul.

Taylor, N. (1993) Ability grouping and its effect on pupil behaviour: A case study of a Midlands comprehensive school, *Education Today, 43(2),* pp. 14–17.

Topping, K. (1992) Cooperative learning and peer tutoring, *The Psychologist, 5,* pp. 151–7.

Tough, P. (1977) *The Development of Meaning: a Study of Use of Language.* London: Allen and Unwin.

Valli, L. (1986) Tracking: can it benefit low-achieving students? Paper presented at the annual meeting of the American Educational Research Association, San Francicso.

Vanfossen, B. E., Jones, J. D. and Spade, J. Z. (1987) Curriculum tracking and status maintenance, *Sociology of Education, 60 April,* pp. 104–22.

Veenman, S. (1995) Cognitive and noncognitive effects of multigrade and multi-age classes: a best evidence synthesis, *Review of Educational Research, 65(4),* pp. 319–81.

Vernon, P. E. (ed.) (1957) *Secondary School Selection.* London: Methuen.

Walberg, H. J. (1984) Improving the productivity of America's schools, *Educational Leadership, 44(1),* pp. 19–27.

Waxman, H. C., Wang, M. C., Anderson, K. A. and Walberg, H. J. (1985) Synthesis of research on the effects of adaptive education, *Educational Leadership, 43(1),* pp. 27–9.

Webb, N. (1983) Predicting learning from student interaction: defining the interaction variable, *Educational Psychologist, 18,* pp. 33–41.

Webb, N. (1985) Verbal interaction and learning in peer directed groups, *Theory into Practice, 24(1),* pp. 32–9.

Webb, N. (1991) Task-related verbal interaction and mathematics learning in small groups, *Journal of Research in Mathematics Education, 22,* pp. 366–89.

Willig, C. J. (1963) Social implications of streaming in junior schools, *Educational Research, 5,* pp. 151–4.

Willms, J. D. and Cuttance, P. (1985) School effects in Scottish secondary schools, *British Journal of Sociology of Education, 6,* pp. 289–306.

Wilson, B. J. and Schmidts, D. W. (1978) What's new in ability grouping? *Phi Delta Kappan, 59,* pp. 535–6.

Wragg, E. C. (ed.) (1984) *Classroom Teaching Skills: the Research Findings of the Teacher Education Project.* London: Routledge.

Wylie, R. C. (1979) *The Self Concept (Vol. 2).* Lincoln: University of Nebraska Press.

Yeomans, A. (1983) Collaborative groupwork in primary and secondary schools: Britain and USA, *Durham and Newcastle Research Review, X, (51),* pp. 99–105.

Index